KU-544-723

Richard III

DAVID BALDWIN

LIBRARIES NI
WITHDRAWN FROM STOCK

AMBERLEY

Cover illustration: *Front*: Richard III courtesy of Ripon Cathedral.
Background: Medieval painted rood screen © Jonathan Reeve.
Back: Richard's face, reconstructed by Caroline Wilkinson based on his
skull discovered at Grey Friars. Dr P. T. Stone.

This edition first published 2013

Amberley Publishing
The Hill, Stroud,
Gloucestershire, GL5 4EP

www.amberley-books.com

Copyright © David Baldwin, 2012, 2013

The right of David Baldwin to be identified as
the Author of this work has been asserted in
accordance with the Copyrights, Designs and
Patents Act 1988.

ISBN 978 1 4456 1591 2 paperback
ISBN 978 1 4456 1820 3 ebook

All rights reserved. No part of this book may
be reprinted or reproduced or utilised in any
form or by any electronic, mechanical or other
means, now known or hereafter invented,
including photocopying and recording, or in any
information storage or retrieval system, without
the permission in writing from the Publishers.

British Library Cataloguing in Publication Data.
A catalogue record for this book is available
from the British Library.

Typesetting and Origination by Amberley Publishing.
Printed in the UK.

CONTENTS

DRAMATIS PERSONAE

Persons whose names are identical or similar:

Anne Neville, Warwick the Kingmaker's younger daughter and Richard's wife.

Elizabeth Woodville, Edward IV's wife.

Elizabeth of York, Edward IV's eldest daughter, Richard's niece.

Edmund, Earl of Rutland, Richard's brother, killed in 1460.

Edward IV, Richard's eldest brother.

Edward V, Edward IV's son, the elder of the 'Princes in the Tower'.

Edward of Middleham, Richard's only legitimate son.

Edward of Westminster, 'Prince Edward of Lancaster', Henry VI's son.

George, Duke of Clarence, Richard's brother, executed in 1478.

George Neville, Archbishop of York, Warwick the Kingmaker's youngest brother.

George Neville, Duke of Bedford, Warwick the Kingmaker's nephew.

Henry VI, the last king of the House of Lancaster.

Henry VII, the first king of the House of Tudor.

Isabel Neville, Warwick the Kingmaker's elder daughter and George, Duke of Clarence's wife.

John Neville, Marquis Montagu, Warwick the Kingmaker's brother.

Margaret of Anjou, Henry VI's wife.

Margaret Beaufort, Countess of Richmond, Henry Tudor's mother.

Margaret, Duchess of Burgundy, Richard's youngest surviving sister.

Richard, Duke of Gloucester, afterwards King Richard III.

Richard Neville, Earl of Salisbury, Richard's uncle and Warwick the Kingmaker's father.

Richard Neville, Earl of Warwick, the 'Kingmaker', Richard's cousin.

Richard, Duke of York, Richard's father, killed in 1460.

Richard, Duke of York, Edward IV's son, the younger of the 'Princes in the Tower'.

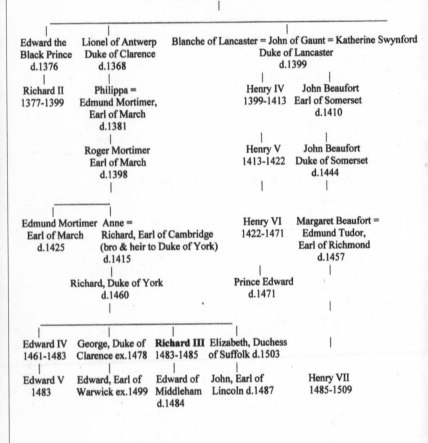

Edward III 1327-1377

Edward the Black Prince d.1376

Richard II 1377-1399

Lionel of Antwerp Duke of Clarence d.1368

Philippa = Edmund Mortimer, Earl of March d.1381

Roger Mortimer Earl of March d.1398

Edmund Mortimer Earl of March d.1425

Anne = Richard, Earl of Cambridge (bro & heir to Duke of York) d.1415

Richard, Duke of York d.1460

Blanche of Lancaster = John of Gaunt = Katherine Swynford
Duke of Lancaster
d.1399

Henry IV 1399-1413

John Beaufort Earl of Somerset d.1410

Henry V 1413-1422

John Beaufort Duke of Somerset d.1444

Henry VI 1422-1471

Margaret Beaufort = Edmund Tudor, Earl of Richmond d.1457

Prince Edward d.1471

Edward IV 1461-1483

George, Duke of Clarence ex.1478

Richard III 1483-1485

Elizabeth, Duchess of Suffolk d.1503

Edward V 1483

Edward, Earl of Warwick ex.1499

Edward of Middleham d.1484

John, Earl of Lincoln d.1487

Henry VII 1485-1509

1. The Houses of York, Lancaster and Tudor.

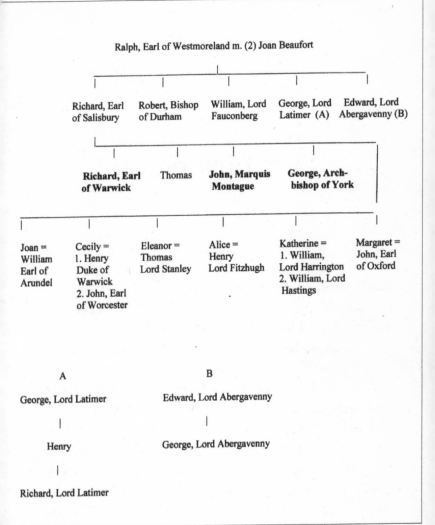

Ralph, Earl of Westmoreland m. (2) Joan Beaufort

| Richard, Earl of Salisbury | Robert, Bishop of Durham | William, Lord Fauconberg | George, Lord Latimer (A) | Edward, Lord Abergavenny (B) |

| Richard, Earl of Warwick | Thomas | John, Marquis Montague | George, Archbishop of York |

| Joan = William Earl of Arundel | Cecily = 1. Henry Duke of Warwick 2. John, Earl of Worcester | Eleanor = Thomas Lord Stanley | Alice = Henry Lord Fitzhugh | Katherine = 1. William, Lord Harrington 2. William, Lord Hastings | Margaret = John, Earl of Oxford |

A

George, Lord Latimer

|

Henry

|

Richard, Lord Latimer

B

Edward, Lord Abergavenny

|

George, Lord Abergavenny

2. The Junior Nevilles.

INTRODUCTION

Most of the books written about Richard III portray him as either very good or very bad. A man who was either a villain or who has been unjustifiably vilified throughout history. Modern works such as Annette Carson's *Richard III. The Maligned King*, and Desmond Seward's *Richard III. England's Black Legend*, stand on opposite sides of a debate that has already lasted for five centuries, and it is possible to wonder how two authors working from the same body of evidence could reach such widely differing conclusions. Surely, the contemporaries who produced the evidence – and who knew Richard or talked with those who remembered him – would have known what sort of man, and king, he was?

It is not quite that simple, however. Late medieval authors were sometimes no better informed than their modern counterparts, and could just as easily fall victim to their own prejudices. The detailed, personal information that informs modern biographies is seldom available for the medieval period, and Richard's defenders may have misrepresented him as much as his critics. It seems improbable that any human being could be as evil – or alternatively as misunderstood – as Richard, and my starting point is that somewhere behind all the conflicting argument stands a real man who had both qualities and failings. Neither black nor white, but – like all of us – somewhere in between.

Richard III is an enigma because for most of his life he worked loyally and diligently to support his royal brother King Edward IV. At first glance it appears that it was only in the three months which elapsed between Edward's death and his own accession that he behaved atrociously and out of character. But first glances can prove deceptive. Was the man who deposed the nephew he should have protected really a 'different' Richard, or were the traits that appear to manifest themselves in this short period always part of his make-up? Taking the throne was his most dramatic decision, but it was only one incident in a life that spanned almost thirty-three years. We need to see him in the round, to examine episodes in his career both before and after he became king, to try to understand his mindset. Only then can we tell if the Richard who seized the Crown was the same Richard who had played a leading, and generally commendable, role in the politics of the late 1460s, 1470s and early 1480s, or if his character had changed over time.

When Jonathan Reeve at Amberley Publishing suggested I write about Richard, I hesitated. There seemed to be so many books about him available already that I wondered if another one was needed. But the more I read the more I concluded that, half a century after Paul Murray Kendall's pioneering work, there was room for a new, concise *biography* as opposed to a thesis dealing with some aspects of his life and reign. It has become fashionable to start with a particular episode in the subject's life even if he/she is only born one or two chapters later, but this invariably involves repetition – as well as being potentially more confusing – and I have chosen to 'begin at the beginning and finish at the end'.

There are occasions when my approach has been more thematic – sometimes, it seemed better to follow a topic to its logical conclusion than to return to it in succeeding chapters – but my overriding aim has been to approach the subject dispassionately without preconceptions. I hope that the book offers a fairer, more balanced, portrait of him than some others, and that it will interest students familiar with the period as well as those coming to it for the first time.

Historians are often torn between retaining the original medieval spelling when quoting from contemporary documents and turning them into modern English. The medieval form helps to convey something of the flavour of the period, but I have decided, for the sake of clarity, to use modern English here. Like everyone who has studied Richard, I owe a vast debt to the industry of others, and am grateful to Peter Hammond and Geoffrey Wheeler for reading my manuscript and suggesting a number of improvements. Mistakes which remain are entirely my own.

The first edition of this book was published several months before the excavation of part of the Franciscan friary in Leicester and the unearthing of Richard III's skeleton, twenty-six years after I first predicted in a journal article titled 'King Richard's Grave in Leicester' that his remains would be found on the site at some point in the twenty-first century. My initial thought was that it would be necessary to rewrite some of the original text in the light of this, but on reflection it seemed preferable to leave the body of the book unaltered and to gather the new material into a new final chapter.

David Baldwin,
7 February 2013

PROLOGUE:
CONFLICTING OPINIONS

Richard III is an enigma. His reign of only twenty-six months is one of the shortest in English history, yet few other kings have had so much calumny heaped upon them or been subjected to such intense scrutiny. Edward II may, or may not, have been murdered at Berkeley Castle on the orders of Roger Mortimer and Queen Isabella, and King John may, or may not, have killed his nephew Prince Arthur: but these 'crimes' are somehow less notorious than King Richard's alleged involvement in the deaths of Henry VI and Prince Edward of Lancaster, and the disappearance of his own nephews, the Princes in the Tower.

So why this fascination with a king who, most would agree, brought about the ruin of his dynasty and who died more than five hundred years ago? Was he a man of ability and courage who has been misunderstood by History, or are his apologists guilty of trying to excuse the inexcusable? Ability and ruthlessness often walk hand in hand of course, and the most successful rulers are not always the most popular. Perhaps the real problem is that we know that Edward II and King John had more failings than virtues, but there are too many apparent contradictions in Richard III's life for him to be neatly pigeonholed as 'good' or 'bad'.

Some contemporary writers are often quoted for their apparent praise of Richard while others are cited by his critics for the opposite reason; but they cannot always be taken at face value and few are quite as pro- or anti- as they may appear at first glance. One of the King's earliest admirers was Thomas Langton, a career clergyman whose good service to Edward IV had been rewarded with a number of religious sinecures and who had Richard to thank for his promotion to the bishopric of St David's in July 1483. Langton accompanied Richard on his royal progress, or tour, of his kingdom that summer, and found time between the receptions and entertainments that punctuated their travels to write to his friend William Selling, the prior of Christ Church, Canterbury. His letter is concerned mainly with obtaining wine from Bordeaux and with recent diplomatic contacts, but concludes with this ringing tribute to his new royal master:

> He [Richard] contents the people where he goes best that ever did prince; for many a poor man that hath suffered wrong many days have been relieved and helped by him and his commands in his progress. And in many great cities and towns were great sums of money given him which he hath refused. On my truth I liked never the conditions of any prince so well as his; God has sent him to us for the weal of us all.[1]

Langton assumed that his words would remain private, so he was clearly not engaged in a propaganda exercise; but it is apparent from other evidence that King Richard admired him as much as he admired King Richard. When, in December 1484, Richard asked the dean and chapter of Salisbury cathedral to accept him as their next bishop, he referred to 'the laudable merits, high virtues, and profound cunning [learning]' of 'the right reverend father in God our right trusty and right well beloved counsellor the bishop of St. David[s]'. And for his 'continued truth and faithful services to us in sundry wises done to our singular pleasure [we] desire and heartily pray you that in your said election you will have him to the said pre-eminence and pastoral dignity before all other, especially recommended and preferred'.[2] Langton was a northerner (from Appleby in Westmoreland), and it has been suggested that his comments would have been endorsed by many other residents of northern England; but it would be unwise to rely too much on the opinion of a man who, for all his undoubted qualities, basked in the glow of royal approval and owed a great deal to the king he praised.

Nearest in time to Langton, but very different in outlook, was an Italian clergyman called Dominic Mancini who came to England late in 1482 or early in 1483. He was probably hoping to obtain snippets of information that his patron Angelo Cato, Archbishop of Vienne, could pass on to the King of France, Louis XI, and as luck would have it found himself ideally placed to record the events that followed Edward IV's death in April. It is unlikely that he could speak or read English and admits that his memory may be defective in some particulars; but he had at least one good informant in John Argentine, the young Edward V's doctor, and his work flatly contradicted the claim that Richard III's accession was greeted with almost universal approval. Unfortunately (from our viewpoint), Cato ordered Mancini home shortly after Richard's coronation, and he concluded his memoir at Beaugency in Orleans on 1 December 1483.

Mancini could not verify the accuracy of his information, but he had no personal or vested interest in what happened in England and would not have fed Cato deliberate falsehoods. Dr Argentine told him that the deposed boy-king (the elder of the Princes in the Tower) 'like a victim prepared for sacrifice, sought remission of his sins by daily confession and penance because he believed that death was facing him', and there is no reason to doubt his assertion that 'I have seen many men burst forth into tears and lamentations when mention was made of him [Edward] after his removal from men's sight'. Already, there was a rumour that he had 'been done away with', and Mancini laid the blame for this and the other events of that dramatic summer squarely at Richard of Gloucester's door.[3]

Mancini thought that Richard had aimed at the throne from the moment of his brother's death, perhaps earlier: but he was careful not to allow his imagination to run away with him or deny that Richard had some redeeming qualities. He qualifies his remark that Edward V had been 'done away with' by adding 'whether, however, he has been done away with, and by what manner of death, so far I have not at all discovered', and admits that 'the good reputation of his [Richard's] private life and public activities powerfully attracted the esteem of strangers. Such was his renown in warfare that, whenever a difficult and dangerous policy had to be undertaken, it would be entrusted to his discretion and his generalship.' An able man, but, in Mancini's opinion, a ruthless one. 'Some ... who understood his ambition and deceit, always suspected whither his enterprises would lead.'[4]

The House Books of the City of York contain two comments written shortly after Richard's death that are often cited as further proof of his popularity in northern England. The clerk, John Harrington, recorded how 'King Richard, late mercifully reigning upon us ... was piteously slain and murdered to the great heaviness of this city' when he heard the news of Bosworth, and described the late King as 'the most famous prince of blessed memory' when recalling a grant he had made to the city some two months later.[5] Harrington's admiration for Richard appears to have been as genuine as Langton's, but it was not shared by some of his fellow citizens. In 1482 one Roger Brere, 'saddiller', had allegedly remarked that 'as touching my lord of Gloucester, what might he do for the city? Nothing but grin of us', and when Richard asked the council to surrender rights of common over land belonging to St Nicholas's hospital two years later, he provoked a riot.[6] John Burton, the schoolmaster of St Leonard's, was held to have said that the late King was 'an hypocrite, a crouchback, and buried in a dike like a dog' in 1490, a slur his accuser John Painter challenged by asserting that, on the contrary, King Henry had buried him 'like a noble gentleman'.[7] Curiously, Painter did not dispute that Richard was both a crouchback and a hypocrite, a claim not unlike the earlier accusation that there were times when he would 'grin' at their plight.

One of our most authoritative sources for the Yorkist period is the so-called 'second continuation' of the Croyland Chronicle, a work composed at Croyland (modern Crowland) Abbey in the Lincolnshire fen country in April 1486. Its author does not identify himself, and it is unclear if he visited Croyland personally or if the monks acquired a copy of his memoir; but a marginal note indicates that he was a doctor of canon law who was sent on a diplomatic mission to Burgundy in 1471. Unfortunately the record of precisely who went to Burgundy on that occasion is missing, and the writer could have been any one of perhaps no fewer than six individuals.[8] But whoever he was, he was clearly at the heart of both Edward IV's and Richard III's governments and knew a great deal about what was going on.

The continuator's view of Richard is that he obtained the throne by first deceiving and then eliminating all who would have opposed him (they were removed 'without justice or judgement'), and that terror was one of the principal weapons in his armoury. Elizabeth

Woodville, Edward IV's widow, surrendered her daughters to him only 'after frequent entreaties as well as threats had been made use of', and his letters summoning his subjects to join him before the battle of Bosworth made it clear that 'whoever should be found in any part of the kingdom after the victory had been gained, to have omitted appearing in his presence on the field, was to expect no other fate than the loss of all his goods and possessions, as well as his life'. His instruction to execute Lord Stanley's son Lord Strange when his father failed to commit himself is condemned as 'this cruel order of the king', and there is a distinct note of sarcasm in the writer's observation that 'from this day forward, as long as he lived, this man was *styled* [my italics] King Richard, the third of that name'.[9]

Richard was safely dead when the chronicler penned his memoir and he could speak the truth without fear or favour; but he does not accuse Richard of the Princes' murder and acknowledges that he possessed some more admirable qualities. His 'great activity and vigilance' meant that he was always one step ahead of his treacherous former ally, the Duke of Buckingham, and he was as devastated as any parent when his eight-year-old son Edward died suddenly in April 1484. The continuator, who was present, reported that 'you might have seen his father and mother in a state almost bordering on madness, by reason of their sudden grief'; but he added that Richard quickly pulled himself together and 'took all necessary precautions for the defence of his party'. He is careful to state that the King was slain at Bosworth 'while fighting, and *not in the act of flight*' (my italics), and 'fell in the field like a brave and most valiant prince'.[10]

Another writer whose view of Richard is usually assumed to be entirely negative is the Warwickshire ecclesiastic John Rous. Rous, a chantry priest at Guy's Cliff, was a great admirer of the earls of Warwick, and described them in two pictorial rolls, one in English and the other in Latin, which he may have completed by the summer of 1483. Both versions included a ringing tribute to King Richard, the husband of Anne Neville, the younger daughter of 'Warwick the Kingmaker'; but at some point after August 1485 he excised this from the Latin copy and replaced it with *'Ricardus tertius Rex Anglie … infelix maritus'* ('Richard the Third King of England … unfortunate husband'). One drawing of Richard was replaced by a picture of Edward III, a representation of Prince Edward of Lancaster (Anne's first husband) was inserted into a later family grouping, and Richard's wife and son were shorn of their royal regalia. Rous would, presumably, have done the same to the English version if he could have got his hands on it, but fortunately, it had passed beyond his reach.[11]

Rous's neat handiwork would make it impossible to say what he *really* thought of Richard III if this was all we had to go on, but we also possess his *Historia Regnum Angliae*, written at some time between the battle of Bosworth and his death in 1491 or the beginning of 1492. His account of Richard's reign has been appositely described by Alison Hanham as a 'rag-bag of gleanings', although some of them are assertions, or scraps of information, not found elsewhere. Perhaps the best known is the statement that the King was 'retained within his mother's womb for two years, emerging with teeth and hair to his shoulders', an allegation as fanciful and as mistaken as the claim that he was born under the sign of Scorpio 'and like a scorpion he combined a smooth front with a stinging tail'. He was also 'excessively cruel', his reign 'ended with no lamentation from his groaning subjects', and 'like the Antichrist to come, he was confounded at his moment of greatest pride'.[12]

Rous is more strident, more damning in his condemnation of Richard, than any of the other writers we have considered, but even he is prepared to concede that some of the late King's actions were commendable and that he had at least two personal qualities. He was 'praiseworthy for his building ... at Westminster, Nottingham, Warwick, York, Middleham and many other places', for founding 'a noble chantry for a hundred priests in the cathedral of York', together with colleges at Middleham and in the chapel of St Mary at Barking by the Tower of London, and for endowing Queens' College, Cambridge, with 500 marks' annual rent. 'The money which was offered him by the peoples of London, Gloucester and Worcester he declined with thanks, affirming that he would rather have their love than their treasure' (q.v. Langton), and at Bosworth 'bore himself like a noble soldier, and honourably defended himself to his last breath, shouting again and again that he was betrayed'.[13]

Remarkably perhaps, there was at least one former servant of Richard who owed his living to the Tudors but who was still prepared to defend his late master after 1485. When in 1554 Henry Parker, Lord Morley, produced a work entitled *Account of Miracles performed by the Holy Eucharist* for the edification of Queen Mary, he recalled that half a century earlier, when he had been in service to Henry VII's mother Margaret Beaufort, he had heard Sir Ralph Bigod challenge anyone who 'dispraised' Richard in his presence. Bigod had been carver to Richard's wife Queen Anne (the capacity in which he was then serving Margaret), and had joined the King's household after her death. He had been wounded fighting for Richard at Bosworth and would have died if Henry had 'taken him in that heat' of battle; but his good fortune in being able to continue his career under the new dynasty had not changed his opinions. Fortunately (and perhaps surprisingly), Lady Margaret praised his stance because, in the opinion of Retha M. Warnicke, 'whatever she thought about Richard III's actions, he had been crowned king, an event she had witnessed and which had placed him by her reckoning above the criticism of his social inferiors'. Alternatively, Margaret had herself experienced many vicissitudes of fortune, and may have approved of loyalty even when it was 'misplaced'.[14]

We could continue this survey by considering the views of slightly later writers, but perhaps enough had been said to give the flavour of the mixed messages we would continue to encounter. Sir Thomas More, who wrote his *History of King Richard III* about 1513, and Polydore Vergil, whose *Anglica Historia* was completed at about the same time, both talked with people who had known Richard; but More was only seven when Richard was killed at Bosworth, and Vergil (Henry VII's court historian) did not come to England until 1502. Already, we have reached a point where the author's knowledge is wholly second-hand, and while both writers have much to tell us they were not present when the events they described happened. If there is a single comment that sums Richard up in a nutshell, it is perhaps that of the *Great Chronicle of London*:

and thus ended this man with dishonour as he that sought it, for had he continued still protector and have suffered the children [the Princes] to have prospered according to his allegiance and fidelity, he should have been honourably lauded over all, whereas now his fame is dirked and dishonoured ... but God that is all merciful forgive him his misdeeds.[15]

I

'RICHARD LIVETH YET', 1452–1461

Richard was born at Fotheringhay Castle in Northamptonshire on 2 October 1452, the eleventh child of Richard, Duke of York, and his wife Cecily Neville, and the youngest to survive infancy. His earliest memories would have been of the great stone castle by the River Nene founded by the Norman knight Simon de Senlis, and of the magnificent collegiate church dedicated to St Mary and All Saints a short distance away. He would have seen – and perhaps marvelled at – the expensive memorials of his great grandfather, Edward III's son, Edmund of Langley, the first Duke of York, and his great uncle, Edward of Norwich, the second Duke, who had died at Agincourt. Today, the chancel has gone, the tombs are Elizabethan replacements, and all that remains of the castle is a grassy mound and a single block of masonry by the river. But shades of greatness still linger and evoke the sense of a lost medieval world.

No one would have supposed that Richard would one day become the head of his family, still less King of England, and contemporary writers seldom noticed him in his father's lifetime. The first to do so was the compiler of an armorial history of members of the Clare family and their association with Clare Priory in Suffolk. Richard,

Duke of York, was descended from the Clare earls of Gloucester, and his children are described in the following poem:

> After the time of long barrenness, [the Yorks had remained childless
> for some years after their marriage]
> God first sent Anne, which signifyeth grace,
> In token that at her heart's heaviness,
> He as for barrenness would from them chase.
> Harry, Edward, Edmund, each in his place
> Succeeded; and after twain daughters came
> Elizabeth and Margaret, and afterwards William.
> John after William next born was,
> Which both be passed to God's grace:
> George was next, and after Thomas
> Born was, which son after did pace
> By the path of death into the heavenly place.
> *Richard liveth yet;* [my italics] but the last of all
> Was Ursula, to Him who God list call.

The 'Clare Roll', as it is known today, was drawn up in May 1456 when Richard would have been between three and four years old. The author goes on to explain that Anne has been married to the Duke of Exeter 'in her tender youth', that Henry (Harry) has also died, presumably (although not certainly) since the above was written, and that Edward and Edmund have been created earls of March and Rutland. He has no doubt that the Duke and Duchess will provide their four youngest children with appropriate titles and marriage partners when the time comes.

The phrase 'Richard liveth yet' led the Victorian scholar James Gairdner and some later commentators to assume that Richard was a sickly child whose life was sometimes despaired of, but a straightforward reading of the poem does not imply this. All the writer says is that Richard is still alive – unlike four of his brothers and one of his sisters, who have all predeceased him. The writer does not mention the state of health of any of Richard's surviving siblings, and was, apparently, concerned only to record how many offspring the Duke and Duchess had at that moment and what advantages had been obtained for them. Richard may have been smaller, and less robust, than his elder brothers, but there is no evidence for it here.[1]

It would be fascinating to know how Richard spent his earliest years, where he lived and who may have influenced him, but all this is unfortunately lost to us. Paul Murray Kendall surmises that he remained at Fotheringhay with Margaret and George, the two children nearest him in age, and that he did not meet his two eldest brothers, Edward and Edmund, until he was in his seventh year or venture north of the River Trent until he was nine. None of this is certain, however. It is perhaps more likely that he was moved at different times to his father's other strongholds at Sandal in Yorkshire and Ludlow and Wigmore in the Welsh Marches, and that the whole family came together at Christmas and on great occasions until the political situation deteriorated towards the end of the 1450s. Richard, Duke of York, was a member of the royal family, the reigning King Henry VI's heir apparent until the Queen, Margaret of Anjou, gave birth to a son in 1453. In normal circumstances he would have been the Crown's first counsellor, but Henry was a weak man who allowed his wife and certain noblemen who enjoyed her favour to dominate him to their own advantage. York found himself all but excluded from the royal presence and drawn into conflict with some who, in happier circumstances, would have been both colleagues and friends.

Richard of York undoubtedly believed that liberating the King from the control of a small faction and reforming his policies was in England's, as well as his own, best interests, but medieval monarchs were their own masters and could not be overruled whatever the circumstances. He found himself in the same position as earlier rebels against royal authority, men like Simon de Montfort and Thomas of Lancaster, who had both failed to persuade incompetent rulers to govern more wisely and who had lost their lives when they resorted to arms. At the beginning of 1452, the year Richard was born, York followed in their footsteps when he confronted King Henry and his supporters at Dartford in Kent. He may have hoped that the threat of civil war would bring the court party to its senses; but few people who mattered politically were willing to back him and he was left with no alternative but to disband his army and promise not to oppose the royal will in future. He was lucky: some kings would have beheaded him for less.

It was against this background, a steady, almost inexorable, slide into conflict, that Richard spent his infancy and boyhood. When he grew a little older he would have learned that on two occasions, the first when King Henry suffered a severe mental illness in August 1453, and again in the aftermath of the Yorkist victory at the first battle of St Albans two years later, his father had finally been brought into the government, but these appointments lasted only until the King recovered or the Queen regained the initiative. In March 1458 Henry arranged what became known as a 'loveday' in the course of which York and Queen Margaret walked arm in arm together to St Paul's Cathedral, but it was a charade that did nothing to mollify the ill-feeling between them. The situation again deteriorated, and York, his two elder sons, and his principal allies – his brother-in-law Richard Neville, Earl of Salisbury, and Salisbury's son, Richard, Earl of Warwick – were forced into exile after they were confronted by a much larger royal army at Ludford Bridge, near Ludlow, in October 1459.

The three great lords who fled into the night from Ludlow were all called Richard: but they left behind them another Richard, the Duke of York's youngest son, now just seven. He had been staying in the castle with his parents, and was captured by the triumphant royalists together with his mother, Duchess Cecily, and next brother, George.[2] Wives and children were not normally punished for their husbands' and fathers' misdemeanours, but the close family of a convicted traitor could expect few favours.[3] Cecily and her boys were placed in the custody of her sister, the Duchess of Buckingham, where, according to a chronicler, she (and presumably George and Richard) was 'kept full straight [with] many a great rebuke'.[4]

The Duke of York and his second son Edmund made their way to Ireland while Salisbury, Warwick, and Edward of March found refuge in Calais. They spent the next eight months planning their return and co-ordinating strategy, but it was only the three Calais-based lords who landed at Sandwich in Kent on 26 June 1460. Making their way rapidly northwards, Warwick and Edward found the King's army still assembling near Northampton, and on 10 July won a decisive victory. Duchess Cecily and her younger children were released from custody, and on reaching London in mid-September were accommodated in the late Sir John Fastolf's house at Southwark. When, shortly afterwards, the Duke of York returned from Ireland he summoned Cecily to meet him at Hereford, and she left George, Richard and their sister Margaret in the care of Edward, who, we are told, visited them every day.[5]

Fastolf Place, where Richard was to spend the next few months of his life, was a mansion on the south bank of the Thames just opposite the Tower of London, a world away from his father's cold, isolated Norman castles. Sir John Fastolf had spent more than £1,650 (over £600,000 in today's money) on the purchase and development of the site in the years after 1439, and it now boasted a substantial dwelling surrounded by a walled moat a quarter of a mile in circumference. It was approached by a stone causeway leading to a drawbridge, the numerous outbuildings included two granaries, a bakehouse, stables and a larder house, there was a wharf on the northern (river) side, and to the south a pleasant garden with elm trees. Of the house itself only a few particulars can be gleaned from the surviving records, but the features mentioned include 'my lord's chamber and closet', lodgings for the yeomen of the chamber, the hall, the 'great gallery', the buttery, the kitchen, and the cellar. Richard must have spent many hours watching the boats on the river or playing in the garden in the autumn sunshine, and would have eagerly anticipated trips into the bustling city beyond the wall.[6]

All this was to be short-lived, however. When the Duke of York returned to London he surprised everyone – his friends as much as his opponents – by declaring that he, not Henry VI, was the rightful king. It was true that he was descended from an elder son of King Edward III in the female line whereas Henry was the offspring of a younger son of King Edward in the male line; but Henry was an anointed sovereign whose father and grandfather had been kings before him and who had already reigned over his subjects for thirty-eight years. The Earl of Warwick brokered an uneasy compromise by which Henry would remain king for his lifetime and would then cede the throne to York and his successors; but Queen Margaret had no intention of allowing her son's birthright to be given away.

On 9 December, the Duke of York, his son Edmund of Rutland, and the Earl of Salisbury left London to confront the army the Queen was assembling in northern England, while Edward of March made for Wales to deal with royalist sympathisers who were recruiting men there. Details are sketchy, but on the last day of the month the Duke and his men were enticed or tricked into leaving the safety of Sandal Castle, and were overwhelmed by their enemies' superior numbers. The three Yorkist leaders were all killed in the battle or executed afterwards, and a few days later the eight-year-old Richard would have learned that he had lost his father, an uncle, and a doubtless admired elder brother. He may not have understood much of what had happened at Ludlow, but he would have been deeply affected by this.

Queen Margaret's victorious army now headed for London, her hardy northern soldiers taking whatever they needed to sustain them and bringing fear to every place they approached. The Earl of Warwick, who was organising resistance in the capital, issued calls to arms emphasising the threat posed by 'the misruled and outrageous people in the north parts of this realm, coming towards these parts to the destruction thereof, of you, and subversion of all our land',[7] while the prior of Croyland described them still more colourfully as 'locusts' who 'swept onwards like a whirlwind' destroying everything in their path.[8] On 17 February they routed Warwick's forces at the second battle of St Albans, and the Yorkist cause seemed lost.

The leading citizens of London sent a deputation of noble ladies to beg the Queen not to unleash her undisciplined forces on the city, and Duchess Cecily took steps to ensure that her two youngest sons, George and Richard, did not share the fate of their brother Edmund. She had already asked Philip, Duke of Burgundy, to give them refuge when the news of her husband's death was brought to her, and in the meantime, perhaps when she heard of Margaret's approach or in the aftermath of Warwick's defeat at St Albans, arranged for them to be lodged with a local widow, Alice Martyn. We know almost nothing of Alice or precisely where she resided, but the grant of a hundred shillings a year she received from their eldest brother, Edward, after he became king, described how she had been responsible for 'receiving and keeping our right entirely beloved brethren, the dukes of Clarence and Gloucester [George and Richard] from danger and peril in their troubles unto the time of their departing out of this our realm into the parts of Flanders'.[9]

Alice's house would have given the boys a degree of anonymity and protection they would not have enjoyed in the great mansion at Southwark, but they were still sent to the greater safety of Utrecht, in the Low Countries, probably as soon as a favourable reply was received from Duke Philip and arrangements could be made for their safe passage. Philip's authority in Utrecht was informal – his illegitimate son David was the town's bishop – and the implication is that although he was willing to help the Duke of York's family he was not prepared to receive George and Richard personally. There was no reason to suppose that the Yorkists would recover from these setbacks or that Henry and Margaret would cease to be King and Queen.

But this is precisely what did happen. Queen Margaret was persuaded not to force an entry into London, and was left with little alternative but to allow her army to retire northwards. In the meantime Edward of March had defeated the Welsh royalists at Mortimer's Cross on 2 or 3 February, and moving eastwards linked up with the remnants of Warwick's forces in the Cotswolds. They were welcomed into London a few days later (the Londoners did not fear them as they had Margaret's soldiers), and rapidly took stock of the situation. Henry VI had been their prisoner in the period between the battles of Northampton and second St Albans, and this had allowed them to claim that they were acting with royal approval; but now that Margaret had 'recaptured' him their only realistic course of action was to declare that he had never been their lawful sovereign. Edward, Earl of March and titular Duke of York since the death of his father, was proclaimed King Edward IV, the first king of the House of York, on 4 March 1461.

King Edward mustered his forces and destroyed his rival's army at Towton (Yorks.) on 29 March, Palm Sunday, in what was destined to be the largest, and bloodiest, battle of the entire civil conflict. Word of his accession reached Burgundy about 9 March; but it was only when he heard of the victory of Towton almost a month later that Duke Philip felt able to treat George and Richard as members of a new royal family. They arrived in Sluys on 9 April accompanied by twenty-three persons, and were entertained there for a week (perhaps to allow time for confirmation of their brother's victory to reach the Low Countries), before being conducted to the ducal court at Bruges. There, the Milanese ambassador noted that 'the two brothers of King Edward have arrived, one eleven [*sic*] and the other twelve years of age. The duke, who is most kind in everything, has been to visit them at their lodging, and showed them great reverence.' The town accounts record that 'a banquet was given to our dread lord [Philip] and the children of York in the alderman's hall, where the ladies of the city were invited and where also many other noble lords of our aforesaid dread lord's blood and council were present'.[10]

Duke Philip left Bruges for St Omer on 22 April, and George and Richard were escorted to English-held Calais by a distinguished entourage that included Philip, the Bastard of Brabant and many gentlemen. They crossed the Channel shortly after the 28th, and were conducted to Canterbury, where they were feted by the leading citizens. The mayor and aldermen of London formally received them at Billingsgate on 2 June, and ten days later they knelt before their brother Edward when he arrived at Greenwich. They knew his success was entirely responsible for the dramatic upturn in their own fortunes, but had no inkling of how it would change the course of both their careers.

Richard was still only eight years old when he returned to England, but already his experiences must have begun to condition his outlook on life generally. It would be pointless to speculate how much the violent deaths of three of his closest relatives – and the time he had spent under house arrest, in hiding, and in exile – had affected him personally; but he now knew how violently the wheel of fortune could spin both for and against him and how few things could be taken for granted. Had this boy who would one day be king already decided, albeit in his own childish way, that when he grew up he would do everything in his power to ensure that nothing like this ever happened to him again?

2

THE KING'S BROTHER, 1461–1469

If Richard had remained the youngest son of a duke he might have entered the Church and ended his days as an abbot or bishop: but now he was the brother of a king and second in line to the throne. He was bound to become a major player in both war and politics, and the honours he received reflected his new status. On Friday 26 June 1461, two days before Edward's coronation, he rode to the Tower with his brothers, escorted by the mayor and aldermen dressed in scarlet, and next day was dubbed a knight of the Bath. He became Duke of Gloucester some four months later (George had been created Duke of Clarence immediately after the coronation), and they were both then elected to the Order of the Garter. Soon, he was being nominally commissioned to levy troops to subdue pockets of resistance to the new government, and became titular Admiral of England, Ireland and Aquitaine, the territory in south-western France from which the English had been driven in 1453.

Richard did not undertake these responsibilities in person: instead his royal brother appointed deputies, experienced men who would act for him. Kendall has him riding into Leicester at the age of eleven wearing full armour and leading a body of men he had raised in south-western England,[1] but he is unlikely to have done anything of the sort. There is no evidence that he attended the Parliament that met at Westminster in April 1463, nor was he asked to perform any formal duty at the Queen's coronation two years later – unlike George, three years his senior, who acted as Steward. War, politics and ceremony could be left to others for the moment, but his turn would come soon enough.

The years of waiting may have seemed dull, frustrating even on occasion, but King Edward was mindful of his little brother and was already planning to endow him with the lands he would need to maintain his status in society. A new and insecure ruler could not always do as he wished, however, and the grants Richard received in August 1462 proved to be less permanent than those given to George and to some of Edward's supporters who were not members of the royal family. The lordship of Richmond in Yorkshire was soon transferred to George, who coveted it, while that of Pembroke in Wales remained firmly under the control of William Herbert, who became its earl in 1468. The de Vere estates forfeited by the twelfth Earl of Oxford in 1462 were lost when his son was restored to the title in January 1464, and although Edward gave Richard lands in Berkshire and Wiltshire that had formerly belonged to Robert, Lord Hungerford, to compensate him for the loss of Richmond, he repossessed them only six months later. A grant of the recently attainted Duke of Somerset's manors in December 1463 did not help much (the Duke had been poorly endowed and there were two widows to be provided for), and although the Hungerford lands were restored to Richard in October 1468 they yielded him perhaps only £500 a year. A grant of the Duchy of Lancaster lordships of Bolingbroke in Lincolnshire, and Pickering and Barnoldswick in

Yorkshire, augmented his annual income by £1,000 from 1465 onwards, but it was no great sum for a royal duke.[2]

Richard was also given his own household, an establishment that included – or came to include – four 'henchmen' (well-born boys of his own age who would be brought up with him), servants, and even minstrels. We know something of this because King Edward, or, more precisely, the Great Wardrobe, met many of the expenses, partly perhaps because his brother lacked the means to pay them himself. It is sometimes difficult to distinguish between items supplied to Richard and those intended for George or their sister Margaret; but in the period covered by the two surviving accounts (17 April 1461 to 4 April 1465) he received woollen cloths, linen, silks and furs (large quantities of ermine, miniver, sable and marten), from which to make shirts, hose, gowns, doublets and other garments and bedding. There was also a harness (a suit of armour), bowstrings, three 'Irish mantles' (heavy cloaks), gloves, and no fewer than 222 hats and bonnets and 204 pairs of shoes. It is a reasonable assumption that many of these were for members of his household rather than for his own personal use.[3]

The goods were sent at various times to Greenwich, Westminster and even Leicester, and the fact that they included spurs, saddles, bits, reins and other riding equipment leaves little doubt that Richard and his household sometimes travelled with the King. He was at Christ Church Priory, Canterbury, with both his brothers in August 1463, and at St Mary's church, Warwick, probably with the Earl of Warwick and his family, at some time in 1464–5. These and other journeys would have allowed him to observe the country he would one day rule over, perhaps with greater understanding than when he had been a small child. Late fifteenth-century England was a land of small cities and smaller towns – only

London, York, Bristol and Coventry had populations of more than a few thousand – and beyond them, in the vast, often empty, rural areas, were abbeys, manor houses, villages with thatched cottages and great open fields, sheep farms, woodlands, and the remains of settlements depopulated by the Black Death. Like everyone, Richard would have been impressed by some sights, the grandeur of the great cathedrals for example, but inconvenienced or disturbed by others. The ancient, pitted roads could turn into quagmires when they were not frozen solid, and a glance at the quarters of traitors impaled on town gates would have reminded him that he had not always been a prince and might not always be one in the future. He could not have failed to notice the contrast between the privileged existence of his own class and the poverty and squalor that characterised the lives of most Englishmen, but his companions would have laughed at any suggestion that this was unfair or intolerable. The ordering of society was a matter for God, not men.

Later generations would shield lads of Richard's age from some of the world's starker realities, but this was an era in which life expectancy was short and children grew up quickly. Roughly half the population died before reaching the age of twenty, and although there were some notable exceptions (Bishop Richard Bell of Carlisle was eighty-five when he died in 1495 for example), not many could expect to live beyond forty or fifty. A boy as young as seven was deemed to be criminally responsible and could be hanged for theft; children who had married in accordance with their parents' wishes often began to cohabit at fourteen; and Richard would find himself commanding a division of his brother Edward's army when he was still only eighteen. He was little more than a youth, but it was a young person's world.

By 1464 Richard had begun to accustom himself to his new life and put the memories of his earliest years behind him, but he was about to encounter a problem that, in one form or another, would never quite leave him. When the royal council met at Reading Abbey in September his brother King Edward startled the assembled notables by announcing that he had contracted a secret marriage with Elizabeth Woodville, the daughter of a Northamptonshire baron, Lord Rivers. English kings had traditionally married foreign princesses to secure the large dowries and political and military alliances they invariably brought with them (advantages that were lost if monarchs wedded one of their own subjects), and to make matters worse Elizabeth was already a widow and the mother of two young sons. Edward could have taken her as his mistress without anyone blinking an eyelid; but his marriage was a matter of public policy and his friends were appalled that he had deceived them to please himself.

The now eleven-year-old Richard may or may not have been present when Edward made his shocking admission, but he would soon have become aware of its consequences. The new Queen was a member of a large family – she had five brothers and six, or possibly seven, sisters besides her two sons[4] – and would expect her husband to provide them with noble marriage partners and give them appropriate offices and titles. Members of other families who had hoped to secure these appointments, or wed their own children to the young heirs and heiresses siphoned off by the Woodvilles, were inevitably disappointed, and none more than the Earl of Warwick, who had been negotiating Edward's marriage to a French princess and who had been made to appear foolish. It may have been partly to appease Warwick's injured feelings that he was given the honour of taking Richard into his household to complete his education, probably at some time in 1465.[5]

Richard's early schooling and training is another aspect of his life that is completely hidden from us, but he would have been taught to read and write (in English, French and Latin), while acquiring some knowledge of arithmetic, the law of property and, most importantly, good manners. His education would have been badly disrupted in the months that separated his capture at Ludlow from his return from exile in Holland, and Kendall suggests that he spent part of this period studying in the household of the Archbishop of Canterbury, Thomas Bourchier. He might have done, but King Edward's grant to the Archbishop a decade later says only that 'in time past and at the King's request he [Bourchier] supported the King's brothers the dukes of Clarence and Gloucester [George and Richard] for a long time at great charges'.[6] It seems likely that it had already been decided that Richard would be deemed to come of age when he turned sixteen in 1468 (the age at which the 'childhood' of his elder brother George had formally ended), and Warwick's task was to spend the next three years teaching him to be a leader, a warrior, and a 'veray parfit gentil' knight.[7]

It is not known precisely where Richard went. Kendall's suggestion that he spent most of his time at Middleham in north Yorkshire may be accurate, but it is not improbable that there were sojourns at Warwick's other great castles at Sheriff Hutton (Yorks.), and even Warwick itself. King Edward gave the Earl £1,000 to defray his 'costs and expenses', and Richard, and, presumably, members of his small company, were then embedded in his cousin's far greater household. How he fared is again a matter for conjecture, but bullying, and homesickness, were probably as common then as they are in modern society. It was not many years since his brothers Edward and Edmund had written to their father complaining of the 'odious rule and demeaning' of Richard Croft and his brother, who were probably slightly older members of the establishment in which they were all serving their knightly apprenticeships.[8] Richard would have to stand up for himself and learn to take knocks as well as give them: but that, of course, was the whole point.

The Earl of Warwick was frequently absent on the King's business, but Richard would have spent much time in the company of his countess, Anne Beauchamp, and their two daughters, Isabel and Anne. John Rous, who almost certainly knew the Countess, describes her as a caring lady, 'ever companionable and liberal and in her own person seemly and beauteous … glad to be at and with women that travailed of child, full comfortable and plenteous then of all thing[s] that should be helping to them'.[9] She had no son of her own, and may have gone out of her way to befriend Richard and treat him as one of the family. When, in September 1465, a great banquet was held at Cawood Castle in Yorkshire to celebrate the enthronement of Warwick's brother George as Archbishop of York, Richard was seated in the 'chief' chamber with his sister Elizabeth, Duchess of Suffolk, the Neville countesses of Westmoreland and Northumberland, 'and two of the Lord of Warwick's daughters'[10] – the only two, in fact.

It would be fanciful to suppose that there was any romantic attachment between Richard and Isabel, who was about his own age, or with Anne, who he would later marry and who was some four years younger, but he undoubtedly formed friendships that would stand him in good stead in later years. One was with Francis Lovell, the heir to five baronies, who would serve him as his chamberlain and who remained loyal to his cause even after the battle of Bosworth. Lovell and his estates had come into the King's hands following the death of his father in 1465, and Edward had already used the income from his lands to pay Warwick to maintain Richard. He was married to Anne Fitzhugh, the Earl's niece, in or before February 1466, and was probably already living in Warwick's household when the King formally relinquished his wardship in November 1467. He was three or four years younger than Richard, but perhaps the older boy could empathise with a newcomer who had also lost his father and who was trying to find his feet in an unfamiliar, and larger, world.[11]

It is also likely that it was at Middleham or Sheriff Hutton that he first encountered Thomas Parr and Thomas Huddleston, who would both die at his side in the great battles of 1471. The Parrs of Westmoreland and the Huddlestons of Cumberland were closely associated with the Earl of Warwick, whose 'good lordship' would have included training their offspring; and since Richard held no land in either county at this period their devotion to him must have been essentially personal. We only know of them because when Richard, many years later (in July 1477 to be exact), endowed four fellowships within Queens' College, Cambridge, he instructed the new priest-fellows to pray for the well-being of his own family, for the souls of a number of deceased members of the Houses of York and Neville, and for the souls of Thomas Parr, John Milewater, Christopher Worsley, Thomas Huddleston, John Harper 'and all other gentlemen and yeomen, servants and lovers [i.e. friends and well-wishers] of the said Duke of Gloucester [Richard], the which were slain in his service at the battles of Barnet or Tewkesbury'. Milewater, Worsley and Harper were older men. Worsley had been nominated as sheriff of Somerset and Dorset on three occasions in the 1460s, while Milewater, who had served Richard's father, and Harper were experienced estate officials. It is some testimony to Richard's own loyalty to his close followers that he still remembered them by name and wanted to ensure they entered paradise almost six years after their deaths.[12]

Richard's years with Warwick were largely uneventful, but trouble was brewing behind the scenes. It was almost inevitable that King Edward would assert himself and depend less on the Earl as he grew older, but what irked Warwick was that the Queen's Woodville relatives were superseding him in the royal favour. In 1467 Edward abruptly deprived his brother George, Archbishop of York, of the chancellorship, and then rubbed salt in the wound by allowing his sister Princess Margaret to marry the Duke of Burgundy, Charles the Bold. Warwick had long favoured an alliance with France – there had even been talk of marrying Richard into the French royal family[13] – and a union between a royal sibling and Duke Charles, the King of France's enemy, was another blow to his ambitions. It was, in the opinion of the well-informed Croyland writer, 'really the cause of the dissensions between the King and the Earl'.[14]

Warwick could do nothing to change Edward's policy or repair the damage done to his own reputation as a statesman, but he had other irons in the fire. The French chronicler Jean de Waurin recorded that as early as 1464 he had enticed both the King's brothers to Cambridge, and proposed that George should marry his elder daughter Isabel. Edward learned that they were secretly discussing a matter that he alone could determine, and when George and Richard returned to court he gave them a thorough dressing-down before ordering four knights to arrest them.[15] This was a story that had grown with the telling long before it reached Waurin's ears, but there can be no doubt that

Warwick *did* want to marry Isabel to George, and that he was again mortified when Edward's answer was a firm 'no'.

Warwick bided his time for the moment, even helping to escort Princess Margaret to Margate, from where she was to embark for her marriage to Duke Charles, but he had little love for the Woodvilles and avoided them whenever possible. Richard, who rode with him to Margate, was now approaching sixteen and nearing the end of his formal tutelage; but no writer suggests that the Earl was still actively cultivating him or regarded him as a potential ally. With hindsight, it is clear that George had been wholly won over, but that Richard, who had no reason of his own to dislike the Woodvilles,[16] had made it clear that he was not going to take sides in a dispute between rival court factions. His first loyalty was to his brother, the King.

Richard's first taste of real authority – at least the first that we know of – was when he attended the trial of the traitors Henry Courtney and Thomas Hungerford at Salisbury in January 1469, and served as the leading member of the commission that condemned them to death. Hungerford's father, Robert, had been executed after the battle of Hexham in 1464, and this latest treason placed Margaret, his mother, in a potentially ruinous situation. Richard could have tried to seize everything when the Hungerford lands were restored to him in 1468 (see above), but the terms of the settlement agreed between them were remarkably generous. Margaret surrendered the 'prize' castle and manor of Farleigh Hungerford in Somerset immediately, but in return Richard allowed her to retain a life interest in nineteen manors in Wiltshire and Cornwall and to continue to receive the profits of other lands held in trust. The income from a further six manors was to be used to found a chantry in Salisbury Cathedral and to establish an almshouse for twelve poor men in Haytesbury (Wilts.), Richard undertaking to apply for the appropriate royal licences within a year.[17] If he was to behave harshly later, there is no evidence of it here.

Richard was now almost seventeen and taking an interest in the opposite sex, but few details of his liaisons have come down to us. He subsequently acknowledged two illegitimate children: a son, John of Gloucester (or of Pontefract), who was knighted in 1483 and appointed Captain of Calais two years later, and a daughter, Katherine, who married William Herbert, Earl of Huntingdon, in 1484. Nothing is known of their mother (or mothers), or when, precisely, they were born; but if John was old enough to be knighted and given a responsible position (admittedly, without the right to make appointments) by 1485, he was probably by then in his mid-teens. Katherine was presumably of marriageable age in 1484, so the implication is that she was by then thirteen or fourteen and had also been conceived near the end of the 1460s. John was initially favoured by Henry VII but seems to have been executed in 1499 after a long period of imprisonment, while Katherine's husband was described as a widower in November 1487. Neither left children so far as is known.[18]

3

THE YEARS OF CRISIS, 1469–1471

The Earl of Warwick was not, as yet, seeking to unmake the king he had 'made' only eight years earlier, but he thought Edward thoroughly ungrateful and was determined to recover what he considered to be his rightful place in the royal counsels. In the spring of 1469 a man calling himself 'Robin of Redesdale' stirred a local uprising in Yorkshire, and although this was quickly suppressed another Robin, this time 'of Holderness', caused trouble in the East Riding shortly afterwards. Both disturbances were essentially protests against excessive taxation, or, in the latter case, a demand that the earldom of Northumberland which had been given to Warwick's brother John Neville should be restored to the heir of the local Percy family; and it was John Neville who confronted the rebels and executed Robin of Holderness when he fell into his hands.

Warwick would not have inspired a campaign against his own brother or (presumably) allowed John to suppress rebellions he had himself instigated; but the discontent that was obviously bubbling beneath the surface of northern England may have suggested a way out of his own difficulties. In June Robin of Redesdale reappeared in Lancashire and this time, it seems, no one moved to intercept him. King Edward had left London for Norfolk at the beginning of the month taking with him Richard, the Queen's father Earl Rivers and her brothers Anthony Lord Scales and Sir John Woodville, and it was from Norwich that he despatched letters ordering his friends to assemble their forces. But he saw no reason to postpone his pilgrimage to the shrine of Our Lady at Walsingham,[1] and subsequently spent a week with the Queen at Fotheringhay before finally reaching Newark about 10 July.

Edward and his companions had not supposed that a new uprising was imminent when they left the capital, and Richard, for one, found himself short of money to pay the men he had summoned personally. He was at Castle Rising (Norfolk), when, on 24 June, he wrote what is now his earliest surviving letter to the Chancellor of the Duchy of Lancaster, Sir John Say:

Right trusty and well beloved, we greet you well. And forasmuch as the King's good Grace hath appointed me to attend upon his Highness into the North parts of his land, which will be to my great cost and charge, whereunto I am so suddenly called that I am not so well purveyed of money therefore as behoves me to be, and therefore pray you as my special trust is in you, to lend me a hundred pounds of money unto Easter next coming, at which time I promise you you shall be truly thereof content and paid again, as the bearer hereof shall inform you: to whom I pray you to give credence therein, and show me such friendliness in the same as I may do for you hereafter, wherein ye shall find me ready. Written at Rising the xxiiij day of June. R. GLOUCESTER

The above was dictated to a secretary (it was perhaps one of a number of similar requests), but Richard added in his own hand:

Sir J Say I pray you that ye fail me not at this time in my great
need, as ye will that I show you my good lordship in that matter
that ye labour to me for.[2]

In other words, he would not only repay the money, but would
respond positively to an earlier request from the lender for help.

It was probably just before the royal party reached Newark that
King Edward received two pieces of very disturbing news. The first
was that the army commanded by 'Robin' was almost three times as
large as his own, and the second was that Warwick had announced
that his daughter Isabel was to wed George of Clarence in defiance
of the King's wishes. Edward had not previously suspected Warwick
and George and wrote to them, rather plaintively, asking for
confirmation that they were not 'of any such disposition towards
us as the rumour here runneth';[3] but he was left in no doubt when
he learned that George and Isabel had been married at Calais by
Archbishop Neville on 11 July and that a number of the Earl's
relatives had joined 'Robin'. Indeed, 'Robin' himself was probably a
member of the Conyers family, Warwick's cousins by marriage, and
not the man who had rebelled earlier in the year.

Edward's response was to retire to the safety of Nottingham
Castle and to urge the earls of Pembroke and Devon, who were
both recruiting large contingents, to join him as quickly as possible.
He knew the Woodvilles would be given short shrift if things
turned out badly, and sent Earl Rivers and his sons to seek safety
in more distant parts of the kingdom. The wisdom of this became
apparent when Warwick issued an open letter setting out the rebels'
grievances and complaining specifically that Earl Rivers, his wife
Jacquetta, their sons, the newly promoted earls of Pembroke and
Devon, and others, had 'caused our said sovereign lord and his said

realm to fall in great poverty of misery, disturbing the ministration of the laws, only intending their own promotion and enriching'. He drew ominous parallels with Edward II, Richard II and Henry VI, who had all been deposed when they 'estranged the great lords of their blood from their secret counsels', and called on all who agreed with him to join him at Canterbury the following Sunday (16 July) in order to 'show the same to his [Edward's] good grace'.[4]

Warwick and George of Clarence were well received on their return from Calais, and were soon marching northwards from Canterbury at the head of an army. They intended to link up with Robin of Redesdale's men, who had now bypassed the King in Nottingham, but on 26 July Robin defeated the forces of the earls of Pembroke and Devon at Edgecote, near Banbury. The Earl of Pembroke and his brother were executed next day, Devon escaped only to be killed at Bridgewater (Somerset), and Earl Rivers and Sir John Woodville were hunted down and beheaded outside Coventry on 12 August. Edward, who was unaware of what had happened at Edgecote, left Nottingham on 29 July and began to make his way southwards. Nearly all his men deserted when news of the battle reached them, and he was taken into custody by Archbishop George Neville at Olney, in Buckinghamshire. The Nevilles treated him respectfully, but sent him first to Warwick Castle and then to Middleham in the distant north.

Warwick thought that he could now issue orders in the King's name and that everyone would obey them, but found that few would respond to instructions that did not emanate from Edward personally. There was serious rioting in London, magnates seized the opportunity to settle old scores with rivals in other parts of the country, and when the Earl tried to raise troops to suppress an uprising on behalf of Henry VI on the Scottish border he was met with indifference. Faced with a serious situation he had no alternative but to restore Edward to liberty, and was unable, or unwilling, to object when the King summoned other lords to join him. By mid-October Edward was back in his capital and again in full command of affairs.

Where was Richard during this time? The chroniclers do not mention him, but it is reasonable to suppose that he had previously enjoyed a good personal relationship with Warwick and that there was accordingly no threat to his safety. He was probably still with the King when he was captured at Olney, and may have subsequently shared his imprisonment, either voluntarily or because no one knew what else to do with him. He was no stranger to Warwick and Middleham castles – indeed, he would have felt more at home there than in most other places – and Edward rewarded his loyalty by appointing him Constable of England for life (17 October), and granting him the Duchy of Lancaster honours of Clitheroe (Lancashire) and Halton (Cheshire), with the castle and lordship of Sudeley in Gloucestershire. He had not (as yet) been required to choose between his old tutor and his brother, but it had been a close call.

Many supposed that King Edward would punish Warwick and the Nevilles for murdering his friends and usurping his authority; but they were powerful, influential men who were closely related to him and he decided to give them another chance. Some of the offices they had misappropriated during the recent troubles were taken from them, but their gains of earlier years were respected and they attended conciliatory meetings of the royal Council. The King even went so far as to create Warwick's nephew George (his brother John's son), Duke of Bedford, and promised his father and uncle that he would marry him to Elizabeth, his own eldest daughter, in due course.

Warwick and his friends may have been partially mollified by this generosity, but the reality was that Edward was still able to favour the surviving Woodvilles and pursue his own policies. Within months the Earl's frustration had again boiled over, and he seized on a violent dispute in Lincolnshire between the Yorkist Sir Thomas Burgh of Gainsborough and his local rivals the Welles family to foment more trouble. King Edward decided to restore the peace in person, and news that he was coming north with an army gave rise to rumours that he intended to punish those who had joined Robin of Redesdale's uprising the previous year. It is unclear if Warwick actually fanned local fears that 'the king's judges should sit and hang and draw [disembowel] a great number of the commons',[5] but he was almost certainly behind Sir Robert Welles's decision to summon the men of the county to resist the royal forces. He intended to rendezvous with Welles's men at Leicester while drawing in other supporters from the north and the West Country; but on the 12 March 1470 the Lincolnshire rebels were defeated at Empingham in Rutland. Welles's men threw away their padded jackets and other heavy equipment as they tried to escape the pursuing royalists, giving the battle its popular name of 'Lose-Cote Field'.[6]

Sir Robert Welles confessed that Warwick's aim had been to depose Edward in favour of George of Clarence, a revelation that placed both their lives in jeopardy. The King ordered them to appear before him and hinted that if they disbanded their remaining forces and promised to be loyal an accommodation was still possible; but he was bound to reject their demand for safe-conducts and pardons for themselves and all their supporters before they would agree to obey him. The royal army grew in strength as the risings in the north and the West Country faded, and Warwick and George fled towards Manchester (in the vain hope that Thomas, Lord Stanley, one of the Earl's brothers-in-law, would help them), before taking ship for Calais and ultimately France.

Richard of Gloucester would normally have been at his brother's side when soldiers were needed, but was preoccupied on this occasion with new responsibilities in Wales. Edward had decided that he should fill the vacuum left by the untimely death of the Earl of Pembroke, and had appointed him chief justice of North Wales, chief steward of all the Duchy of Lancaster lordships in South Wales and chief steward and surveyor of the principality of Wales and of the earldom of March in November 1469, and chief justice and chamberlain of South Wales in February 1470. His immediate task was to retake the rebel-held castles of Carmarthen and Cardigan, and it was only belatedly that he led a force of men into England to support his brother. He seems to have clashed with some of Lord Stanley's retainers in Lancashire, and his intervention may have helped to dissuade Stanley from assisting Warwick. It is curious to reflect that if the Earl of Warwick had remained loyal after the troubles of 1469 much of Richard's future career would, in all probability, have been spent in the principality rather than in the north.

Warwick and George of Clarence were warmly received in France and their arrival gave Louis XI an opportunity to promote a scheme that had been lurking in his mind for some time. If Louis could use Warwick and his friends to restore Henry VI to the throne in place of King Edward, then England would become France's ally and the Duke of Burgundy would be effectively isolated. He accordingly brought the Earl face to face with his old enemy, Henry's wife Queen Margaret, at Angers on 22 June 1470, where, after some initial difficulty – Margaret kept Warwick on his knees for a full fifteen minutes pleading forgiveness for the wrong he had done her

– they were formally reconciled and it was agreed that Henry and Margaret's son, Prince Edward, would marry Warwick's younger daughter Anne. What George of Clarence thought of this is not recorded, but he must have been at least dimly aware that if his brother lost power in England he would not now become king in his place.

Part of Warwick's plan was to arrange for his brother-in-law Henry, Lord Fitzhugh, to organise a minor uprising in northern England to draw Edward away from the south at the crucial moment, and although Fitzhugh, in the event, showed his hand too early Edward was still in Yorkshire when Warwick and George landed in the West Country in mid-August. He presumably thought he had the means to deal with them, but was surprised by their popularity and ability to draw over men who had supported him in previous conflicts. Lord Stanley was one of those who now joined them, but the most serious defection was that of John Neville, Warwick's brother, who this time, it seems, put family loyalty before his obligations to his sovereign. Edward had deprived John of the princely earldom of Northumberland to appease local demands for the restoration of the heir of the Percies to his ancestral title a year earlier, and although he had received a handsome 'compensation package' – elevation to a marquisate (of Montagu), broad estates in Devon, the dukedom of Bedford and the promise of a royal marriage for his infant son George – it was still, apparently, not enough.

Edward still had with him Richard, Anthony Woodville (now Earl Rivers), William, Lord Hastings, and other loyal followers, but John Neville's defection was a body blow. Flight seemed the only option, and after dismissing most of their company they made a dash for the Wash (where Edward was almost drowned), before finding ships at King's Lynn. Their little flotilla was chased and nearly captured by hostile Hanseatic vessels, but managed to reach the coast of Holland, where they fell into the friendly hands of Louis de Gruthuyse, Duke Charles's governor, who provided them with food, clothes and money. Before long they heard that Warwick had brought Henry VI out of the Tower of London and set him back on his long-lost throne.

It has been assumed that although Edward and Richard sailed for Holland in separate ships they arrived there at more or less the same time, but recent research has suggested another possibility.[7] Two messengers who reached the ducal court at Hesdin on 13 October (ten days after the exiles had arrived in Holland) informed Duke Charles that Edward was then at The Hague with Anthony Woodville and William Hastings. Richard was not mentioned – it is unlikely that he was merely one of the 'several other great lords' in Edward's company – and he was also omitted from a letter written by the Duke on 1 November which referred specifically to Woodville, Hastings, Lord Say, Lord Mountjoy's son and five knights. Both documents would surely have noticed him had he been present, and an entry in the town accounts of Veere for the second week of the month seems to imply that he had only reached Holland very recently. Adrian le But, a Cistercian monk who lived at Les Dunes Abbey (between Bruges and Calais), heard that 'the younger brother of the now fugitive King Edward ... [had] put up as much resistance as he could', and remarked later that 'the Duke of Gloucester came to him from England with many men'. There is nothing to corroborate this in English chronicles, but it seems possible that Richard had remained in England for some weeks acting as a focus for those who wanted to join his brother in exile before escaping himself. Edward and Anthony Woodville could expect little mercy if they were captured, but Richard may have thought it a risk he could take.

King Edward had reached the island of Texel on 3 October, and proceeded via Alkmaar, Noordwijk and Leyden to The Hague, where he was welcomed with wines and sweetmeats eight days later. He hoped that Duke Charles would invite him to Hesdin, but Charles was afraid of the combined might of Warwick and King Louis and decided to keep his brother-in-law at arm's length. Letters and messengers passed between them at regular intervals until Christmas (long after Richard, who had experienced similar Burgundian prevarication ten years earlier, had rejoined his brother), but when Louis began hostilities by seizing St Quentin Charles realised he could hedge no longer. On 31 December he gave Edward £20,000 'for his and his brother Gloucester's expenses ... and for their departure from my lord the duke's lands to return to England',[8] and they met on several occasions in the first half of January, at Aire and latterly at St Pol, home of the Queen's kinsman Jacques de Luxembourg, before the King went to stay at Bruges.

Preparations for Edward's recovery of his kingdom now began in earnest. More money was borrowed from five towns in Holland and from individuals including English merchants; ships were hired, principally from the Hanse with the promise of commercial privileges; and a force of 1,200 mercenaries was assembled. Messengers and letters were sent to potential supporters in England, not least to George of Clarence, who was coming under increasing pressure to desert Warwick, and help was sought from dignitaries in other countries including the Duke of Brittany and the Earl of Ormond. Richard was kept very busy, but still found time to visit his sister Margaret (Duke Charles's wife) at Lille on 12 February. It was almost four years since he had last seen her, and they would not meet again until she visited England in 1480. We know nothing of what passed between them, but she could not have failed to notice that the youth who had escorted her to Margate in the summer of 1468 had become a man.

Edward, Richard and their little army left Flushing on 11 March 1471. They hoped to make landfall in East Anglia, where Anthony Woodville had influence and where the dukes of Norfolk and Suffolk were well disposed towards them, but they found the region well defended and decided to sail further north. Their fleet was hit by storms and scattered, and although Edward came ashore at Ravenspur on the Humber on 14 March other contingents put into nearby harbours and were not able to rejoin him until the following day. Hull refused them entry, and although Edward and a few followers were admitted to York when he claimed that he had come only to recover his father's duchy, their situation remained precarious. Both John Neville and Henry Percy, Earl of Northumberland, could have contained them in Yorkshire; but Northumberland made no move to intercept them and Neville apparently decided that he could not, or would not, intervene while Percy remained uncommitted. Edward had sent a personal envoy, Nicholas Leventhorpe, one of his yeomen of the Chamber, to England during the exile to beg the Earl to at least remain neutral, and Leventhorpe's persuasiveness paid rich dividends now.[9]

Edward and Richard moved south, gathering troops as they went, and found that luck, and boldness, both favoured them. The combined forces of their enemies were far greater, but the Duke of Exeter and the Earl of Oxford, who were at Newark, withdrew when Edward moved towards them, and Warwick shut himself up in Coventry and refused to fight. George of Clarence, who was in the West Country, may still have been waiting on events before committing himself; but on 3 April the brothers met on the road to Banbury and were formally reconciled. Edward now decided to make a dash for London which he entered, unopposed, on 11 April. His first acts were to secure the person of his rival King Henry, and to see his son, now five months old, for the first time. Queen Elizabeth had taken sanctuary at Westminster when Warwick invaded, and there had been occasions when she had feared for her life.

Warwick belatedly drew together his various forces – his own, his brother John's, and Exeter and Oxford's contingent – and approached London on 12 April, Good Friday. Next day King Edward, Richard and their friends marched out to confront them, and found them drawn up about half a mile north of Barnet astride the main road to St Albans. Richard's precise role in the ensuing battle is uncertain, but the loss of at least one and probably more of his close personal servants proves that he was in the thick of the fighting.[10] Warwick's army was larger than the King's, and for a long time the outcome was in the balance. A mist that had allowed Edward to close in on his enemies also helped to conceal Oxford's routing of the left wing of the Yorkist army, and when the Earl's men returned to the battle they came under fire from some of their comrades who, according to one account, mistook their 'star with streams' badges for Edward's 'sun in splendour'. They fled crying 'treason', and the King pressed home his advantage. Warwick and John Neville were both killed, the former as he fled and before Edward or Richard could intervene to save him. It was an ignominious ending to an exceptional career.

Queen Margaret belatedly landed at Weymouth on the day Barnet was fought, and was soon joined by the Duke of Somerset and the Earl of Devon, who had declined to fight alongside their old enemy Warwick. A considerable force was raised from the West Country, and Margaret advanced northwards through Taunton, Bath and Bristol intending to link up with other supporters in Wales and, eventually, Lancashire and Cheshire. King Edward realised that it was essential to prevent them from crossing the River Severn, and ordered his governor, Sir Richard Beauchamp, to bar the bridge at the nearest crossing point at Gloucester. His enemies had no alternative but to press on to the ford at Tewkesbury, and it was here that he caught up with them after marching his men for a remarkable thirty-six miles in twenty-four hours on 3 May.

Richard commanded the vanguard of his brother's army when battle was joined the following morning, and was again in the thick of the conflict. The Queen's forces were driven back and dispersed in fierce hand-to-hand fighting, and when it was all over Richard, as Constable, and the Duke of Norfolk, as Earl Marshall, sat in judgement on Somerset and others who had been captured or removed from the sanctuary of Tewkesbury Abbey. Death sentences were inevitable, and Richard must surely have reflected that if the tide of battle had flowed differently he would now be the condemned traitor and Somerset and the rest his judges. This latest cycle of killings, exile, and of victory against the odds had been a stark reminder of the traumas of a decade earlier, and can only have increased his determination to control his own destiny. He knew that he could expect no mercy himself in future, and that there would be times when he would have to strike first and decisively in order to survive.

But it was not all over yet. No sooner had Edward triumphed at Tewkesbury than he heard that Thomas Neville, the 'Bastard of Fauconberg' (an illegitimate son of Warwick's late uncle, William Neville, Lord Fauconberg and Earl of Kent), had raised the flag of rebellion in Kent and was threatening London. Fortunately, the citizens put up stout resistance, and a counter-attack from the Tower led by Anthony Woodville successfully secured the capital until a detachment from Edward's army arrived a few days later. The King made his triumphant entry into the city on 21 May with Richard, George of Clarence, a long train of noblemen, and the captured and forlorn Queen Margaret. Margaret's only son, Prince Edward, had been slain at Tewkesbury, and her husband King Henry would die in the Tower that same night.

The deaths of Prince Edward and his father are among the 'crimes' sometimes attributed to Richard, but both are stories that have grown with the telling. The author of the pro-Yorkist *Arrivall* says that 'Edward, called Prince, was taken, fleeing to the town wards and slain, in the field', a view endorsed by John Warkworth, the master of Peterhouse, Cambridge, who wrote that 'there was slain in the field Prince Edward, which cried for succour to his brother-in-law the Duke of Clarence'.[11] The story that that the young man was captured and brought before King Edward, who struck him when he boldly stated that he had come to England to claim his birthright, first appears in the illuminated late fifteenth-century Besançon manuscript, but it is only when we come to the Tudor era and the chronicles of Robert Fabyan and Polydore Vergil that we are informed that it was Richard, George of Clarence and William Hastings who then attacked and killed him – a lurid story concocted, we may assume, after all the alleged perpetrators were dead and their cause lay in ruins.

Henry VI had been allowed to live quietly in the Tower since his capture seven years earlier because judicial murder or a fatal 'accident' would only have transferred his claim to the throne to his son. But now that Prince Edward was dead his father could also be silenced, and the threat to King Edward and his House ended. The *Arrivall* says that the old King died 'of pure displeasure and melancholy' when word of the defeat of his armies and the death of his son was brought to him, but Dr Warkworth was in no doubt that he had been 'put to death, the twenty-first day of May, on a Tuesday night, between eleven and twelve of the clock, being then at the Tower the Duke of Gloucester, brother to King Edward and many other'.[12] Tudor writers, most notably Thomas More and his copyists, carried this a step further by alleging that since Richard was present he was responsible for whatever happened to Henry, although More is careful not to vouch for the accuracy of the story:

> He slew with his own hands King Henry the sixth being prisoner in the Tower of London, *as men constantly say* [my italics], and that without commandment or knowledge of the king, which would undoubtedly, if he had intended that thing, have appointed that butcherly office to some other than his own born brother.[13]

Richard was arguably staying at the Tower (a royal palace) because he had no town house of his own in London, and the 'many other' who were there included, in all probability, Queen Elizabeth, her children and members of the Council. The order to kill Henry could not have come from anyone but King Edward, and while Richard could have supervised or verified the execution he would not have struck the fatal blow personally. His subsequent reburial of the ex-king's remains at Windsor has been seen as an act of contrition, but an alternative reason is that he wanted the gifts left by pilgrims visiting the shrine to enrich St George's Chapel. There could be two kings in England no longer, and Henry's fate was already sealed.[14]

4

WARWICK'S HEIR, 1471–1475

The Earl of Warwick had always loomed large in Richard's life, and the memory of him would linger long after. King Edward urgently needed a reliable deputy who could fill the power vacuum the Earl's death had created in northern England, and Richard, who had already been appointed warden of the West March towards Scotland in 1470, was asked to exchange his responsibilities in Wales for a larger role in this frequently violent region. He was appointed to Warwick's office of chief steward of the Duchy of Lancaster in the north parts as early as 4 July 1471, and ten days later was granted all the estates the Earl had held north of the River Trent, including Middleham and Sheriff Hutton in Yorkshire and Penrith in Cumberland. He replaced the unreliable Lord Stanley as the Duchy's chief steward in the county palatine of Lancashire, superseded the Earl of Northumberland as keeper of all the northern royal forests, and added Warwick's position as Great Chamberlain of England to his existing appointments of Constable and Admiral. The Earl's northern lordships would serve as his power base in the region, and additional revenues were provided by a grant of lands forfeited by the Earl of Oxford and the leaders of the Lincolnshire rebellion worth in excess of £1,000 annually. It was a considerable undertaking for a young man not yet nineteen years old.

The 'Bastard of Fauconberg' had retreated into Kent after being driven from the Tower of London, and Edward and Richard spent little more than a day in the capital before setting off in pursuit. The Bastard's great strength was his fleet of some forty-seven ships moored at Sandwich (what had until recently been Warwick's navy), and Edward accepted that he had no alternative but to try to persuade him to surrender peacefully before he sailed away and engaged in piracy. Envoys shuttled between them, and it was agreed that the Bastard and his captains would submit on the promise of pardon and that he would then enter the King's service. Richard, as Admiral, accepted his formal capitulation on 27 May.

The Bastard was pardoned on 10 June, and six days later was given a safe-conduct to accompany Richard into Yorkshire. Richard had to win acceptance among men who had formerly acknowledged Warwick as their overlord, and the presence of the Earl's (albeit illegitimate) cousin in his retinue could only bolster his credentials. What happened next is uncertain, but by the summer of 1472 the Bastard had apparently gone absent without leave and returned to the south coast. His pardon had been revoked by 11 September, shortly before or after he was arrested at Southampton, and he was returned to Richard's custody at Middleham and executed. His head was fixed on a spike on London Bridge 'looking into Kent-ward', the scene of his earlier crimes.

Richard dealt with the Bastard because he had been under his immediate authority, but there is no doubt that King Edward was aware of, and approved of, his execution. The commission to seize his goods was issued under the royal letters patent, and the

Exchequer paid one Henry Cappe the considerable sum of £30 to return the Bastard's head to the capital. Curiously, there is no mention of what specific crime he had committed since his pardon, and some writers have argued that the brothers simply found an excuse to be rid of him. But Edward knew only too well that men he had forgiven had afterwards betrayed him, and the Bastard's flight, whatever its purpose, implied that he was about to do likewise. He forfeited his life when he stepped out of line.[1]

The Bastard was the first problem arising out of his tenure of part of northern England that Richard had to deal with, and the second was the long-running dispute between Lord Stanley and the brothers James and Robert Harrington. The Harringtons' father Sir Thomas and eldest brother John had died fighting with the Duke of York at Wakefield in 1460, leaving two infant heiresses, John's daughters, to inherit the family properties. James and Robert had taken possession of their nieces and occupied their lands; but in 1468 King Edward granted their legal wardship to their distant relative Lord Stanley. Stanley married them to one of his younger sons and a nephew; but the Harringtons refused to surrender Hornby Castle and the other estates that had belonged to their father and brother. The Earl of Warwick was in the process of sending ordnance to Hornby to help Stanley (his brother-in-law) besiege it when he fell at Barnet, a battle in which the Harringtons – unsurprisingly – fought on Edward IV's side.

Lord Stanley made his peace with King Edward after the battle of Tewkesbury, and this meant that the Crown could not side openly with either party. In 1473 Edward asked Richard, who was on notably good terms with the Harringtons, to find a solution to the problem, and a compromise was reached by which the latter agreed to surrender Hornby but were allowed to retain and fortify two other manors, Farleton and Brierley, that were also on Stanley's shopping list. The agreement held for more than a decade, but Stanley's simmering hostility towards the fiercely loyal Harringtons may help to explain why – crucially – he failed to support Richard at the battle of Bosworth in 1485.

There can be little doubt that Lord Stanley resented Richard's intrusion into northern England, and the same was true of Henry Percy, Earl of Northumberland, whose equivocation in 1471 had proved so critical. Richard had persuaded a number of knights and gentry to enter his service as part of the process of establishing himself in northern England; but some of the men he retained were also members of Northumberland's affinity and the Earl did not care to share their allegiance with him. The ill-feeling between them intensified when Richard recruited John Wedrington, the Earl's master forester of Alnwick, and an alarmed King Edward decided to intervene personally. An agreement brokered when they appeared before the Council at Nottingham in May 1473 took the heat out of the situation, and a formal indenture signed a year later assured Northumberland that Richard would be his 'good and faithful lord' and that he would not 'ask or claim any office or fee that the Earl hath of the King's grant or of any other person or persons ... or take any servant retained by the Earl'. Northumberland for his part undertook to be Richard's 'faithful servant', and to 'do service to the Duke at all times lawful and convenient when he ... shall be lawfully required'.[2] The accord was not retrospective, however, as it specifically stated that John Wedrington was to remain in Richard's service. Northumberland is unlikely to have been entirely satisfied, and there are suspicions that he, too, failed his royal master in 1485.

Richard's main task in the north, as already noted, was to replace the Earl of Warwick, and securing the allegiance of the

Earl's regional affinity was a crucial part of the process. It was by no means easy – some of the men involved had fought against him in the campaigns of 1469–71 – but a surviving account for Middleham indicates that many had accepted him as Warwick's successor by 1473–4. Middleham was not merely a village and castle but a lordship of some twenty-five properties – manors, parks and forests scattered over the fertile dales and barren moors of Richmondshire. It yielded £936 13s 6d in 1473–4, of which a total of £75 14s 2d was spent on fees and wages paid to senior servants, foresters, auditors and other officials, and a further £175 6s 8d on annuities granted to twenty-two local worthies who were retained for life.[3] These included Sir Robert Danby, Chief Justice of the Common Pleas, who was 'retained of council' in the sum of £6 13s 4d, but the most prominent was Sir John Conyers, who, according to some accounts, may have been 'Robin of Redesdale', and who had succeeded his father as steward of the lordship before Michaelmas 1465. He received £20 (with the addition of £5 6s 8d for his stewardship and £6 13s 4d for serving as constable of the castle), and was joined in Richard's service by his son Richard, his brothers Sir Richard and Sir Roger, his brother-in-law William Burgh, his sons-in-law Sir Thomas Markenfield, Roland Pudsay and Robert Wycliffe, and his wife's half-brother Thomas Tunstall. Tunstall, who received the largest retainer (£33 6s 8d) and his brother of Sir Richard Tunstall of Thurland Castle (Lancs.), had both supported Henry VI's restoration, and a similar deal was struck with Robert Clifford, whose father Thomas had died fighting for Henry at the first battle of St Albans. Former enemies would not always find it easy to work together, but Richard needed their local influence as much as they needed his patronage. Mutual respect, even comradeship, would bring them together, but in the meantime they all had to live in the real world.

Richard clearly had his 'targets', individuals whose support would enhance his influence in the region, but men also sought to enter his service and not always for the best of reasons. A petition presented to Parliament by one Katherine Richardson described how her husband, Richard Williamson of Howden in Yorkshire, had been attacked and killed by Robert, Richard and John Farnell (or Foster), the three sons of Thomas Farnell 'late of Newsholme near Howden' as he waited for the ferry at Hemingborough on 1 October 1472. The assailants were clearly bent on violence: they were equipped with 'jacks and sallets' (padded jackets and helmets), and cut off both Williamson's hands and one of his arms above the elbow before stealing his possessions. There was presumably some 'bad blood' between the two families, and there are numerous examples of men like the Farnells taking the law into their own hands when it suited them: but this case is interesting because Thomas Farnell, the brothers' father, 'immediately after the said felony, murder and robbery had thus been committed, made approaches to the most high and mighty prince and most honourable lord Richard, duke of Gloucester, to take and accept him and all his said wicked sons into his service'. The Farnells clearly hoped that if they became Richard's men he would use his influence to frustrate any attempt to bring them to justice, but they were to be disappointed. Richard,

> having afterwards been reliably informed and notified of the said felony, murder and robbery, when the said Thomas was calling himself a servant of the said duke and wearing his clothing [livery] which he had obtained and received by crafty and devious means,

commanded that the said Thomas should be brought to the gaol at York to remain there until he was lawfully acquitted or attainted [convicted] of the aforesaid felony, murder and robbery.[4]

The record of Richard's interaction with his followers is scanty, but there were certainly occasions when he intervened to settle disputes between them. When Richard Clervaux and Rowland Place quarrelled over land boundaries, their pews in church and rights of game, he imposed a settlement 'tendering the peace and weal [well-being] of the country the said parties inhabit, and also willing good concord, rest, [and] friendly suite to he had from henceforth between them'.[5] His influence also extended into the wider community. On one occasion he was approached by the parishioners of Snaith, who claimed that the abbey of Selby had failed in its obligation to provide their church with books, vestments and a chalice. Richard ordered the abbey to make good the deficiency by the following Easter, but ruled that the parishioners should supply the various items themselves thereafter. Both parties were to abandon their lawsuits and neither was to act provocatively towards the other.

Most medieval lords would have automatically sided with their own followers and their associates when differences brought them into conflict with men outside the retinue, but there was at least one occasion when Richard put justice and the protection of the weak before self-interest. In 1480 a humble husbandman, John Randson of Burntoft in County Durham, complained to him that Sir Robert Claxton of Horden, who was the father of one of his retainers and the father-in-law of another, was preventing him from working some land in which they both had an interest. Richard could have ignored Randson or fobbed him off with vague promises, but instead wrote to Claxton instructing him to make concessions to his rival. Claxton prevaricated, but the matter was settled after Richard, 'marvelling greatly' that his first letter had been disregarded, left his correspondent in no doubt that he meant to 'provide his [Randson's] lawful remedy in this behalf'.[6]

The overriding impression is that Richard dealt with these several matters both fairly and firmly, and in a way calculated to earn him respect in northern political society. It was inevitable that, from time to time, he would have to contend with local ambitions and rivalries, but none of these disputes was as intractable or as potentially far-reaching as his clash with his brother George of Clarence over the Warwick inheritance. Anne Neville, the Earl of Warwick's younger daughter, had been widowed when her husband, Prince Edward of Lancaster, fell at Tewkesbury, and Richard made it clear that he wanted to marry her and take possession of her notional half-share of her parents' properties. This did not suit George, who was acting as Anne's guardian and who had apparently assumed that everything would fall to him as the husband of her elder sister Isabel. He tried to frustrate his brother's plans by concealing her somewhere in London, but Richard discovered her (disguised in the habit of a cookmaid, according to the Croyland chronicler), and lodged her in St Martin's sanctuary. He had to tread carefully because a union was only valid if both parties consented to it. Taking Anne into his own custody would have allowed George to claim that he had abducted her and forced her to marry him against her will.

Richard appealed to King Edward and Sir John Paston told a correspondent that 'the King entreateth my Lord of Clarence for my Lord of Gloucester', but Edward had to be more even-handed in public. In February 1472 he invited his brothers to discuss the matter in Council, and may have been as surprised as the Croyland writer by the 'many arguments ... [that] were, with the greatest acuteness, put forward'. Richard and George presented their cases so eloquently that 'all present, and the lawyers even, were quite surprised that these princes should find argument in such abundance by means of which to support their respective causes', and the inevitable compromise pleased neither of them. Richard was given permission to marry Anne and was confirmed in possession of the northern Warwick lands the King had already given him; but he had to surrender his office of chamberlain of England to George, who was to receive the rest of the inheritance and who was created earl of Warwick and of Salisbury on 25 March.[7]

Richard wed Anne at a date variously estimated to have been as early as March 1472 or as late as May 1474, but this was by no means the end of the matter. Many of the estates promised to George belonged to the widowed Countess of Warwick, who had been in sanctuary at Beaulieu in Hampshire since her husband's death at Barnet. She tried desperately to protect her rights, appealing to the King, George and Richard among others; but it was not until June 1473 that Richard ordered his retainer Sir James Tyrell to escort her to Middleham 'men say by the King's assent, whereto some men say that the Duke of Clarence is not agreed'.[8] Richard knew the Countess Anne well and may have been repaying her earlier kindness to him; but he may also have calculated that with the legal owner of so many of the lands in his possession he would find it easier to bring pressure to bear on his brothers. He would have been a fool merely to shrug his shoulders and allow George to take more than his share.

What precisely happened next is uncertain, but by November all pretensions of harmony had been abandoned. Sir John Paston reported that

the world seemeth queasy here [in London]; for the most part that be about the King have sent hither for their harness [armour], and it [is] said for certain that the Duke of Clarence maketh him big in that he can, showing as he would but deal with the Duke of Gloucester; but the King intenteth, in eschewing all inconvenients, to be a big as they both, and to be a stifler between them.[9]

Edward apparently leaned heavily on his brothers, particularly on George, who was threatened with the loss of some of the estates he held by royal grant, and his success allowed a relieved Paston to express the hope that 'the two dukes of Clarence and Gloucester shall be set at one by the award of the King'[10] only sixteen days later. In May 1474 Richard was allowed to add Barnard Castle in County Durham and a group of Welsh Marcher lordships to his existing portion, and Isabel and Anne's title (and that of their husbands) was secured by an Act of Parliament that declared the Countess of Warwick to be legally deceased. This was manifestly unjust, but Richard had at least reunited his mother-in-law with her younger daughter, and ensured that his wife would be a great lady again.

The Act that disinherited the Countess contained several other important clauses. Richard was allowed to retain his wife's lands for his own lifetime if she predeceased him (normally, they would have reverted to her own heirs), and, more unusually, to keep them if he and Anne were either temporarily or permanently separated:

It is ordained by the same authority that if the said Richard, duke of Gloucester, and Anne shall subsequently be divorced, and then lawfully married, this present act shall still be to them as good and valid as if no such divorce had taken place, but that the same Anne had continued as the wife of the said duke of Gloucester.

And:

It is ordained by the said authority that if the said duke of Gloucester and Anne shall subsequently be divorced, and he then does the very best he can, by all appropriate and lawful means, to be lawfully married to the said Anne, the daughter, and during the lifetime of the same Anne is not wedded or married to any other woman: that the said duke of Gloucester shall still have and enjoy as much of the foregoing as shall appertain to the said Anne during the lifetime of the said duke of Gloucester.[11]

'Divorce' in this context means annulment, the marriage being deemed to be invalid because the couple were related within the prohibited degrees. Richard's mother and Anne's paternal grandfather were brother and sister, his great-grandfather Edmund of Langley was her great-great-grandfather (making them first and second cousins, once removed), and he was also her first husband Prince Edward of Lancaster's second cousin once removed. This meant that they were related by blood (consanguinity) in the second and third, and in the third and fourth, degrees, as well as by marriage (affinity) in the third and fourth degrees, and could only wed lawfully if all three impediments were 'dispensed' by an appropriate papal licence or licences. A document discovered in the recently opened archives of the Papal Penitentiary has shown that Richard and Anne sought – and obtained – a dispensation for the relationship created by her marriage to Prince Edward, but there is no mention of the blood ties between them. They would not have requested – nor would the Papacy have issued – a document that was effectively worthless because it only addressed some of the issues, and there must, logically, have been an oversight or misunderstanding. This could have happened when the petition was being drawn up in London, or alternatively (and more probably) when the formal consent was prepared in Rome.

All Richard and Anne could do in this situation was to submit a second application to dispense their blood relationships, and place their marriage on hold until permission was granted. There is no direct evidence that George of Clarence interfered in the process, but he would have been quick to realise that if Richard was not, and did not become, Anne's legal husband he would not have to share the Warwick inheritance with him. Richard clearly feared that a full dispensation would be denied him (perhaps because George was secretly 'lobbying' against him at Rome), and so he ensured that Parliament gave him a life interest in Anne's properties even if their marriage was frustrated. This seems to have been the end of the matter (it was not even raised when Richard later called King Edward's marriage into question), so we may assume that George's efforts failed and a licence was obtained.[12]

The final piece of the jigsaw was put in place in February 1475 when another Act of Parliament barred John Neville's son George's claim to his uncle Warwick's entailed northern properties and made it less likely that he would be able to wrest them from Richard at some time in the future. Throughout this episode Richard had shown himself to be articulate and persuasive (particularly when laying his case before his brothers and the Council), but also both clever and determined. They were characteristics he would display on other occasions, not least when he seized the Crown in 1483.

It has been suggested that Richard was a hard man who was becoming yet harder, and some have found further evidence of this in his dealings with Elizabeth Howard, the elderly dowager Countess of Oxford. Richard had been granted most of the forfeited estates of her son, the Earl of Oxford, in 1471, and made it clear that he expected to inherit the Countess's own lands which would have passed to Oxford on her death.[13] Elizabeth tried to forestall him by conveying her properties to a group of feoffees (trustees) who became their legal owners and who would distribute them in accordance with her will or other instructions: but Richard believed that he had a moral – if not a strictly legal – right to them and reacted vigorously. According to later accounts he compelled the Countess to leave the nunnery at Stratford le Bow (Essex) where she was then staying, took her to his own lodgings in Stepney, and held her prisoner until she agreed to surrender the lands to him. He allegedly threatened to send her on a long (and potentially fatal) journey to Middleham in the middle of winter unless she co-operated, and witnesses testified that they had often seen her reduced to tears.

The 'problem' with these allegations is that they were all made twenty and more years later when Richard was long dead and the now restored Earl of Oxford wanted to confirm his right to his late mother's properties. Oxford had recovered all his former possessions after the battle of Bosworth, but feared that if his mother had legally disposed of her assets he would face claims from those who had subsequently bought them. He argued that her actions were invalid because she had acted under duress, and petitioned Cardinal Morton, the Chancellor, to take depositions from six former (presumably hand-picked) deponents who would corroborate his story. Oxford had breezily claimed that Richard's behaviour was 'openly and notoriously known' when he was first restored to his earldom, but by 1495 death had thinned the ranks of potential witnesses and memories were fading. He clearly thought it prudent to obtain formal, written testimony while there was still time.

So did Richard behave particularly badly towards the Countess, or was he merely trying to protect his own interests? Elizabeth formally released her rights in her estates to him in deeds dated 9 January 1473, a transaction he afterwards claimed was 'at the desire of the said countess, and by the advice of her council'. He undertook to allow her an annuity of 500 marks (£333 6s 8d) for life, to pay debts totalling £240, to provide a younger son studying for the priesthood with a benefice, and to honour bequests to her children, grandchildren and others in accordance with her wishes. Professor Hicks has argued that 'there is no evidence that Gloucester paid any of Elizabeth's bequests, provided for her children or grandchildren, or promoted any of her sons to benefices', but perhaps not even his Richard would have perjured himself by making false statements or given assurances he had no intention of keeping. William Tunstall, one of Oxford's witnesses, testified that he had comforted the weeping Countess by telling her that 'the said duke [Richard] was a knight and a king's brother, and [he] trusted that he would do her no wrong'.[14]

Seven of the thirteen feoffees initially refused to seal the Countess's deeds – because they were not certain they reflected her true wishes – and Richard had to haul them before the Chancellor to oblige them to comply. A hearing before Chancellor Stillington was aborted when he was replaced by Laurence Booth in June 1473,[15] and it was Booth who subsequently pronounced in Richard's favour. This does not suggest that he found the Duke's arguments unjust or unconvincing (Hicks's claim that he 'was a highly partial judge and one certainly cannot accept his decree without question as just' again reflects his view of the whole matter), and the same is true of King Edward, who could have intervened but chose not to. One deponent, Sir John Risley, said that the King had warned him against buying the dowager's London town house from Richard some years later because although 'the title of the place be good in my brother of Gloucester's hands' it would be hard for a lesser man to 'keep it and defend it'. He did not say that Richard's title was bad – only that some might claim that it was.

It would be fascinating to have a full, impartial account of this episode, but medieval evidence is seldom complete or unbiased. Richard may have been economical with the truth when he implied that he had reached an amicable settlement with the old lady, but whatever she *feared* might happen to her, none of the witnesses claimed to *know* that she had been abused or threatened while in his custody. They stated as much as they remembered – or thought they remembered – but may not have appreciated that persuasion is one thing and coercion another.

Richard could certainly manipulate a situation when he chose to, but his dealings were not always contrary to the other party's interests. By early 1476 the payments due to him as warden of the West March were in arrears, and King Edward proposed that he accept the wardship of the sixteen-year-old Thomas, Lord Scrope of Masham, in lieu. This would have allowed him to farm the boy's lands to his own profit, but inquiries revealed that they were burdened with the widow's jointure, with a trust created to provide for Thomas's brothers and sisters, and with a debt due to Sir Richard Strangeways. Richard accordingly entered into negotiations with Lady Elizabeth, Thomas's mother, who agreed to pay him 200 marks annually from the revenues of the Scrope properties and to accept that her son and their affinity would be ruled by him. This was more, perhaps much more, than Richard would have earned by administering the lands directly, but he did not renege on his undertaking 'to be good and loving lord to the said Elizabeth, Thomas her son, and all her said servants, tenants and inhabitants'.[16] He gave Thomas a place in his household, facilitated his marriage to a daughter of Marquis Montagu as his late father had intended, and after he became king allowed his brother Ralph Scrope to wed King Edward's now 'illegitimate' daughter Cecily. Both sides benefitted from the arrangement, and for the Scropes there was the added advantage that their lands were not given to a guardian who might have wasted them for a quick profit. Richard saw an opportunity to augment both his wealth and his northern following and did not allow it to pass him by.

There can be no doubt that, when it came to protecting and extending his interests, Richard was as aggressive as any other medieval nobleman, but was he *unusually* so? Professor Hicks has drawn attention to a register of grants, deeds and other memoranda (now British Library Cotton Julius BXII), compiled by Richard's secretariat in the years before 1483.[17] It was apparently intended to furnish evidence of his title to his various lands and offices, and included not only the estates and appointments he held at the time of writing but others he had surrendered or which the King had granted to third parties. The implication is that he hoped to recover these one day if and when the opportunity presented itself, and that he personally directed the quite considerable efforts of the researchers and lawyers who were charged to seek out anything that might work to his advantage. Clearly, no chance to increase his acres or extend his influence was to be allowed to go begging, but was he more avaricious or just more efficient? Because he was a King's brother his activities were always likely to be on a larger scale than those who ranked beneath him in the social pecking-order, and even Professor Hicks concedes 'that Richard was acquisitive needs no emphasis and no justification. He had to be, if he was to achieve the level of resources ... considered appropriate for a royal duke and to endow a ducal dynasty.' One is reminded of the late Bruce McFarlane's observation that 'a lord needed to look well to his own if he were to keep it ... the indolent, the vacillating, or the feeble good-intentioned would not long have had any estates to enjoy'.[18]

5

WAR & PEACE, 1475–1482

King Edward was determined to punish Louis XI for backing Warwick and Queen Margaret against him in 1470–1, and the settlement with his brothers removed a major obstacle to what has been called his 'Great Enterprise'. His decision to invade France in Edward III's and Henry V's footsteps was a bold one given that the English had been ignominiously expelled from Normandy and Gascony only twenty years earlier, and it would be interesting to know if he really expected to be crowned King of France at Rheims after he had deposed Louis or if privately, his sights were set much lower. It took several years to negotiate alliances with Burgundy and Brittany (Brittany was the other semi-independent duchy that feared absorption into France proper), and to secure peace with Scotland and the Hansards; but friendships had been cemented and potential enemies neutralised by the summer of 1475.

Funding an army of invasion was a very expensive business, and although Parliament allowed Edward to raise large sums through taxation (more than in all the earlier years of the reign put together), he still had recourse to 'benevolences', gifts from wealthy subjects who he charmed or intimidated into increasing their contributions. The money was spent on hiring and repairing a fleet of transports, various pieces of ordnance (including 779 stone cannon balls), food and equipment (at least 10,000 sheaves of arrows), and on wages for the near 20,000 soldiers and non-combatants such as craftsmen and sappers. It was a larger army than any previous English king had led across the Channel, and included a force of ten knights, one hundred men-at-arms and a thousand archers recruited by his brother Richard, who received a mark (13s 4d) for each day he served.[1]

King Edward crossed to Calais on 4 July but the campaign did not go according to plan. The Duke of Brittany failed to assist him, while Charles of Burgundy brought only a small personal escort and refused to allow the English to enter his towns. Edward did not relish the prospect of fighting alone or spending the winter in hostile territory, and accepted King Louis's suggestion that envoys from both sides should meet to discuss a treaty. The English terms were rigorous – Louis was to pay Edward £15,000 within fifteen days, £10,000 each year for their lifetimes, and provide a dowry of £60,000 when the Dauphin married one of his daughters – but the French king took the view that paying his enemies to go home was better than waging a costly and potentially devastating war against them. The two monarchs held a friendly meeting on the bridge at Picquigny, near Amiens, and the English army retraced its steps to Calais as soon as the first instalment of the money had been paid.

The Duke of Clarence, the Earl of Northumberland, Lord Hastings and other peers accompanied Edward to his meeting with Louis, but Richard was among those who absented themselves. He was 'not pleased by the peace' – to quote the Franco-Burgundian writer Philippe de Commynes, who was present – presumably because he thought financial and political gains a poor substitute for military glory. Commynes says that, in the end, he accepted the situation, and that 'shortly afterwards the duke of Gloucester came to visit the King [Louis] at Amiens and the King gave him some very fine presents, including plate and well-equipped horses'.[2] He was bound to concur with his royal brother's decision, but would, possibly, have preferred to join those who took the view that they had come to France to do some fighting and who now offered their services to the Duke of Burgundy. Louis had donned sheep's clothing to beguile Edward, but Richard knew that beneath it he remained a wolf.

The French campaign had taken Richard away from home and England for some three months, perhaps longer, and it was at about this time – possibly at the beginning of 1476 or a little earlier – that Anne Neville gave birth to their son Edward. Not much is known of this boy – he only achieved prominence of a sort when his father became king and he was briefly Prince of Wales – and his earliest years were spent entirely at Middleham, where Isabel Burgh was employed to nurse him and 'our right well beloved servant Anne Idley' was appointed 'Mistress of the Nursery'. His parents doubtless hoped that siblings would soon join him, but he was destined to remain their only child.[3]

Richard and the rest of the army arrived back in England in September, and he was able to spend the winter months at Middleham with his family before duty again called him away. His father Richard, Duke of York, and brother Edmund, Earl of Rutland, had been buried perfunctorily at Pontefract after being killed at Wakefield in 1460, and King Edward decided that now was the moment to transfer their remains to the family church at Fotheringhay. He could, presumably, have done this at any time in the 1460s or even more recently, and it is difficult to avoid the conclusion that it was King Louis's pension that funded what was both an act of piety and an opportunity to display his new wealth and authority. Richard was designated chief mourner and charged with supervising the day-to-day arrangements as the cortège made its way south.

The bodies were exhumed about 21 July 1476 and placed in coffins within elaborate hearses decorated with heraldic and religious symbols. An effigy of the Duke wearing a dark blue royal mourning gown, a purple cap of maintenance, and with an angel holding a crown behind his head was placed above his casket, and Richard, the Earl of Northumberland, Lord Stanley and other noblemen knelt before it 'within the rails'. When the cortège left Pontefract the following day it was led by Richard riding immediately behind the carriage at the head of his father's effigy, accompanied by a large party of peers, bishops, abbots, heralds, the singers of the Chapel Royal, and 400 poor men on foot carrying large torches. Their route took them through Doncaster, Blyth, Tuxford, Newark-on-Trent, Grantham and Stamford, and at each stopping place the clergymen rode on ahead to ensure that everything was in readiness. Local worthies welcomed them, services were held both on arrival and departure, and alms given to the poor.

When the cortège reached Fotheringhay on 29 July Richard and his brothers Edward and George received the bodies and the Duke's effigy into the church with great ceremony. The coffins were again placed on hearses, and after 'Placebo' and 'Dirige' had been said the assembled nobles each laid a number of pieces of cloth of gold over them. Next day, the day of the funeral, three masses were celebrated, the Bishop of Lincoln preached the sermon, and the Duke's knightly 'achievements', his coat of arms, shield, sword and helmet, were offered at the altar together with his harness. The harness was brought into the church by Lord Ferrers, riding a black warhorse, displaying the full royal arms and holding an axe, point downwards, the emphasis throughout being on the validity of the Duke's claim to the throne and that of his son Edward after him.

After the bodies had been buried a great feast was held in tents specially erected for the occasion. Prodigious quantities of food and drink were provided, enough to feed as many as 2,000 guests and members of staff, and five times as many people who came seeking charity were given a penny. Everyone was presumably served in order of rank – another triumph of organisation – although on this occasion we have no knowledge of who sat where. The occasion had been a great success, and Richard could reflect that this had been in no small measure thanks to him.[4]

King Edward had done his best to heal the rift between Richard and George of Clarence, but their relationship may have been one of tolerance rather than friendship. They had worked together to promote the French expedition and to jointly rebury their father, but George may have envied Richard's rewarding, vice-regal role in northern England, and dreamed of securing a similar, or greater, position for himself. His prospects seemed decidedly limited until, by a remarkable coincidence, his wife Isabel died on 22 December 1476, and Duke Charles of Burgundy was killed in battle at Nancy thirteen days later. Charles left an only daughter, Mary, to defend the Burgundian lands against King Louis, and his widow Duchess Margaret proposed that her stepdaughter should marry George, her brother. George was delighted by the prospect of cutting a figure on the stage of Europe, but King Edward refused even to consider it. He knew that direct English involvement in Burgundy would inevitably jeopardise his French pension, and may have been influenced by rumours (spread, probably, by King Louis) that George would use the duchy as a springboard to the throne of England when Edward died.

George, angry and frustrated, withdrew from Court, and began to behave as though he was a law unto himself in his own territories. He had Ankarette Twynho, a servant of his late wife, hanged on the absurd charge that she had poisoned her mistress (everyone knew that Duchess Isabel had died after childbirth), and challenged the validity of the royal justice by declaring that Thomas Burdet, a supporter who had been executed for treason, was entirely innocent. King Edward could not tolerate such insubordinate behaviour and was almost bound to punish his brother: but contemporaries were surprised when George was executed on 18 February 1478. Medieval rulers were more inclined to imprison troublesome brothers than eliminate them,[5] and George had done little more than make a nuisance of himself. The implication is that Edward saw him as a danger either to himself or to the succession, perhaps because he had threatened to question the legality of the royal marriage. It would be questioned again in 1483.

Richard may have been glad to see the back of George or he may have thought that King Edward was overreacting. The Italian Dominic Mancini heard that 'at that time Richard Duke of Gloucester was so overcome with grief for his brother, that he could not dissimulate so well, but was overheard to say that he would one day avenge his brother's death';[6] but he was content to recover the great chamberlainship of England he had surrendered to George six years earlier, to exchange manors in the south for his brother's castle and fee farm of Richmond (Yorks.), and to accept the earldom of Salisbury for his infant son. Richard had, in fact, continued to add to his northern estates and offices throughout the 1470s. We have already noted that he acquired Barnard Castle in County Durham as part of his share of the Countess of Warwick's inheritance, and lands in Derbyshire and Hertfordshire which came to him from the same source were exchanged for the royal castle and lordship of Scarborough. In February 1475 he was appointed sheriff of Cumberland for life, a grant which included, or came to include, the profits of the shrievalty, the demesne lands of Carlisle Castle and the city's fee farm; and a few months later the King gave him the forfeited barony and estates of the Clifford family based on Skipton Castle in the West Riding. These had initially been conferred on Sir William Stanley, Lord Stanley's brother, but he now surrendered them and Richard released his interest in Chirk, in the Welsh Marches (where Stanley was influential), in return. Richard was consolidating his northern hegemony at the expense of lands in other parts of the country, and from time to time resided at Barnard Castle, Skipton and Scarborough. It was essential to see and be seen.

Another way in which Richard promoted his influence in the region was through his stewardship of the northern lands of the Duchy of Lancaster. These consisted of the lordships of Pickering and Tickhill in the north and south of Yorkshire together with estates in the Aire valley (including Pontefract, the steward's official residence), and the forest of Knaresborough. Across the Pennines the steward administered the county palatine of Lancashire, land in north Cheshire and the Forest of Bowland, and was also responsible for the north midlands lordships of Tutbury in Staffordshire and the High Peak in Derbyshire. They had become royal property when the Duke of Lancaster, Henry Bolingbroke, had seized Richard II's throne in 1399, but had remained a separate entity within the Crown estate, a situation Edward IV saw no reason to alter. In theory, it was the King who made appointments, granted annuities and leases, and commanded the loyalty of those who lived and worked in the various territories: but much of this patronage lay in the hands of the steward who dispensed it on a day-to-day basis. Richard was the man in charge of the Duchy and Richard had the ear of the King.

Part of Richard's strategy was to win the goodwill of institutions and individuals through what may be termed 'good lordship', and nowhere is this more evident than in his dealings with the city of York and with the Earl of Westmoreland's heir Ralph, Lord Neville. The mayor and aldermen of York sought his assistance on matters ranging from the potential loss of their charter of liberties to the removal of illegal fishgarths (traps that restricted navigation on the river Ouse and reduced the number of fish available to ordinary people), and found him ready to use his influence to intercede for them. The result was that he was always honourably received in the city, feted and given presents, but it was a relationship founded on mutual respect rather than on the domination of one by the other. When, in 1482, Thomas Redeheid, a servant of Richard's treasurer, abused a citizen who was visiting Middleham Castle, Richard had no hesitation in sending Redeheid to York to be punished,[7] and his ability to influence mayoral elections was limited. When the question 'who shall we have for our mayor this year?' was posed in an alehouse at the beginning of 1483, one Stephen Hoghson answered that 'if it please the commons I would that we had Master [Thomas] Wrangwysh for he is the man that my lord of Gloucester will do for'. The parties could not agree on what followed, but Richard Rede, a girdler, allegedly retorted that 'if my lord of Gloucester would have him mayor the commons would not have him mayor ... for the mayor must be chosen by the commonalty, not by no lord'. Witnesses claimed afterwards that Rede had said only that 'my lord of Gloucester would not be displeased whomsoever it pleased the commons to choose for their mayor' – clearly, they were anxious not to offend Richard, but their 'rights', as they saw them, came first.[8]

Ralph, Lord Neville, belonged to the 'senior' Durham branch of the family, whose members had long been at loggerheads with the Earl of Salisbury and his son Warwick, their 'junior' relatives of the half-blood. Ralph Neville, Earl of Westmoreland (d. 1425), had sired twenty-three children, nine by his first wife Margaret Stafford, and fourteen by his second, Joan Beaufort. His heir was his grandson by the eldest son of his first wife (John, his eldest son by Margaret Stafford, had died in his father's lifetime), but he settled the bulk of his estate on Joan, who was closely related to the royal family. The young Earl of Westmoreland tried desperately to recover these lands – the Council struggled to keep the peace and find a solution for most of the 1430s – and the dispute entered a new phase when Joan was succeeded by her eldest son, Richard, Earl of Salisbury, in 1440. Salisbury was an able soldier who served the Crown in France and on the Scottish border – unlike his half-brother whose fifty-nine-year tenure of his earldom was marked by a singular lack of involvement in war and politics – and Westmoreland finally admitted defeat in 1443.

The 'agreement' reached in 1443 settled the dispute, at least in theory, but there was little love lost between the 'senior' and 'junior' branches of the family thereafter. Westmoreland remained largely aloof from the Wars of the Roses, but John, his younger brother, fought for King Henry and was perhaps partly responsible the deaths of the Duke of York and the Earl of Salisbury at Wakefield in 1460. One account says that he offered to raise men for York but then joined the opposition, and he was to die at Towton three months later. He left a five-year-old son, another Ralph, who now stood to inherit his childless uncle's earldom if he could secure the reversal of his father's attainder. There was little prospect of this in the short term – his cousin Warwick 'the Kingmaker' dominated the north throughout the 1460s – but his father's barony was restored to him in 1472, a year after Warwick's death at Barnet. When Richard of Gloucester was granted the Kingmaker's northern lands and married his younger daughter he became in effect the head of the 'junior' branch of the Neville family in the region, and reached an understanding with young Ralph soon after the latter attained his majority in 1477. Ralph renounced his residual claim to some of the family estates held by Richard, and by entering his service finally 'ended the long-standing feud between the junior and senior Neville lines'.[9]

Another Neville who needed to be neutralised was young George, Duke of Bedford, whose lands – the lands he had expected to inherit from his uncle, the Earl of Warwick – had been confirmed to Richard in 1475. George, who had been born *c.* 1457, was approaching his twenty-first birthday, and Richard may have feared that he would seek to recover some of the properties, either now or at some time in the future. The result was that he was degraded from the peerage (on the basis that his wealth was insufficient to support the dukedom of Bedford or any other title), and Richard was granted his custody and marriage two years later. Paul Murray Kendall writes of how Richard took pity on a young man who by this time had lost both parents: but there can be little doubt that Richard felt safer with his rival firmly in his own hands.[10]

Richard had made the long journey south at the end of 1477 or the beginning of 1478 partly to attend George of Clarence's trial but also to help celebrate the marriage of the King's second son, Prince Richard, to the late Duke of Norfolk's heiress, Anne Mowbray. This was another piece of dynastic gerrymandering by King Edward – the bride and groom were only five and four years old respectively and her lands were to remain with her young husband even if she died childless – but the magnificence of the occasion rivalled that of the reburial of his father eighteen months earlier. After the marriage 'was there great number of gold and silver [coins] cast among the common people, brought in basins of gold, by the high and mighty Prince, the Duke of Glouc[ester]',[11] and Richard afterwards escorted the little bride to her wedding breakfast. A great tournament was held a week later in which several of the Queen's Woodville relatives participated, but Richard (apparently) remained a spectator. There is no evidence from any period of his life that he enjoyed these mock battles or joined his peers in the lists.

The money Richard literally 'threw away' at his nephew's wedding may have been his royal brother's, or was quite possibly his own. Largesse, what K.B. McFarlane called 'conspicuous waste', was a mark of gentility, and Richard would have remembered how, when the Earl of Warwick came to London, 'six oxen were eaten at a breakfast, and every tavern was full of his meat, for who that had any acquaintance in that house, he should have had as much sodden and roast [boiled and roast meat] as he might carry upon a long dagger'.[12] Wages, fees and annuities absorbed a significant part of Richard's income, but there was more than enough left over to buy both the things he needed and the things he liked. Some of his purchases are recorded in a single surviving account containing details of his East Anglian and nearby lands for the year 1476/77.[13] They included saddles, horses, cloth of arras, woollen cloth, silk and velvet, furs and the cost of furring robes, together with other silks and furs 'delivered by command of the said duke to his most dearly beloved consort'. A total of £209 14s was spent in this way and fees and wages accounted for another £75, leaving a surplus of only £86 5s 9d in ready cash.

Richard also spent money on books: volumes that men in his position were expected to own and others that (we may assume) reflect his personal tastes and interests. Four of his known texts were religious works, four others were romances, five were histories (if we include Lydgate's *Siege of Thebes*, which was really a romance but which passed for history), four were books of instruction for princes and soldiers, and finally, there was *The Prophecy of the Eagle*, which emphasised the right of the House of York to the throne. They are only identifiable as his because he signed them, or because they bear his arms, or because they were dedicated to him, and it is likely that they once formed part of a much larger collection. Some volumes may have been destroyed while his autograph may have been erased or lost from others.

Richard certainly acquired five of these texts while he was king – four bear his royal signature, *Ricardus Rex*, and a fifth has his crowned arms – but the others were very possibly bought while he was Duke of Gloucester or even earlier. The religious works are his personalised Book of Hours, an English New Testament, *The Booke of Gostlye Grace* by Mechtild of Hackeborn, and a verse paraphrase of several Old Testament stories, while those which may be defined as 'romances' are *Palamon and Arcite* and *Griselda* by

Chaucer, a prose *Ipomedon*, and the opening section of the *Prose Tristan*. Lydgate's *Siege of Thebes*, Guido delle Colonne's *Historia Destructionis Troiae* [Troy], Geoffrey of Monmouth's *Historia Regum Britanniae*, the *Grandes Chroniques de France* and the Anonymous or Fitzhugh Chronicle (a history of England to 1199) made up a strikingly catholic history section, and practical advice was obtained from Giles of Rome's *De regimine principum* ('*On the Guidance of Princes*'), Caxton's translation of Ramon Lull's *Order of Chivalry*, Vegetius's *De Re Militari* ('*On Military Matters*'), and William Worcester's *Boke of Noblesse*. With the exception of the Vegetius they were all obtained second-hand. Richard also owned two heraldic rolls of arms depicting many hundreds of shields (which he presumably found useful in his role as constable), and would have been familiar with three illustrated family manuscripts – the *Salisbury Roll*, the *Rous Roll*, and the *Beauchamp Pageant* which portrayed him with his wife and son. His copies of the rolls of arms no longer exist, but they were noted and partially copied by Sir Thomas Wriothesley, Garter King of Arms 1505–34. The collection reveals a range of interests, but there are no works that could be described as medical or alchemical, or any dealing with estate management.[14]

Richard also used his wealth to patronise and found religious fraternities, On 21 February 1478 he obtained a royal licence to establish colleges at Barnard Castle and Middleham, but the cost was perhaps more than he had anticipated and only the Middleham foundation came into being. It consisted of a dean, six chaplains, five clerks and six choristers whose prime task was to pray for the King and Queen, Richard's parents, his brothers and sisters, and his wife and son. He took a close personal interest in the project and was almost certainly responsible for dictating the preamble to the statutes governing its constitution and organisation. No one else could have described him as a 'most simple creature, nakedly born into this wretched world, destitute of possessions, goods and inheritaments', and there is great depth of feeling in his admission that 'it hath pleased Almighty God ... of his infinite goodness not only to endow me with great possessions and of gifts of His divine grace, but also to preserve, keep and deliver me of many great jeopardies, perils and hurts'[15] – surely a reference to his two periods of exile and the battles of Barnet and Tewkesbury. Regrettably, the college was always underfinanced, perhaps partly because after Richard became king he conceived a greater plan to establish a foundation of a hundred priests in York Minster. The focus shifted away from Middleham and further endowment was curtailed by his death.

Richard also wanted to convert the chapel of St Mary which stood in the churchyard of Allhallows, Barking (London) into a royal free chapel, but again time did not allow him to bring his plan to fruition. St Mary's had first come to prominence in the thirteenth century when Prince Edward, the future Edward I, had a dream, or vision, in which he was told that if he and his successors patronised it they would always defeat the Scots and their other enemies. Edward IV had continued the tradition by founding a chantry there in 1465; but whereas Edward had made provision for two priests to pray for the well-being of members of the Yorkist royal family, Richard purposed a college consisting of a dean (Edmund Chaderton, his treasurer of the chamber) and six canons, all M.A.s. In March 1485 he endowed it with lands worth approximately £250 (there are, in fact, two grants of different properties worth roughly this amount, one presumably superseding the other), but the gift was cancelled by the Act of Resumption passed in Henry

VII's first Parliament and no more is heard of the canons. The only small consolation was that King Edward's chantry survived until the Reformation, and Richard would have been remembered by name in the daily prayers.[16]

It is impossible to estimate how much money Richard was spending or how it related to his annual income, but it is possible to believe that there were times when he found himself in debt. His lordship of Middleham and, presumably, his other northern estates were burdened with fees, his wardenship of the West March may have cost him more than the salary, and his agreements with Lady Hungerford and the Countess of Oxford required him to meet obligations from the monies he received from their former properties. Endowing the colleges was a major, although by no means the only, drain on his resources, but Richard never allowed financial considerations to overshadow his political and religious ambitions. Professor Hicks has suggested that by selling certain lands and by compounding with former owners he was effectively dissipating his capital to meet current expenditure,[17] a situation that could hardly continue indefinitely. A reluctance to reduce his outgoings, coupled with an inability to increase his income, may have given him an added reason for taking the throne in 1483.

Richard was able to spend some time in the south in 1478 because relations with Scotland were good and raids across the northern border less frequent. King Edward had betrothed his second daughter Cecily to James III's heir in 1474, and four years later James proposed that his sister Margaret should marry Queen Elizabeth's brother, Earl Rivers. Quite why or how the accord collapsed is uncertain – King Louis may have encouraged James to cause trouble to make it more difficult for Edward to interfere in Burgundy – but by 1480 it was business as usual. Edward demanded the return of Berwick which King Henry and Queen Margaret had surrendered to the Scots in return for aid twenty years earlier, and Richard was appointed lieutenant-general, with power to assemble the levies of the northern counties, on 12 May.

It was at about this time that King Louis sent Richard a 'great bombard', a large siege cannon, presumably in the hope that he would persuade his brother to maintain the Treaty of Picquigny and give the French a free hand in Burgundy. The gift was generous – one commentator has compared its value to that of a modern light aircraft – and Richard was singularly appreciative. His letter of thanks, written in London on 16 June, refers to the 'great pleasure … I have always taken and still take in artillery' (something Louis must already have known and was deliberately playing on), and added that 'I assure you it will be a special treasure to me'.[18] We do not know if the 'bombard' was ever fired in anger, but it would be somewhat ironic if Richard subsequently used it to take Berwick from Louis's allies, the Scots.[18]

Louis's strategy worked well because by the summer of 1481 all England's naval and land forces were poised to launch a major invasion of Scotland. The English fleet, commanded by John Howard, raided into the Firth of Forth, but the land campaign was delayed and all but abandoned when King Edward failed to come north in person. Some critics have suggested that he no longer had the taste, or the energy, for such enterprises, but English fortunes revived when Alexander, Duke of Albany, King James's disaffected brother, arrived in England in April 1482. It was agreed that Edward would promote Alexander's claim to the throne of Scotland, and that Alexander would return Berwick, perform homage to Edward, marry Princess Cecily if he could secure the annulment of his existing marriage, and cancel whatever agreement King James had reached with France.

Richard led a raid into south-west Scotland, burning Dumfries and other towns, in the late spring of 1482, and then joined Edward and Albany at Fotheringhay, where the accord between them was signed in June. Again Edward had announced that he intended to lead the campaign in person, but one source hints that his health was deteriorating and Richard's commission as lieutenant-general was renewed on 12 June. By mid-July a large army, including forces raised by the Earl of Northumberland, Lord Stanley and Lord Neville, had been assembled on the border, and Richard used it to devastate large areas of Roxburghshire and Berwickshire. The Scots offered little resistance – many members of their nobility were hostile to King James and his low-born favourites – and Edinburgh fell to the invaders before the end of the month.

The Scottish lords had taken King James into custody as their army moved south to engage the English, and the Duke of Albany lost no time in renouncing his claim to the throne in return for a promise that he would be restored to all his property. His defection left Richard without an obvious objective – there was little point in capturing towns that could not be occupied permanently – and the latter decided to return to Berwick, where he disbanded most of his army. Some writers have argued that Richard abandoned Edinburgh too readily and should have held out for more than the cession of Berwick and an undertaking that the Scots would adhere to the marriage treaty – if King Edward still wished to proceed with it – or repay Cecily's dowry. But none suggest what, precisely, he might have obtained or achieved.

The campaign had cost the English treasury large sums of money without winning lands or military glory for the combatants, and its success was not universally applauded. King Edward could boast to the Pope that Berwick was again an English possession, but garrisoning and guarding it proved so expensive that the Croyland writer 'knew not whether to call it "gain" or "loss"'.[19] Richard gained in prestige – Dominic Mancini wrote soon afterwards that 'such was his renown in warfare, that whenever a difficult and dangerous policy had to be undertaken, it would be entrusted to his discretion and his generalship'[20] – but there were still rumblings of disapproval in some quarters. The Stanleys blamed him rather than Edward for the failure to mount a land attack to complement Lord Howard's naval operations in 1481, and complained that their own contingent had been left isolated and in danger outside Berwick. It is impossible at this distance in time to seek to apportion blame or to guess what might have happened in other circumstances. The Stanleys' comments were made after Richard's overthrow and hindsight may have played a part.[21]

King Edward had never doubted his youngest brother's loyalty and ability, but now his confidence in him knew no bounds. A new county palatine was created for Richard in Cumberland, he was given the right to retain and bequeath any territory he could conquer in south-west Scotland, and his wardenship of the West March was made hereditary. Such rewards were perhaps not unreasonable in the circumstances, but imply that Edward had not really considered their longer-term implications. Richard was an energetic leader and administrator, but who could say that his son or grandson would display similar qualities; and the King's experiences in 1470–1 should have alerted him to the danger of placing too much power in the hands of a single 'overmighty' subject. But Edward's life was now drawing towards its conclusion, and he doubtless believed that he had acted in the best interests of the realm.

6

'THE KING IS DEAD', APRIL–JUNE 1483

King Edward IV died at Westminster after a short illness on 9 April 1483. The precise reason for his early demise remains a mystery – one contemporary thought he had caught a chill on a fishing trip and there were the inevitable hints of poison[1] – but it is perhaps more likely that a life of womanising and overeating had finally caught up with him. Philip de Commynes had noticed that he was growing fat when they met at Picquigny in 1475, and the last years of his life were characterised by a growing lethargy and a readiness to leave matters in the hands of others. He was only forty and his death would have surprised many: but perhaps there were also those who had noted his decline and wondered what the future might bring.

King Edward indisputably wanted his twelve-year-old son Edward, Prince of Wales to succeed him and to begin to rule when he was old enough, but his arrangements for the interim are less certain. His last will, and the deathbed codicils he added to it, almost certainly named Richard guardian of his heir and kingdom, but it is unclear what role he envisaged for his wife Elizabeth and her brother, Anthony, Earl Rivers. Queen Elizabeth had been entrusted with arranging their children's marriages in the will he drew up before leaving for France in 1475, while Rivers had mentored the Prince at Ludlow for a decade. They were presumably to retain some influence, an influence that would have limited Richard's role to some degree.

Richard was on his estates in Yorkshire when he learned of his brother's death, and went to York, where he required the notables present to take an oath of loyalty to the young King and swore the oath himself first. He had already written to Queen Elizabeth assuring her of his 'duty, fealty, and due obedience'[2] to his nephew, and another letter had been sent to the councillors present in London asking them to grant him the position his brother had desired for him. This ought to have been no more than a formality, but the Council was divided between those who, in Mancini's words, thought 'that the Duke of Gloucester should govern', and others who wanted the government 'carried on by many persons among whom the duke, far from being excluded, should be accounted the chief'.[3] The protectorship was probably not an issue, since Richard's authority in this capacity would last only until his nephew was crowned a few weeks later. What really mattered was whether he would then be installed as regent, with power to act as another king, or become merely the senior member of a regency council. Unsurprisingly, the majority preferred an arrangement in which they themselves would retain some say.

The Council's decision would normally have been regarded as final in these circumstances, but there were personal issues involved here as well as the good of the kingdom. We saw how King Edward's secret marriage to Elizabeth Woodville in 1464 had allowed members of her numerous clan – her brothers, the sons of her first marriage, and her sisters' husbands – to rise to positions of authority, and there had been much ill-feeling between them and some members of the 'older' noble families. Dislike of the Woodvilles had been one reason why the Earl of Warwick had rebelled in 1469, and William, Lord Hastings, had quarrelled with them – over disputed offices and shared mistresses – in the course of the 1470s. The young King had been brought up by his uncle Rivers and his mother's family, and at twelve was old enough to give them precedence over men he perhaps neither knew nor liked.

There is no evidence that Richard was on bad terms with the Woodvilles in his brother's lifetime – on the contrary, his relations with them seem to have been entirely amicable – but he would have been sensitive to any arrangement that placed him at the mercy of others. His main concern was that his title in his Neville lands, from which he derived most of his wealth and influence, was not as secure as if he had inherited them from his father. He was assured of his wife Anne's estates only as long as she and their son Edward lived, and his grant of young George Neville's patrimony would similarly revert to a life interest if George died without issue. This was all well and good if Edward and George married and had children; but there was a real possibility that other members of the Neville family would lay claim to the inheritance if they – and Anne – died prematurely and Richard was politically weakened. In the event Anne, Edward and George all expired between 1483 and 1485, but by then Richard was king.

William, Lord Hastings, clearly feared a Woodville-dominated government, and wrote to Richard to advise him of the Council's decision and to urge him to come to London with a well-armed retinue as soon as possible. He threatened to retire to Calais unless the escort bringing the boy-king from Ludlow to the capital was limited, and Queen Elizabeth, who 'most beneficiently tried to extinguish every spark of murmuring and disturbance',[4] agreed that her son and his guardian Earl Rivers would be accompanied by no more than 2,000 men. Richard himself contacted Rivers, and also the Duke of Buckingham, apparently arranging to meet them in the vicinity of Northampton on their way to London. Buckingham was descended from Edward III's youngest son, Thomas of Woodstock, and was one of England's most senior noblemen. Eloquent but shallow, Edward IV had not rated him highly, but Richard clearly thought him a man he could trust.

When Richard reached Northampton on 29 April he learned that Rivers and the King were already at Stony Stratford, seventeen miles nearer London. Contact was soon established, and Rivers, together with Lord Richard Grey, one of the Queen's sons by her first marriage, and others, rode back to Northampton to greet him. The Duke of Buckingham also arrived and the four noblemen passed a pleasant evening together; but next morning Rivers, Grey and two other members of their company were abruptly arrested and sent under guard to Richard's northern strongholds.[5] The two dukes then rode to Stony Stratford, where Richard informed the young King that he had uncovered a plot aimed at denying him the government, and that the perpetrators had been dealt with. The youth replied spiritedly that the men Richard accused had been appointed by his father and he had found them 'good and faithful';[6] but he realised that the dukes were demanding, rather than requesting, his compliance and that he was now, effectively, in their power.

Richard paid his nephew every respect and emphasised his own loyalty to him; but he had taken the first step down a road that would lead him inexorably to the throne. Some contemporaries supposed that this had always been his objective, but it is highly improbable that, at this stage, he foresaw the events of the next few months clearly. He had undoubtedly realised that whoever controlled the young King would dominate both the Council and the kingdom, but may not have grasped (yet) that securing the protectorship and regency would not guarantee his own long-term future. English boy-kings had taken the reins of government long before they reached legal adulthood – Henry III at nineteen, Henry VI at fifteen – and it would only be a very few years before Edward V would do likewise. Richard had time to win his nephew's friendship, to make himself all but indispensable to him: but in the last resort a king was entitled to choose his own counsellors and was not obliged to consult even a former regent. Richard would have known how his predecessor as Duke of Gloucester, Duke Humphrey, had been disgraced and possibly murdered by Henry VI's Beaufort relatives at Bury in 1447. Perhaps the more he thought about it, the more he feared that Edward V's Woodville relations would eliminate him if they had their way.

When word of the events at Northampton and Stony Stratford reached London, Queen Elizabeth and the Marquis of Dorset, the eldest son of her first marriage, tried to persuade other lords to help them oppose Richard's takeover. But they had never quite won acceptance – some still regarded them as upstarts – and when letters were received from Richard explaining that he had acted for his own safety and in the young King's best interests 'all praised the Duke of Gloucester for his dutifulness towards his nephews and for his intention to punish their enemies'.[7] The terrified Queen realised that resistance was hopeless, and used the short time she had before Richard reached London to install her family in the Westminster sanctuary. Sir Thomas More's *History of King Richard III* is not the most reliable of sources – it is unclear if More was writing history or telling a moral story – but his description of Elizabeth's distress is too realistic to be pure invention. The Chancellor, the Archbishop of York, is said to have found her 'sat alone low on the rushes all desolate and dismayed, whom he comforted in the best manner he could, showing her that he trusted the matter was nothing so sore as she took it for', while all around them was 'much heaviness, rumble, haste and business, carriage and conveyance of her stuff into sanctuary, chests, coffers, packs, bundles, trusses, all on men's backs, no man unoccupied, some lading, some going, some discharging, some coming for more, some breaking down the walls to bring in the next way'.[8]

Richard, Buckingham and the young King reached London on 4 May, the date originally proposed for the coronation, and although this was now, inevitably, postponed (until 22 June), there was no hint of cancellation. The gorgeously dressed mayor and aldermen turned out to welcome their new sovereign, and Richard was quick to show them four cartloads of weapons and armour which, he said, the Woodvilles had been planning to use against him. The vast probability is that if these really were Woodville arms they had been hastily assembled in the aftermath of the coup at Stony Stratford and Northampton rather than before it, the clear implication being that Richard felt it necessary to justify his actions to the political nation. Perhaps he was also trying to convince himself.

The Council duly recognised Richard as protector, but refused to consider capital charges against those arrested on 30 April because he had not then been vested with vice-regal authority. The unreliable Archbishop of York, who had briefly surrendered the Great Seal to the embattled Queen Elizabeth, was replaced as

Chancellor by Bishop John Russell of Lincoln, and Buckingham was rewarded with great authority in Wales; but these changes apart, Richard seems to have aimed at continuity and to have resisted the temptation to give as many offices as possible to his own followers. He clearly wanted to create an impression of normality, and to assuage the fears of those who, in Mancini's words, 'always suspected whither his enterprises would lead'.[9]

Our knowledge of the next few weeks is scanty – perhaps there was little outwardly to engage the chroniclers' interest – but dramatic events were unfolding behind the scenes. Richard, we may suppose, worried constantly about the future, searched his conscience many times over, and sought the advice and opinions of senior noblemen: and it was perhaps only after a considerable period of uncertainty that he finally decided that he had no alternative but to make himself king. This, however, was no easy matter. He would have to secure the person of Prince Richard, his younger nephew, who was in sanctuary with his mother; neutralise powerful men like William, Lord Hastings, who would not countenance Edward V's deposition; and, perhaps most importantly, find a reason that would allow him to claim the throne *legally*. It was not enough to argue that he would prove a more able ruler than young Edward, or that he was afraid of what the future might hold.

Richard may have been reluctant to set a revolution in motion, but the decision, once made, was executed with all his usual determination and thoroughness. On 10/11 June he wrote to Ralph, Lord Neville, the City of York and other supporters asking them 'to aid and assist us against the Queen, her blood adherents and affinity, which have intended and daily doeth intend, to murder and utterly destroy us and our cousin, the duke of Buckingham, and the old royal blood of this realm'.[10] There was no immediate threat – it would be some time before northern troops could reach the city and the Queen's party had already been decimated – but Richard clearly thought that soldiers might be needed as the situation unfolded. Two days later, on Friday 13 June, he arranged for the Council to be divided and to meet in two separate places. Some members assembled at Westminster to consider arrangements for the boy-king's coronation, while others were summoned to the Tower to discuss more political matters. Richard attended the latter gathering, and at some point accused William, Lord Hastings, of conspiring with the Woodvilles against him. Armed men concealed in readiness rushed into the chamber, and Hastings was seized and beheaded without even the formality of a trial.

Hastings's sudden death, and the arrest of the Archbishop of York, Lord Stanley (who was slightly wounded in the fracas), and other supporters of Edward V, spread fear and alarm in the streets of the capital. Richard tried to calm the citizens by claiming that a conspiracy against the King had been uncovered and that Hastings, the perpetrator, had paid the penalty; but there were many who, according to Mancini, 'believed that the plot had been feigned by the duke to escape the odium of such a crime'.[11] Hastings was well liked – 'a good knight and a gentle … a loving man and passing wellbeloved' in Thomas More's words[12] – and had welcomed the establishment of Richard's protectorate. His poor relationship with Elizabeth Woodville and her family could be traced back to his dealings with her in Leicestershire before she became queen – when he had agreed to take her part in a dispute with her mother-in-law but on his own somewhat harsh terms – and time had done nothing to improve it. She thought him 'secretly familiar with the King in wanton company', in More's phrase, and there had been more friction when he superseded her brother Anthony as Captain of Calais and quarrelled with her son the Marquis of Dorset over mistresses. It has been suggested that Hastings had hoped to be as close to Richard as he had been to King Edward and resented Buckingham's intrusion: but, logically, the only thing that would have brought these old enemies together was their mutual loyalty to their new sovereign and the realisation that Richard wanted his throne.

Three days later, on 16 June, Richard sent the Archbishop of Canterbury and other senior figures to the Westminster sanctuary to persuade Queen Elizabeth to surrender her younger son to him. The Queen stalled as much as possible, rejecting the lords' arguments that Prince Richard did not need to be in sanctuary because he had committed no crime and that his elder brother was lonely and wanted him for a playfellow. But she was aware that Richard's father and brother had both forced sanctuaries when it suited them, and was dismayed by the Archbishop's threat that he and others who wished her well would abandon her if she refused to co-operate. The Archbishop assured her that he would personally guarantee the boy's safety, and with that she reluctantly released him into Richard's hands.

Events now moved quickly. On Sunday 22 June Richard tackled his third and final difficulty by arranging for Ralph Shaw, a Cambridge doctor of theology, to preach a sermon at St Paul's Cross. What, precisely, Shaw said is open to question, but according to Mancini he claimed that Edward IV had been fathered on Cecily of York by a French archer and that neither he nor his offspring had any right to the kingdom. This was an old story, based probably on nothing more than the fact that Edward had been born in France at Rouen, and so angered Duchess Cecily that the focus switched to the validity of Edward IV's marriage.[13] Robert Stillington, the bishop of Bath and Wells, is said to have informed Richard that when Edward secretly married Elizabeth Woodville in 1464 he was already pre-contracted to Lady Eleanor Butler, the widowed daughter of the late Earl of Shrewsbury. A pre-contract was more binding than a modern-day engagement – it effectively precluded marriage with another person – and, if true, meant that Edward and Elizabeth had never been more than partners. Their children could not succeed to the throne because they were illegitimate, and Richard was *ipso facto* the rightful king.

There can be no doubt that Richard found this revelation highly convenient, although if it was the real reason why George of Clarence had been executed five years earlier he may have had it in his pocket all along. The real *question* of course is how true was it, and was Richard acting as he did at least partly because he was convinced of its veracity? Edward IV had had numerous affairs both before and after his marriage, and had probably made casual promises to various ladies. He had no intention of keeping these of course, and had doubtless forgotten most of them, but it is distinctly possible that Lady Eleanor had agreed to have sex with him on the understanding that he would subsequently marry her. She did not complain when he afterwards wed Elizabeth Woodville – her protests would have been music to the ears of Warwick the Kingmaker and others who were dismayed by the marriage – nor did Edward think that whatever undertaking he had given her ought to be formally nullified. Perhaps he only recognised the danger when his difficulties with George came to a head.

It is clear that by 1478 the horse had long since bolted, but Edward could have taken steps to regularise his union with Queen Elizabeth much earlier. The position was, apparently, that if Elizabeth knew in 1464 that Edward was not free to marry her then their marriage was invalid and they could not have become man and wife at any time in the future. But if she did not know (and how could she have known unless Edward himself told her?), she could have married the King legally after Lady Eleanor died.[14] This was important because Eleanor had died in 1468, two years before the birth of the boy who was now Edward V, and although these were difficult times for his parents they would surely have approached the Church if they had genuinely feared for the future. Clearly, they did not do so, and the most likely explanation is that King Edward had not then realised that what was probably no more than an old, casual liaison had the potential to harm his son.

The young King's alleged bastardy did not necessarily disqualify him, of course. Illegitimacy had not prevented William the Conqueror from becoming king in 1066, nor did similar allegations against Henry VIII's daughters, Mary and Elizabeth, bar them from becoming England's first queens regnant in the sixteenth century.[15] If the powers that be had still wanted Edward V to reign over them they could have validated his title in Parliament or, alternatively, just crowned him. Anointing and sacring would have made him a king however questionable his title, and Richard knew that if he allowed this to happen he would not be able to object afterwards. He had to strike now or not at all.

Two days later, on Tuesday 24 June, Buckingham explained Richard's claim to an assembly of London's leading citizens, and tried to persuade them (with much difficulty, apparently) that he was his late brother's rightful successor. The lords and other notables who had come to the capital for the coronation and to attend the now cancelled meeting of Parliament were treated to a similar oration on Wednesday, the day Richard unilaterally ordered the executions of Earl Rivers and the others seized at Stony Stratford and Northampton. Peers who had come to London attended by armed retinues had already been ordered to disperse them, and Mancini was in no doubt that they agreed to accept Richard as their sovereign only because they saw no practical alternative. Guided by Buckingham, they drew up a petition asking Richard to take the crown, and presented it to him at his mother's house, Baynard's Castle, next day. Richard acceded to their request after a token show of reluctance, and the whole party then rode to Westminster Hall, where he formally took his seat on the marble chair, the King's Bench. The reign of Richard III had begun.

Dominic Mancini suspected – and William Shakespeare was certain – that this was what Richard had always wanted, but the slight evidence implies that he was seizing an opportunity rather than fulfilling an expectation. In the years prior to his brother's death he did his utmost first to obtain and then to secure the Warwick inheritance, but his attitude changed markedly after he became king. Individuals who had claims to particular manors were allowed to acquire them – something that would not have been possible when Richard regarded them as part of his and his son's future – and Warwick lands worth £329 annually were given to Queens' College, Cambridge.[16] He could afford to be generous with his personal holdings now that he had the Crown estates at his disposal, and his determination to protect them before 1483 suggests – no more than that – that he had assumed he would always remain Duke of Gloucester. Perhaps the turn of events surprised him almost as much as it surprised others.

Seen with hindsight, Richard's coup was a series of decisive, brilliantly executed manoeuvres which completely wrong-footed his sometimes bewildered opponents. Perhaps they ought to have been more astute, more politically alive to the danger; but they knew him as a colleague – even as a friend in some cases – and assumed that he would do his duty by his juvenile nephew. They either forgot that his old mentor Warwick had deposed a king and executed several royal favourites in 1469–70, or did not think him capable of the same ruthlessness. Richard did not always *want* to act as he did – More says that he 'loved [Hastings] well and loath was to have lost him'[17] – but saw no alternative if he was to secure his own long-term future. What he did not realise was that his deposition of Edward V would alienate so many people that widespread acceptance as king would always elude him. He had 'solved' one problem but replaced it with another.

7

'LONG LIVE THE KING!' JULY 1483

Although Richard only assumed the kingship on 26 June 1483, arrangements for Edward V's enthronement were so far advanced that he was able to stage his own coronation just ten days later on 6 July. His defenders make much of the fact that a majority of the peers and others who mattered politically attended, but this does not necessarily imply that he enjoyed their wholehearted approval. They were effectively leaderless, and were probably overawed by the presence of the soldiers he had summoned from the north before Hastings's execution. Lords and gentlemen who had come to London expecting to acclaim young Edward as their sovereign and who now returned home or excused themselves risked antagonising their new ruler before he had even taken office. Richard, who was still only thirty, might be around for a long time.

The coronation ceremonies began on Friday 4 July when Richard and his wife Anne left Baynard's Castle and, in keeping with tradition, took up residence in the Tower of London.[1] They may have travelled by water, accompanied by the mayor and City livery companies, and after partaking of a modest fish dinner (modest, that is, by royal standards), Richard performed the customary ritual of creating a number of new knights of the Bath. He had been personally inducted into the Order at his brother's coronation twenty-two years earlier, and may have had some sympathy with the young men who served him at table and who were about to be shaved, bathed and instructed before spending the night in prayer. Next day, they made their confessions before hearing matins and mass, and after a short sleep were again brought before him. Their spurs were fastened to their heels, and Richard personally girded on their swords, bestowed the accolade by striking them on their necks, and kissed them with the words 'Be ye a good knight'.

The newly created knights again served the King and Queen at dinner (a more elaborate meal on this day), before the party retired to prepare for the afternoon procession to Westminster. This was a blaze of display and colour designed to allow as many of the citizens as possible to see their new King and acclaim him. Richard, dressed in blue cloth of gold, purple velvet and ermine, rode a horse trapped in decorated purple and crimson cloth of gold beneath a red, green and gold canopy held by four knights, and was accompanied by Buckingham, John Howard, now Duke of Norfolk, and a great company of noblemen. They were joined by the City aldermen, the new knights of the Bath, heralds, clergy, royal officials, henchmen (noble boys being brought up in the royal household), squires and yeomen of the Crown, all sumptuously dressed for the occasion. The Queen followed in an open litter of white damask and white cloth of gold slung on poles between two palfreys, wearing a white cloth of gold robe, her hair loose beneath a circlet of gold and precious stones. A canopy of imperial (a type of silk cloth) was held over her, and she was attended by her servants and ladies including twelve noblewomen riding in three 'chares', horse-drawn vehicles on four wheels. The streets had been cleaned and decorated for the occasion, and the procession paused periodically so that the royal couple could listen to loyal speeches and be entertained by minstrels and choirs.

When the party reached Westminster Hall the King, Queen and noblemen were refreshed with wine and spices before retiring to their chambers to change their clothes before supper. After they had eaten, Richard took a ceremonial bath to cleanse himself before the coronation ceremony, and the abbot of Westminster instructed him on the procedure to be followed. As on all such occasions, final preparations would have continued almost up to the last minute, and it is doubtful if many slept long or well this night.

On rising, the King was ceremonially dressed by the Duke of Buckingham and the Queen by her ladies before dukes and earls accompanied them into Westminster Hall at 7.00 a.m. When they were seated beneath cloths of estate (Richard sitting on the marble chair of the King's Bench), the senior churchmen entered, and after the Bishop of Durham had said a prayer over the King they all joined the procession to the abbey. The King and Queen were 'supported' by the bishops of Bath and Durham and of Norwich and Exeter respectively, their trains being carried by Buckingham and Margaret Beaufort, Countess of Richmond, mother of the Lancastrian claimant to the throne, Henry Tudor. The Duke of Norfolk bore the King's crown (the 'Imperial' crown, not St Edward's Crown which awaited the King on the abbey's altar), and the noblemen carrying other items of regalia included the Earl of Northumberland, the sword Curtana; Lord Stanley (who had evidently recovered from the injuries he received when Hastings was arrested), the mace of Constable; and Lord Lovell, the third sword of justice to the temporality.

The King and Queen entered the abbey by the west door and were conducted to a platform covered in red worsted which had been erected between the high altar and the choir. Richard stood on the platform by his throne (St Edward's Chair) while the Archbishop of Canterbury formally presented him to the people and asked them to assent to his coronation – a request greeted with the traditional 'King Richard, King Richard, King Richard, yea, yea, yea'. He was then led to the altar followed by the Queen, made his first offering, and prostrated himself while prayers were read over him. When he was again seated an unnamed bishop preached a short sermon, after which the King was asked to swear that he would uphold the law, do justice, and support and defend the Church. There were more prayers followed by a brief respite before the King again approached the altar for his anointing. His upper garments were loosened, and he then knelt before the seated Archbishop, who smeared the holy oil of St Thomas (Becket) on his hands, breast, in the middle of his back, on his shoulders and in the crook of his elbows, and finally on the crown of his head in the form of a cross.

The King was then vested in his royal garments, the sword of state was girded on him, and the Archbishop crowned him with St Edward's Crown. A ring was placed on the fourth finger of his right hand, and he then offered his sword on the altar, receiving it back again as a token that his power came from God. The sceptre was placed in his right hand and the orb in his left, and he was blessed. After each bishop present had kissed him he returned to his throne on the platform for the formal pledging of fealty and homage.

It was now the Queen's turn. She was led to the altar, where she briefly prostrated herself while a prayer was said over her, before

an attendant removed the circlet of gold from her head and untied
and opened the front of her kirtle, or dress. She was anointed on
her forehead (again, in the form of a cross), and on her breast
before her kirtle was re-laced and a ring placed on the fourth finger
of her right hand. She was then crowned with the Queen's crown,
the sceptre and rod were placed in her right and left hands, and she
returned to the platform, curtseying as she approached the King.

Mass was then sung by the Archbishop, the bible used in the
reading of the Gospel being carried to the new monarchs for them
to kiss. After the Creed they were again led to the altar, where they
made further offerings, and on returning to their thrones kissed
the Pax, a tablet bearing an image of Christ. They went back to
the altar to make their confessions before receiving the Host (the
consecrated bread) and drinking wine from St Edward's Chalice.
They then again returned to their thrones for a short period while
the service was brought to an end.

The final part of the ceremony required Richard, Anne and
the assembled bishops and nobles to walk to the altar before the
Shrine of St Edward (behind the high altar), where the Archbishop
laid their crowns. They were then conducted to recesses where the
outer garments they had worn during the service were removed,
and where they were dressed in purple robes of estate designed
to emphasise their majesty. After their discarded clothing had
been laid on the altar the Archbishop placed the Imperial and
Queen's crowns on their heads, and they returned to their thrones
on the platform. The procession then reformed for the walk back
to Westminster Hall, where the King and Queen retired to their
chambers to rest and to break their fast.

The coronation banquet commenced at four o'clock, the King,
the Queen and the Bishop of Durham (deputising for the elderly

Archbishop) being seated at the high table, the marble table of the King's Bench, and the assembled notables at four tables set up at right angles to them running the length of the hall. Each course was introduced by trumpeters and escorted by the most senior officers of state and of the household, and the King was served on gold plate, the Queen on gilt, and the Bishop on silver. During the second course Sir Robert Dymock, the King's Champion, rode into the hall and offered to fight anyone who denied Richard's title. But he was met only with shouts of 'King Richard!', and after a covered cup of wine had been brought to him he departed, keeping the cup as his fee.

By now it was so late that torches were required (even though it was July), and the third course was dispensed with. The mayor of London served Richard and Anne with the 'void' (retiring drink) of diluted wine and wafers, and the guests rose and made their obeisance to the monarchs before they departed to their chambers. The guests then retired themselves.

What were Richard's thoughts on this most momentous of occasions, a day which only good fortune coupled with determination and some ruthlessness had allowed him to see? His betrayal of his late brother's trust in him must have sat uneasily on his conscience, but would not Edward, who had stolen inheritances and had men dragged from sanctuary, have acted as resolutely if he had found himself in a similar situation? A Woodville-dominated boy-king might have diminished not only Richard but also the kingdom, and Richard may have genuinely believed that he had taken these steps not only for himself but also for England. He would have been aware that some Edwardian loyalists bitterly resented his actions, but a few years of royal favour and good government would surely mollify them and force them to admit that he had acted prudently. He may not have appreciated that there were some present who could also employ guile when it suited them and who already had agendas of their own.

One problem that must have been on Richard's mind as he surveyed the scene from his throne and as the shouts of acclamation rang in his ears was what was to be done with his two nephews, the deposed Edward V and his brother, the nine-year-old Prince Richard. The fate of these boys, the 'Princes in the Tower', has occasioned no end of speculation (some of it by the present author), but here we will keep strictly to the facts of the matter as far as they are known. Richard's decision to lodge them in the Tower, a royal palace, was not particularly sinister or suspicious, and they were reportedly seen 'shooting and playing' in the Constable's garden on a number of occasions.[2] But Mancini reports that 'after Hastings was removed, all the attendants who had waited upon the king [Edward] were debarred access to him. He and his brother were withdrawn into the inner apartments of the Tower proper, and day by day began to be seen more rarely behind the bars and windows, till at length they ceased to appear altogether.' Dr John Argentine, 'the last of his attendants whose services the king enjoyed', told him that Edward 'sought remission of his sins by daily confession and penance, because he believed that death was facing him'.[3] The presence of a doctor implies that the boy was ill and thought he might not recover, a fear probably exacerbated by what he had learned of the fates of the three other deposed kings of medieval England, Edward II, Richard II, and Henry VI. Edward II had been done to death at Berkeley Castle in Gloucestershire shortly after losing his throne to his queen, Isabella, and her lover Roger Mortimer in 1327, and rumours that he escaped and spent the remainder of his life on the Continent have never been substantiated. Richard II was believed to have survived the revolution of 1399 – as late as 1417 the Lollard knight Sir John Oldcastle told his accusers that they had no right to try him because 'his liege lord, Richard, was alive in Scotland' – but again, there is nothing to suggest that this was anything more than wishful thinking. Henry VI had died in the Tower as soon as Edward IV had returned to London after winning the battle of Tewkesbury, and, again, had almost certainly been killed to prevent him from becoming a focus for opposition. The survival stories spoke of substitute bodies being placed in royal coffins while apologists suggested that the deaths were in part self-inflicted;[4] but whatever their fates it is clear that none of them had simply been allowed to 'retire'.

Richard may have hoped that a policy of 'out of sight, out of mind' would soon erase memories of the Princes; but he had not long left London to begin his royal 'progress' around his new kingdom when he learned of a plot to liberate them from custody. The scheme involved starting fires in the City and gaining access to the Tower in the ensuing confusion; but the fifty or so men involved failed to rouse their fellow citizens and four of them were executed: Robert Russe, serjeant of London; William Davy, pardoner, of Hounslow; John Smith, groom of the stirrup to Edward IV; and Stephen Ireland, the Tower wardrober.[5] Their further intentions are not recorded, but they were surely to restore young Edward to the throne he had so recently lost.

Richard was now on the horns of a dilemma. As long as Edward V and his brother lived and everyone knew their whereabouts, he was likely to face further challenges, but killing them risked alienating even more of his late brother's supporters. He wanted people to believe that he had done the right thing for the right reasons, but was bound to be unfavourably compared with Richard II and Henry VI's uncles, John of Gaunt and John, Duke of Bedford, who had both governed loyally until their young nephews came of age. The depositions of Edward II, Richard II and Henry VI, kings who had reigned for a total of eighty-two years and who had been despised as incompetent and divisive, had been greeted with relief in some quarters; but Edward V had been removed on a pretext without any opportunity to prove his ability or lack of it. Richard had shown that he was perfectly capable of eliminating those who stood in his way politically, but murder could not be justified in this case and risked infamy of an entirely different sort.

The main difficulty facing anyone who tries to probe the fate of the Princes is that those who claimed to know were almost certainly relying on hearsay, while others who undoubtedly did know remained silent. Rumours that they had been 'done away with' were already rife when Mancini left England soon after Richard's coronation, and their deaths were reported as facts by writers as far separated as Caspar Weinrich of Danzig ('Later this summer Richard the king's brother seized power and had his brother's children killed'), the French courtier Commynes ('On the death of Edward [IV], his second brother the Duke of Gloucester killed Edward's two sons, declared his daughters bastards, and had himself crowned king'), and the Spaniard Diego de Valera, who informed Ferdinand and Isabella that 'it is sufficiently well known to your royal majesty that this Richard killed two innocent nephews of his to whom the realm belonged after his brother's life'. English commentators who took the same view included the mayor of Bristol, Robert Ricart ('in this year [the year ending

15 September 1483] the two sons of King Edward were put to silence in the Tower of London'), and John Rous of Warwick ('he [Richard] received his lord King Edward V blandly, with embraces and kisses, and within about three months or a little more he killed him together with his brother'), but were they merely assuming the worst? Commynes rather spoils his argument by declaring elsewhere that 'King Richard did not last long; *nor did the Duke of Buckingham, who had put the two children to death*' (my italics), a possibility echoed by a document preserved among the Ashmolean manuscripts in the Bodleian Library which states that Richard killed the boys 'at the prompting of the Duke of Buckingham, as it is said', and by the jottings of an unnamed London citizen who thought that they had been murdered by Buckingham's 'vise', i.e. on his advice or by his design.[6]

The one writer who must have known most of the answers was the well-informed courtier who contributed to the Croyland Chronicle, but he never really addresses the subject. He implies that the Princes were still in the Tower when Richard was at York in the first half of September, and although he afterwards speaks of 'a rumour ... that King Edward's sons, by some manner of violent destruction, had met their fate',[7] he does not say if he believed it. We sometimes assume that nobody knew what had become of the Princes, but this is, of course, impossible. Whatever their fate, someone had to give the order and someone (perhaps several people) had to execute it, information that must have been available both to Richard and to Henry Tudor, who succeeded him. The boys' mother, Elizabeth Woodville, and their eldest sister Elizabeth, who became Henry's queen, were both in a position to have their inevitable questions answered, and there were few secrets Henry did not share with his mother Margaret

Beaufort or kept from trusted counsellors like Cardinal Morton, his Chancellor and Archbishop of Canterbury. But whatever they knew they all remained officially silent, Henry's belated attempt to blame the deaths on the already executed James Tyrell amounting to no more than a stratagem to discourage future pretenders. Not even Polydore Vergil, his court historian, thought it was true.

One curious matter is why, if Richard was responsible for the Princes' deaths, Henry VII did not use it as a stick with which to beat him. There is a vague reference to the 'shedding of infants blood' in the parliamentary act of attainder passed against the late King and his leading supporters, but this apart, Henry failed to make any political capital from what was easily the worst of his predecessor's alleged offences. Perhaps Henry was sensitive to the fact that since he wanted to be king himself their deaths had benefited him as much, possibly more, than Richard: but the conspiracy of silence could imply that at least one of the boys was still living. Edward V could have succumbed to his malady; but there is no suggestion that Prince Richard was also ill and he might, possibly, have been smuggled away either with his uncle's agreement or without it. Henry would have been obliged to accept the situation as he found it (short of having his brother-in-law executed), and secrecy would have been essential. He would have been happy to let people *think* the boys had been murdered, but not to speculate when or by whose hand.

The mystery might be partially solved if some bones found in 1674 when workmen were removing an external structure and stairs adjoining the White Tower, the central keep of the Tower of London, could be subjected to modern scientific analysis. The remains, which appeared to be those of two children, were found at a depth of ten feet, and appeared to confirm Sir Thomas More's story that the murdered Princes had been buried 'at the stair foot, meetly deep in the ground under a great heap of stones'.[8] Ten feet is a most unusual depth for a grave, however, and while the surface level could have risen by perhaps two feet between 1483 and 1674, the bones could clearly have been in the ground for much longer. They were examined in 1933 by specialists in anatomy and dentistry who concluded that they were the remains of two boys aged approximately twelve to thirteen and between nine and eleven. Edward V was twelve and Prince Richard ten in the late summer of 1483, and while one would not wish to accuse these gentlemen of practising the gentle art of self-deception there is a strong suspicion that they were looking for proof rather than approaching the subject objectively. In practice, estimates of age vary according to the particular bones or teeth being examined (a problem compounded by the fact that children do not all develop at the same rate), and later experts have suggested that the smaller child could have been as young as seven and the larger as old as sixteen. The 1933 specialists assumed that they were dealing with the remains of *boys*, but the sexes of the two individuals could not be determined from their skeletons alone.[9]

A further examination of the bones using techniques not available in 1933 would confirm or deny the existence of a relationship between the two individuals and improve the possibility of their being identified as the children of their putative parents; but no test could tell us precisely when they died or in what circumstances. They remain in the urn in Westminster Abbey where Charles II interred them in 1678, and it is unlikely that the authorities will allow them to be disturbed again in the foreseeable future. The best we can say is that if they are ever proved to be the remains of the Princes all theories postulating their escape or resettlement will have to be abandoned, but if they are *not* the Princes all possibilities remain open until more evidence comes to light.

So where does this leave us and, more importantly, where does it leave Richard? First of all, there is no evidence that the boys were murdered – by Richard or by anyone else. They *disappeared*, and those who knew what had happened to earlier deposed kings drew the inevitable conclusion: but a boy who had never offended anyone cannot be compared with adult rulers who were eliminated after years of disillusionment. It seems incredible that Richard ever supposed that killing his nephews would help to secure his position or make him more acceptable to his subjects, and while he could be ruthless no one has suggested that he was also stupid. He was correct if he thought that placing them in a protected and secret place would prevent his enemies from using them as a focus for opposition; but the downside was that he could not thereafter produce them to scotch rumours they were no longer living. Niclas von Popplau, a Silesian knight who met Richard in 1484, noted that 'King Richard has killed King Edward his brother's sons, so that not they, but he was crowned. However, many people say – and I agree with them that they are still alive and are kept in a very dark cellar.' Von Popplau's prose is often convoluted, and his translator adds, 'I hope that what [he] really meant was that they were imprisoned somewhere very secretly, where nobody could find them.'[10] If only von Popplau had thought – or dared – to ask Richard in the course of one of their talks!

8

RICHARD 'CROOKBACK'?

Whenever Richard is mentioned in Arthur Mee's *The King's England*, he is almost invariably called 'crookback'. This famous series of books, written in the 1930s, reflect the prejudices of their era, but their caricature of the King goes back much further, to William Shakespeare and, ultimately, to Sir Thomas More. Shakespeare has Richard say,

> Why, love forswore me in my mother's womb:
> And, for I should not deal in her soft laws,
> She did corrupt frail nature with some bribe,
> To shrink mine arm up like a wither'd shrub;
> To make an envious mountain on my back,
> Where sits deformity to mock my body;
> To shape my legs of an unequal size;
> To disproportion me in every part ...

while More described him as

> little of stature, ill featured of limbs, crook backed, his left shoulder much higher than his right, hard favoured of visage ... malicious,

wrathful, envious and from afore his birth, ever forward. It is for truth reported, that the Duchess his mother had much ado in her travail, that she could not be delivered of him uncut, and that he came into the world with his feet forward ... and (as the fame runneth) also not untoothed.

More was only seven years old when Richard was killed at Bosworth and may never have seen him; but he was perhaps teased with exaggerated stories during his years in Cardinal Morton's household and could have read John Rous's description of the King, written about 1486:

Richard was born at Fotheringhay in Northamptonshire, retained within his mother's womb for two years and emerging with teeth and hair to his shoulders. He was small of stature, with a short face and unequal shoulders, the right higher and the left lower ...[1]

More, working from memory, confused the shoulders, but modern writers still accept the substance of his account.[2]

Modern medical authorities have suggested a number of conditions which may have been responsible for the disfigurements described by the three writers. A breech presentation would have been difficult and could have resulted in injury, perhaps kyphoscoliosis, curvature of the spine, giving the impression of a raised shoulder and unequal legs. Another possibility is a nerve injury affecting the arm, perhaps Klumpke's Palsy, a wasting of the small muscles of the hand resulting in an inability to grip, or Erb's Palsy, in which the arm hangs limp and is rotated inwards. Erb's Palsy also leads to depression of the shoulder on the side affected, as does Sprengel's deformity, a condition in which the shoulder blade may be underdeveloped or elevated and is sometimes attached to the spinal column. Other suggestions include the very rare Ellis-Van Creveld Syndrome – a phenomenon characterised by shortness of stature, shortened legs and forearms, a malformed pelvis and sometimes extra fingers and toes – and even polio in infancy, which could have resulted in a deformed arm and legs of unequal size. More mundanely, he could have been injured during his years of hard training at Middleham, or met with an accident at an even earlier stage of his life.

Then there is the somewhat curious sequence of events immediately prior to Lord Hastings's arrest and execution. According to More, Richard joined the assembled counsellors at nine o'clock that morning, and asked Bishop Morton of Ely to send him some strawberries from his garden in Holborn. He then excused himself, but returned an hour later between ten and eleven 'all changed, with a wonderful sour angry countenance'. He claimed that Queen Elizabeth and Hastings's mistress Elizabeth 'Jane' Shore had enfeebled him with 'sorcery and witchcraft … and therewith he plucked up his doublet sleeve to his elbow upon his left arm, where he showed a werish withered arm and small'. More remarks that Richard's arm 'was never other' and that everyone knew he was merely using it to pick a quarrel; but would a man who was always careful to act with outward propriety have risked ridicule by resorting to farce?

There must, logically, have been more than this to it, and Dr J. Swift Joly has suggested that the answer lies in the otherwise rather pointless story about the bishop's strawberries. Richard, he suspects, was allergic to strawberries and knew that eating them would produce an urticarial rash on his arms and other parts of his body. The rash had conveniently developed by the time he returned to the Council chamber, and the sleeve he pulled up to convince the onlookers was the sleeve of his normally 'good' arm. The redness, and blotchiness, would disappear quite quickly of course, and it would have seemed that beheading Hastings had also 'killed' the malign influence. Perhaps this is why Richard had him executed with so little delay.

Another possibility is that Richard suffered from coeliac disease, an intestinal disorder associated with the malabsorption of fat resulting in general weakness, delayed growth, secondary skeletal deformity and the passage of large and offensive stools. Dr Gordon Dale has based this diagnosis on several passages in Shakespeare, particularly the remarks that Richard was 'the wretched'st thing when he was young, / So long a-growing, and so leisurely' (*Richard III*, Act 2 Scene 4), and displayed the characteristic naughtiness: 'Tetchy and wayward was thy infancy' (Act 4, Scene 4). Shakespeare would have found it difficult to discuss Richard's bowel movements on stage, but Dr Dale wonders if his repeated use of the adjective 'foul' – 'foul swine', 'foul undigested lump' – is an oblique reference to them. Coeliac disease was a recognised condition, and was known by this name, when the Bard wrote his plays.[3]

These diagnoses are plausible, even ingenious, but they are characterised by one fatal flaw. They all assume that Shakespeare, More and Rous's descriptions of Richard's physical appearance are accurate. It is true that an ill-wisher described him as a 'crouchback' in 1490,[4] but no one implied that he was deformed in his lifetime and the accusation may be no more than a play on words. Richard's badge was a boar, an animal which is naturally humpbacked, and it is possible that the distinction between the symbol and its owner became blurred at the edges. A man who was severely physically handicapped or who suffered from the general weakness associated with coeliac disease could not have ridden a horse, wielded weapons, or distinguished himself in three major battles, and there is nothing to suggest that illness prevented him from attending to any of his other multifarious duties. Two men who undoubtedly saw him and who have left written records – the Croyland chronicler and the Silesian knight Niclas von Popplau – say only that he was comparatively lean and had pale, drawn features. Croyland remarks that, on the morning of Bosworth, 'his countenance which, always attenuated, was on this occasion, more livid and ghastly than usual', while von Popplau describes him as 'three fingers taller than I [i.e. about two and a quarter inches], but a bit slimmer and not as thickset as I am, and much more lightly built; he has quite slender arms and thighs, and also a great heart'. Von Popplau does not say how big he was himself, so his comment is not particularly helpful; but the inference is that he was a rather short, stocky individual while Richard was somewhat slimmer and taller. Richard wanted to know as much about foreign rulers and the situation in other countries as the well-travelled knight could tell him, and, in von Popplau's words, 'hardly touched his food, but talked with me all the time'. When they parted he gave his visitor money and a gold collar 'that he took from the neck of a free or high-born lord'.[5]

The Tudor historian Polydore Vergil never knew Richard personally, and much of what he writes is coloured by the assumption that the late King was 'bad' and his patron King Henry 'good'. His comment that Richard had 'a short and sour countenance, which seemed to savour of mischief and utter evidently of craft and deceit' can be dismissed as so much propaganda; but he adds that 'the while he was thinking of any matter, he did continually bite his nether lip ... also, he was wont to be ever with his right hand pulling [halfway] out of the sheath and putting in again the dagger which he did always wear'. It seems unlikely that Vergil would have bothered to invent such small details, and he may well have been told this by someone who had been in Richard's company and who remembered these characteristics. They do not, of course, prove that 'that cruel nature of his did so rage against itself in that little carcase',[6] as Vergil claims.

The earliest surviving portrait of Richard, now in the possession of the Society of Antiquaries of London and dated to within a few years of 1516, displays no obvious physical deformity, although restoration in 2007 revealed that the lips had been overpainted to make them appear 'tighter' and meaner. X-rays of the well-known picture in the Royal Collection, possibly copied from a now lost original between 1518 and 1523, have shown that the eyes were originally drawn in a less slit-like fashion, and that the right shoulder has been elevated to give the impression of unevenness. The images were clearly being changed to 'fit' the legend, and a copy made in the 1530s or later shows Richard holding a broken sword symbolising that his royal power had been broken in battle. The original artists may have flattered him, but they could hardly have produced portraits that were not tolerably true to life.

The vast probability then, is that Richard displayed no particular physical deformity except, perhaps, for a mild degree of kyphoscoliosis, and possibly some extra development of the muscles around his right shoulder attributable to his military lifestyle. These were unexceptionable defects, but it was easy for Tudor writers to exaggerate them and claim that his wickedness was evident from his appearance. Rous's allegation that he was born with teeth probably derives from the ancient belief that such children were a bad omen, unlucky for themselves, their families, and even for entire communities, and that only extraction – or infanticide in some cultures – could avert disaster. The pain associated with breast feeding a child with teeth may explain how the idea first arose and why it became so widespread; but whatever the circumstances, in Richard's case it provided further proof that he was demonstrably evil. If, of course, it was true at all.

A man's looks may tell us something about him, but they are hardly a guide to his personality. Most of the private letters and other documents that would have given us a real insight into Richard's character have perished, and we have to rely on a few very intimate survivals and the evidence of his dealings with others. We noticed his books in chapter six, but the one we did not discuss there was arguably his most personal and treasured volume, his Book of Hours. This was already second-hand when he acquired it as king, but he personalised it by adding his own prayer, probably written by or with the help of his confessor John Roby, a Franciscan friar and doctor of theology. Quoting many scriptural examples, he asks the Son of God to release him

from the affliction, temptation, grief, sickness, necessity and danger in which I stand, and give me counsel ... deign to free me from every tribulation, sorrow and trouble in which I am placed and from all the plots of my enemies ... deign to assuage, turn aside, destroy and bring to nothing the hatred they bear towards me. I ask you, most gentle Lord Jesus Christ, to keep me, thy servant King Richard, and defend me from all evil ... and from all peril past, present and to come ... and deign always to deliver and help me.[7]

No one could doubt that these are the words of a man who knew that he had his back to the wall and that only divine intervention could save him. His fears can only have increased as his short reign drew to its conclusion, and the pressure of 'putting a brave face on it', of trying to appear confident in public, must have been enormous. Richard's commitment to his religion seems to have been both personal and genuine, a devotion which some allege became more pronounced after he became king and which his critics have dismissed as hypocritical.[8] They suggest that his good laws, his generosity and his acts of faith (most notably his reburial of Henry VI's remains at Windsor and his refusal to fight on holy days – something he had not been able to do while his brother was king) were all designed to salvage his reputation, a reputation which no man of conscience or 'principle' would have acquired in the first place. Richard undoubtedly wanted to bury the past, to 'move on' from the events of the summer of 1483, but it would be wrong to assume his motivation was entirely selfish or that ruthlessness and violence are somehow incompatible with piety. King David is described in the Old Testament as 'a man after God's own heart', but he could still eliminate Bathsheba's husband Uriah the Hittite for the basest of reasons; and the deeply religious Oliver Cromwell justified the slaughter of between two and four thousand Catholics at Drogheda in Ireland with the words, 'I am persuaded that this is a righteous judgement of God upon these barbarous wretches, who have imbrued their hands in so much innocent blood.'[9] One writer has described Richard as a schizophrenic 'whose mission to save himself was readily translated into a divine mission to save his country from moral decadence';[10] but not even the harshest of his contemporary and near-contemporary critics ever questioned his state of mind.

It is not easy to see where this idea comes from unless it originated in Richard's apparent tendency to indulge in wishful thinking and voice thoughts that were impractical or unrealistic. When Niclas von Popplau told him of how the troops of the King of Hungary and the Emperor had defeated the Turks 'before St Martin's Day 1483', Richard became animated and declared that 'I would like my kingdom and land to lie where the land and kingdom of the king of Hungary lies, on the Turkish frontier itself. Then I would certainly, with my own people alone, without the help of other kings, princes or lords, properly drive away not only the Turks, but all my enemies and opponents.'[11] His enthusiasm is commendable, but he cannot have been unaware that Constantinople, the great capital of the Christian Eastern Roman Empire, had been lost to the Muslims within a year of his birth, or that a French-led coalition had been disastrously defeated at Nicapolis in 1396. Von Popplau claimed to be impressed, but the idea that England alone could defeat not just the Turks but anyone else who dared to threaten her was laughable. Was Richard's belief that he could overcome any odds ranged against him partly responsible for his downfall on Bosworth Field?

Faith is a very personal thing, but so too are a man's relationships with those closest to him. Richard seems to have been committed to his eldest brother Edward but resentful and suspicious of George, the younger, not without justification if the events of the late 1460s and early 1470s are anything to go by. He was on good terms with his sister Margaret, Duchess of Burgundy, whom he visited when he was on the Continent in 1471 and 1475, and for whose benefit (to see her for what was to prove to be the last time) he made the long journey to London in 1480. He would scarcely have known his father, who was killed when he was only eight, but his mother Cecily long outlived him. Aristocratic parents did not nurture their children personally – that was the responsibility of nurses and tutors – but that is not to say that they did not care for them. On the contrary, their value as marriage partners for eligible heirs and heiresses made them essential if a family was to forge alliances and add to its lands.

Cecily could have fled with her husband from Ludlow in October 1459 had she chosen, but instead remained with her younger sons, Richard and George, and ensured their safety. She sent them abroad when Queen Margaret threatened London fourteen months later, and, we may suppose, continued to take a close interest in their upbringing after the Yorkist triumph. The surviving documents imply that Richard remained on good terms with her after he grew to manhood, and he held crucial meetings at her town house, Baynard's Castle, when he reached London after Edward IV's death. He would hardly have done this if their relationship had been other than amicable, and it is therefore all the more remarkable that he initially tried to justify his bid for the throne by claiming that King Edward was illegitimate. Cecily resented the aspersion that she had been unfaithful to her husband – Vergil remarked that she 'complained afterwards in sundry places to right many noble men, whereof some yet live'[12] – and although the 'mistake' was quickly rectified it was not easily forgotten. A letter Richard wrote to her after he became king is couched in the formal style that any monarch would affect when writing to a subject and I have argued elsewhere that there was no obvious animosity between them. But it *could* be read in a rather different light:

Madam, I recommend me to you as heartily as is to me possible, beseeching you in my most humble and effectual wise [manner] of your daily blessing to my singular comfort and defence in my need.

Left: 3. Richard III. An early seventeenth-century copy of an original likeness, but displaying the uneven shoulders common to all later portraits. *Above*: 4. A grassy mound and a block of masonry protected by railings is all that remains of Fotheringhay Castle, where Richard was born in 1452.

5. The church of St Mary and All Saints, Fotheringhay (Northamptonshire), from the River Nene. The loss of the medieval choir and Lady chapel has reduced the length of the building by more than half.

Above left: 6. The Elizabethan tomb of Richard's parents – Richard, Duke of York, and Cecily Neville – at St Mary and All Saints, Fotheringhay. Their original sepulchres in the choir were destroyed at the Dissolution of the Monasteries. *Above right*: 8. Ludlow Castle, Shropshire, where Richard was captured in 1459 and where Edward V was brought up, as it would have appeared *c.* 1450. The Great Hall and state apartments are to the north of the round chapel dedicated to St Mary Magdalene, where they would have worshipped.

7. The pulpit of St Mary and All Saints, Fotheringhay, reputedly donated by Edward IV, displays the royal arms in the centre, the black bull of Clarence on the left, and the white boar of Gloucester on the right.

Above left: 9. Richard, Duke of York, and Edward IV portrayed in nineteenth-century stained glass by Thomas Willement in the west window of St Laurence's church, Ludlow. *Above right*: 10. Edward V and Prince Arthur (Henry VII's son) portrayed in nineteenth-century stained glass by Thomas Willement in the west window of St Laurence's church, Ludlow.

11. Claes Visscher's view of London Bridge and the Tower of London (1616). This is the world Richard would have observed when he lodged at Fastolf's Place in 1460–1.

Above left: 12. The gatehouse of Cawood Castle (Yorks.), where Richard attended the great banquet held to celebrate his cousin George Neville's enthronement as Archbishop of York in September 1465. *Above right*: 13. Walsingham Priory church (Norfolk), the remains of the twin-turreted thirteenth-century arch that housed the great east window. Richard and Edward IV came here on pilgrimage in June 1469.

Above centre left: 14. Castle Rising Castle (Norfolk). Richard visited the castle in June 1469 when raising troops to suppress the rebellion of 'Robin of Redesdale', and his earliest surviving letter is dated from here, a request for a loan of £100 because 'I am not so well purveyed of money therefore as behoves me to be'. *Above right*: 15. Crowland Abbey church (Lincs.), the home of the Croyland Chronicle, from the south-west. Richard and Edward IV stayed here in June 1469 while raising forces to combat rebellion in the north. *Above left*: 16. The unique Triangular (or Trinity) bridge at Crowland from which Richard and Edward embarked for Fotheringhay. Before the draining of the fens the main streets were waterways and it was here that the River Welland divided into two streams.

Above left: 17. Henry VI, d. 1471, portrayed as a saint in about 1500 (Ludham church screen, Norfolk). Richard tried to harness his cult by having his remains reburied in St George's Chapel, Windsor, but Henry VII's attempts to have him canonised failed. *Above right*: 18. Richard Neville, Earl of Warwick, the 'Kingmaker', portrayed as a 'weeper' on the tomb of his father-in-law Richard Beauchamp, Earl of Warwick (St Mary's Church, Warwick).

19. Middleham Castle (Yorkshire), where Richard received some of his knightly training and which became his principal residence in northern England after his marriage.

Above left: 20 The 'Swine Cross', Middleham, thought to commemorate the grant of a twice yearly fair and market obtained by Richard in 1479. The heraldic animal may be his own cognisance of the white boar or the bear of Warwick. *Above right*: 21. The church of St Mary and St Alkelda, Middleham, where Richard founded a college consisting of a dean, six chaplains, four clerks and six choristers in 1477.

Left: 22. Memorial window presented to Middleham church by the Fellowship of the White Boar, the precursor of the Richard III Society, in 1934. Richard is depicted in the lower left light with his son Edward kneeling behind him, and his wife Anne is in the lower right. *Below left*: 23. Skipton Castle (Yorks.) was forfeited by the Lancastrian Clifford family in 1461, and was for a time held by Richard. The motto of the Cliffords, 'Desormais' ('henceforth' or 'from now on'), is displayed above the gatehouse. *Below right*: 24. The walls of Skipton Castle as seen from the Leeds & Liverpool canal.

Above left: 25. The Black Horse, Skipton, said to have been built on the site of the castle stables. Inside, a notice claims that 'Richard III stayed here when he was Lord of the Honour of Skipton'. *Above right*: 26. St Mary's church, Careleton in Craven (Yorks.), two miles from Skipton. Richard bought the manor from William Singleton in 1480.

Above left: 27. Micklegate Bar, the southern entrance to York. The heads of Richard's father and brother were displayed here after their disastrous defeat at the battle of Wakefield in 1460. *Above right*: 28. Monk Bar, York's tallest gatehouse, which still has a working portcullis last lowered in 1953. The uppermost room was added in 1484 and today it houses the Richard III Museum.

29. Bootham Bar, the northern approach to York, with the stately Minster rising behind.

30. St Mary's Abbey, York, was the wealthiest religious house in England after Glastonbury. The papal bull authorising Richard to found colleges at Middleham and Barnard Castle was read here in his presence in July 1482.

31. York Minster Library, once the chapel of the Archbishop of York's palace. Richard invested his son as Prince of Wales in the palace on the feast of the Nativity of the Blessed Virgin Mary, Monday 8 September 1483.

32. York's fifteenth-century Guildhall, seen from the south side of the River Ouse. Richard was entertained to two dinners here while on his royal progress in 1483.

33. Jervaulx Abbey, a house of the Cistercian order three and a half miles from Middleham, burial place of Richard's relatives by marriage, the Fitzhughs. Prince Edward offered twenty pence here in 1483.

34. Creake Abbey (Norfolk), the church from the west. Richard was the abbey's patron, and 'moved with pity' gave the monks £46 13s 4d to help rebuild the church and conventual buildings after a disastrous fire in 1484.

Above: 35. 'Richard, Duke of Gloucester respectfully greets his nephews', by H. Sidney (1884), from *Scenes from Shakespeare for the Young*, ed. C. Alias (1885). The Duke of Buckingham (foreground) wears the arms of his son and the collars of the Order of the Garter are later versions, but overall this is a surprisingly accurate portrayal for a children's book. *Left*: 36. The west tower of Kirby Muxloe Castle (Leicestershire), seat of William, Lord Hastings. Work stopped when he was executed in June 1483.

Left: 37. Richard, Duke of Gloucester, is offered the crown at Baynards Castle on 26 June 1483. Mural by Sigismund Goetze in the Royal Exchange, London. *Above*: 39. Brecon Castle (Powys), from the south-east. John Morton, Bishop of Ely, was imprisoned here in 1483, and is said to have persuaded his gaoler, the Duke of Buckingham, to turn against Richard.

38. On 12 October 1483 Richard wrote to the Chancellor, John Russell, ordering him to bring the Great Seal to him at Grantham. The postscript referring to 'the malice of him that had best cause to be true, the Duke of Buckingham, the most untrue creature living' is in his own hand.

Above: 40. Tretower Court (Powys), home of Sir Thomas Vaughan, who helped to frustrate the Duke of Buckingham's rebellion and raided his lands at Brecon. The western range (pictured) was built by Sir Roger Vaughan (Sir Thomas's father), in the mid-fifteenth century. *Below*: 41. The ruins of the mansion built in the outer court of the Abbey of St Mary of the Meadows, Leicester, photographed in the snow on Christmas Day 2010. Richard stayed at the abbey on 31 July 1484. *Right*: 42. Tomb effigy of Bishop William Waynflete in the retro-choir of Winchester Cathedral. He welcomed Richard to Magdalen, his new Oxford college, in July 1483. Painting by G. Wheeler.

Above: 43. Tomb of Bishop Richard Redman in Ely Cathedral. Redman was a staunch Yorkist who first opposed, but later made his peace with, Henry VII. *Right*: 45. Elizabeth Woodville. Perhaps the most intriguing and inscrutable of Richard's contemporaries. An early seventeenth-century copy of an original likeness.

Above: 44. Bishop Redman (detail). *Right*: 46. Elizabeth of York. The younger of the 'Two Elizabeths'. An early seventeenth-century copy of an original likeness.

Above left: 47. Statue of Richard in Castle Gardens, Leicester by James Butler R.A., presented by the Richard III Society in 1980. *Above right*: 48. The story of the old woman's prophecy is immortalised by this plaque on the modern Bow Bridge.

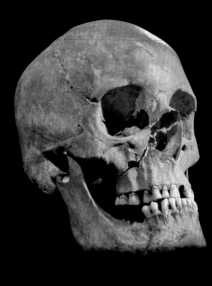

Above left: 49. Commemorative plaque in the chancel of Leicester Cathedral designed by David Kindersley, dedicated in August 1982. *Above right*: Richard's skull. A cut mark on the lower jaw, caused by a bladed weapon, is clearly visible. (UMOA1404. University of Leicester, used with permission) *Below*: Richard's face, reconstructed by Caroline Wilkinson. A younger and less careworn Richard than we are accustomed to seeing in the traditional portraits. (Dr P. T. Stone)

Above: 50. Plaque marking the site of the Franciscan (Grey) friary where Richard was buried, placed by the Richard III Society in 1990. *Left*: 51. Plaque near Bow Bridge recalling the tradition that Richard's body was thrown into the river at the Dissolution of the Monasteries. The plaque was erected by Benjamin Broadbent, a local builder, in 1856.

Above left: 52. Sign above the Richard III public house in Highcross Street. *Above centre*: 53. Richard III Road. *Above right*: 54. 'King Dick's Well' on Bosworth Field, where tradition says Richard took his last drink. The cairn, erected by the Revd Samuel Parr in 1813, was restored in 1964.

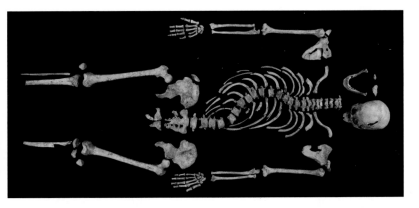

Richard's skeleton, displaying the severity of his scoliosis (curvature of the spine). (UMOA1608. University of Leicester, used with permission)

Above left: 55. 'King Richard's Bed', said to have been left at the White Boar Inn in Leicester when Richard failed to return from Bosworth, and now preserved at Donington le Heath manor house, (Leics.). The present superstructure is Tudor or Jacobean, but the stock may be of late medieval date. *Above right*: 56. Chair with a boar carved into the backrest, said to have come from the White Boar Inn and to have been used by King Richard, now the property of Everards Brewery Ltd.

Above left: 57. Henry VII by E. Folkard, modern sculpture below the castle, Hay-on-Wye, Hereforshire. The plaque reads 'Henry VII – the first Welsh king of the English'. *Above right*: 58. Margaret, Duchess of Burgundy, Richard's youngest sister with whom he enjoyed a particularly close relationship. He visited her whenever possible, and she upheld the Yorkist cause long after his death.

And madam I heartily beseech you that I may often hear from you to my comfort. And madam, I beseech you to be good and gracious lady to my lord, my chamberlain [Francis Lovell], to be your officer in Wiltshire ... I trust he shall therein do you good service and that it please you that by this bearer I may understand your pleasure in this behalf. And I pray God send you the accomplishment of your noble desires. Written at Pontefract the third day of June with the hand of your most humble son, Ricardus Rex.[13]

The words 'madam I heartily beseech you that I may often hear from you to my comfort' could be taken to imply that recent contact between them had been minimal, and that Richard regretted that his ill-chosen allegation had damaged their relationship. When Cecily made her will in April 1495 she described herself as 'late wife to Richard Duke of York and mother to King Edward the Fourth',[14] but her younger royal son was nowhere mentioned. This may reflect the Tudor dogma that Richard had been king in name but not of right; but an alternative explanation would be that she still could not bring herself to speak of him in the same breath as his elder brother. Some wounds never heal, as Richard would learn to his cost.

The 'other' woman who loomed large in Richard's life was his wife and queen, Anne Neville, but we know almost nothing of their personal relationship or whether she encouraged or tried to restrain him in particular circumstances. He knew her from his years in her father Warwick's household and could have married her for herself as well as for her great inheritance; but the only record of a personal, intimate moment between them is when word of their only son's death reached them at Nottingham in 1484. Prince Edward had probably always been sickly – he had travelled from Middleham to York for his investiture as Prince of Wales in a carriage rather than on horseback – but the end, when it came, was apparently sudden. The Croyland writer observed that 'you might have seen his father and mother in a state almost bordering on madness, by reason of their sudden grief', not least because the boy was by now irreplaceable.[15] All kings hope that their offspring will succeed them – Henry VIII more than most, perhaps – and we will see how Anne's lack of fecundity left her vulnerable to the fate that would one day befall Anne Boleyn and Catherine of Aragon. Richard may well have loved her, but not, if Croyland is to be believed, to the extent that he was willing to put her before his duty to his dynasty and his kingdom. His brother Edward's desire for Elizabeth Woodville had nearly cost him everything, but Richard's heart never ruled his head.

A very different sort of lady – but one who can still tell us something about Richard's own personality and attitudes – is Elizabeth Shore, first called 'Jane' by the dramatist Thomas Heywood in 1599. She was the daughter of a London mercer, John Lambert, and wed William Shore, a member of the same company; but her marriage was annulled in 1476 on the grounds that her husband was impotent and she became – if she was not already – one of Edward IV's many mistresses. Thomas More's story that Edward jokingly called her the merriest harlot in his kingdom may be apocryphal, but she undoubtedly had sex appeal and was willing to use her influence with the King to help others:

For a proper wit had she, and could both read well and write, merry in company, ready and quick of answer, neither mute nor full of babble, sometime taunting without displeasure and not without disport. In whom the king therefore took special pleasure. Whose favour, to say the truth ... she never abused to any man's hurt, but to many a man's comfort and relief: where the king took displeasure she would mitigate and appease his mind: where men were out of favour, she would bring them in his grace. For many that had highly offended, she obtained pardon. Of great forfeitures she got men remission. And finally in many weighty suites, she stood many men in great stead, either for none, or very small rewards, and those rather gay than rich: either for that she was content with the deed self well done, or for that she delighted to be said unto, and to show what she was able to do with the king ...[16]

At some point either before or after Edward's death she seems to have transferred her affections to William, Lord Hastings, and after Hastings's execution became the mistress of the Marquis of Dorset. These liaisons identified her with the opposition to Richard's takeover, and although there is no record of precisely how she assisted her lovers she undoubtedly incurred the new King's displeasure. She was called to answer for some of Hastings's goods after his death in June 1483 (her own goods were attached by the sheriffs of London), and Dorset was accused of holding 'the unshameful and mischievous woman called Shore's wife in adultery'[17] when he rebelled in October. She was imprisoned in Ludgate and made to perform public penance 'for the life that she led with the said Lord Hastings and other great estates',[18] but her disgrace only won her new admirers. More describes how she conducted herself 'in countenance and pace demure so womanly, and albeit she were out of all array save her kirtle only: yet went she so fair and lovely ... that her great shame won her much praise'.[19]

Richard probably assumed that this was the end of the matter, but some little time afterwards heard that his solicitor, Thomas Lynom, intended to marry her. He asked Bishop Russell to try to change the 'marvellously blinded and abused'[20] Lynom's mind, but conceded that if he failed she was to be released from prison if she could find sureties for her future behaviour. Her father's will, made in September 1487, makes it clear that they had by then married, presumably while Richard was still king or possibly afterwards. Lynom died some time before 29 July 1518 leaving her a widow, and More claimed, perhaps somewhat implausibly, that she fell into penury and resorted to begging. According to one source she lived until the eighteenth year of Henry VIII's reign, i.e. 1526/27.

Clearly, Richard was less beguiled by 'Jane' than were some of his contemporaries, and his treatment of her may reflect his determination to do the 'right' thing in all circumstances. The problem was that when he wanted something badly, all notions of 'right' and propriety went out of the window. His thoughtless slandering of his mother and his apparent readiness to contemplate the annulment of his marriage represent the worst side of his character, and raise the possibility that he was what we would today call a 'split personality'. He knew the difference between right and wrong, but the terrible uncertainty of his earliest years compelled him to behave in ways he himself would not have thought acceptable in other circumstances. The Richard who was prepared to treat the two women closest to him so callously was the Richard who seized his nephew's throne: not the Richard who was devoted to his religion and who wanted to be remembered for his sense of justice and fairness. Not 'good' *or* 'bad', but both.

9

CONSPIRACY & REBELLION,
JULY–NOVEMBER 1483

Richard, accompanied by many lords, bishops and officials, set out on his royal progress around his kingdom approximately two weeks after his coronation. He was at Reading on 23 July, and next day rode to Oxford, where he was greeted and lodged at Magdalen by the college's founder, Bishop William Waynflete. The next two days were spent listening to disputations and touring the university, before a journey via Woodstock and Lord Lovell's seat at Minster Lovell brought him to Gloucester by 2 August. Here he granted the citizens a charter of liberties, and encountered the Duke of Buckingham, who had apparently stayed behind in London and was now making his way home to Brecon. His next stops were at Tewkesbury, the burial place of his brother George of Clarence, and Worcester, which he reached on 4 or 5 August, after which he turned eastwards towards Warwick. It had been agreed that Queen Anne would join him at Warwick Castle, and the royal party rested in these comfortable and familiar surroundings for almost a week. They were at Coventry on 15–16 August, and spent three days at both Leicester and Nottingham before making their way via Pontefract to York.[1]

The purpose of the tour was to allow people to see – and in some cases to meet – their new sovereign, and for Richard to commend himself to them. The abbot of Tewkesbury was promised that a debt owed by George of Clarence which had been only partially redeemed in King Edward's lifetime would be paid off in instalments, and John Rous reported that at Woodstock the citizens secured the restoration of 'a great area of the country' that Edward had annexed to Wychwood Forest. When London, Gloucester and Worcester offered to contribute towards the cost of the progress Richard told them he 'would rather have their hearts than their money', and there is no reason to doubt his secretary John Kendall's assertion that the King and Queen had 'in all their progress been worshipfully received with pageants and other etc., and his lords and judges in every place sitting, determining the complaints of poor folks with due punishment of offenders [against] his laws'.[2] Bishop Langton, whose letter to the prior of Christ Church, Canterbury, was quoted in the first chapter, uses very similar words.

Some of those who travelled with the royal party may have regarded the jaunt as a holiday, but Richard always had weightier matters on his mind. When he was at Minster Lovell on 29 July he learned of the failure of the conspiracy to liberate Edward IV's sons from the Tower, and immediately wrote to the Chancellor, Bishop Russell, informing him that the plotters had been arrested and instructing him to 'sit [in judgement] upon them and to proceed to the due execution of our laws in that behalf'.[3] At Warwick, he received a Spanish envoy who brought greetings from his royal mistress Queen Isabella together with proposals for an alliance against France. The envoy explained that Isabella 'was turned in her heart from England in time past' because King Edward had rejected her to marry a 'widow of England', but now that he was dead (and now that King Louis had broken his promises to her) she was ready to look to the future. Her natural inclination was 'ever to love and favour England', and she desired 'by all means to her possible to make these alliances and considerations with the King's good Grace',[4]

Richard had no wish to be drawn into a war with France at this particular moment, but he was always obliged to keep a close eye on England's traditional enemy across the Channel. He could not rely on the support of the new Duke of Burgundy (Maximilian, who had married Charles the Bold's daughter Mary, was embroiled in a war with his own subjects), and his attitude towards the Treaty of Picquigny had not endeared him to King Louis. Letters announcing his accession had already been sent to the crowned heads of Europe, and although Louis responded by offering his friendship his brevity betrayed his true feelings:

> My lord and cousin, – I have seen the letters that you have written to me by your herald Blanc Sanglier, and thank you for the news of which you have apprised me. And if I can do you any service I will do it with very good will, for I desire to have your friendship. And farewell, my lord and cousin. Written at Montilz lez Tours, the 21st day of July.

Richard was under no illusions, and his reply, sent from Leicester on 18 August, almost parodied Louis's answer. It may indeed be (as Kendall thought) the only example of his sense of humour to have survived:

My lord, my cousin, I have seen the letters you have sent me by Buckingham herald, whereby I understand that you wish to have my amity, of which I am very glad, in good form and manner; for I do not mean to break such truces as have hitherto been concluded between the late king of most noble memory, my brother deceased, and you, for the term of the same. Nevertheless, the merchants of this my kingdom of England, seeing the great occasions [causes] given them by your subjects by taking vessels and merchandise and otherwise, doubt [fear] greatly to adventure themselves to go to Bordeaux and elsewhere in your obeisance, until they may be assured on your part that they may surely and safely exercise the feat of their said merchandise [trade] in all the places of your said obeisance, according to the right of the said truces. Upon which matter, in order that my said subjects and merchants be not deceived under the shadow of the same, I pray you that by my servant, this bearer, *one of the grooms of my stable* [my italics], you will let me know by writing your full intention, and at the same time if you desire anything that I can do for you, that I may do it with good will. And farewell, my lord my cousin.[5]

The use of such a lowly envoy would have told Louis more about Richard's attitude towards him than any words written on paper, but Louis may never have seen the letter. He died at Plessis-les-Tours on 30 August, leaving an eight-year-old heir who would be unlikely to trouble England in the near future. Richard did not enjoy many strokes of good fortune, but this was undoubtedly one of the few.

Another ruler who breathed a sigh of relief at Louis's passing was Edward IV's perfidious ally Duke Francis of Brittany. Almost as soon as he was crowned, Richard had sent Dr Thomas Hutton to the Duchy to discuss re-establishing friendly relations (there had been differences over unpaid debts and piracy), and to inquire if Francis intended to harbour or actively assist the fugitive Sir Edward Woodville, one of the Queen's younger brothers. Curiously, the letter Hutton carried made no mention of Henry Tudor, who was also living in the Duke's territories, but it is impossible to say if this was because Richard genuinely thought that he posed no threat to him or because the official 'line' was to treat him as a person of no consequence. He may not have appreciated that his decision to depose Edward V had effectively given Henry his chance.

Nearer home there was Scotland, and Ireland, although there was not much that Richard could do about either. In the latter half of August he received what Bishop Langton called 'a courteous and wise' letter from King James proposing an eight-month truce during which commissioners appointed by both monarchs would meet to discuss a more permanent settlement. Richard replied offering to grant safe-conducts to whomever James might appoint for this purpose, but there was no direct mention of the recent conflict between them. On the contrary, James blamed the troubles on 'the workings and means of evil-disposed persons contrary [to] our mind and intention, as God knows', while Richard assured his 'right trusty and well beloved cousin' of his own desire for a 'reasonable and convenient peace'.[6] The regional adventurer of the early 1480s had become king of the entire realm.

Ireland was not, strictly speaking, a 'foreign' country, but a territory where Richard's ability to exercise his lordship depended almost entirely on the willingness of his native-born deputy, the Earl of Kildare, to obey his orders. On 19 July Richard gave the formal lieutenancy to his son Edward, and sent Master William Lacey to Kildare to notify him of the boy's appointment and to effectively confirm him in his own position. He granted privileges to Dublin and charters to the port towns of Galway and Youghal in County Cork, but relations with Kildare were sometimes difficult. When the deputy appointed his brother chancellor (of Ireland) without authority Richard was obliged to withdraw his own candidate, and an attempt to rule that offices should be held at the King's pleasure instead of for unlimited periods also had to be abandoned. Richard hoped that Kildare would use his influence to help him recover the lands of his father's earldom of Ulster, and acceded to his request for the manor of Leixlip and the constableship of Wicklow Castle with a salary of £1,000 per annum. But he baulked when the deputy made his presence in England conditional on the issue of a safe-conduct countersigned by others.

> The king marvels that he can desire any promises, seals or writings of any of his lords more than of his grace only, considering not only that such a surety cannot stand with the king's honour, but also that neither the said Earl nor any other hath seen that his grace hath broken promise or assurance by him made unto any person.[7]

Lacey also carried letters to the other great Irish peer, the Earl of Desmond, and here Richard was at pains to draw a parallel between the execution of the Earl's father in 1464 and the killing of his brother George of Clarence fourteen years later. His point was that both Clarence and Desmond's father had enemies who were determined to destroy them, and later stories claimed that Queen Elizabeth Woodville was responsible for both deaths. But there is nothing to substantiate the allegation that she 'arranged' Desmond's father's execution because he had told King Edward he ought to divorce her in order to marry a well-connected foreigner, and although she undoubtedly feared Clarence would seize the throne if her husband died prematurely it would have required more than feminine wiles to persuade a king to kill his brother. Richard could have named her if he held her responsible, but said only that 'certain persons, then having the governance and rule there [in Ireland]' had murdered Desmond's father, and that much the same thing had overtaken his brother. His commiserations may have been genuine, but he undoubtedly wanted Desmond's support.[8]

John Kendall wrote to York from Nottingham on 23 August to forewarn the citizens that Richard expected to be received there with appropriately regal splendour, and when the royal party reached Pontefract it was joined by seventy-one knights and gentlemen of the north. The aim was clearly to impress the mainly southern-based lords and notables who had accompanied Richard on the earlier stages of his journey, and the King, together with the Queen and their son (who had joined them from Middleham a few days earlier), made their state entry into York on Friday 29 August. The citizens did not disappoint him. The mayor and aldermen wore scarlet and the chamberlains and bridgemasters red when they met Richard on horseback at Brekles Mills outside the walls and conducted him into the city through Micklegate. Cheering crowds clad in blue and grey awaited him, and he was entertained by 'sights' (pageants), one just inside the gate and two others at the Ouse bridge and at Stayngate. The streets were hung with tapestries, and after the mayor had presented the King with a hundred marks in a golden cup (or perhaps in a pair of silver-gilt basins), and Queen Anne with a hundred pounds in gold on a plate, they processed to the Minster to meet the assembled clergy. Here, they were sprinkled with holy water and censed before attending divine service and then retiring to the Archbishop's palace for the remainder of the day.[9]

Richard was presumably delighted with his reception, because next day he sent to London for a number of items of rich clothing together with spurs, banners and coats of arms. The Croyland chronicler thought he intended to hold a second, 'northern' coronation in York Minster, but if the idea ever crossed Richard's mind it was abandoned in favour of a ceremony at which his son would be created Prince of Wales. The King and Queen were provided with various entertainments in the week that followed, and on Monday 8 September, the feast of the Nativity of the Blessed Virgin Mary, walked in procession to the Minster accompanied by Edward and the lords spiritual and temporal. After mass they returned to the Archbishop's palace, where the boy was formally invested, Richard girding him with a sword before presenting him with a gold rod and ring and placing a coronet upon his head. The King and Queen wore their crowns and regalia (perhaps thereby giving rise to the story that they had been crowned again), and there was much cheering and merrymaking. Even the sometimes hostile Vergil recorded that 'with so great honour, joy and congratulation of the inhabitants, as in show of rejoicing they extolled king Richard above the skies'.[10]

The new Prince of Wales returned to Middleham accompanied by the Queen shortly after the middle of September, and before Richard took his own leave of the citizens he summoned them to the chapter house of the Minster, where he thanked them for their devotion and remitted more than half the taxes they paid to the Crown. He then retraced his steps southwards via Pontefract and Gainsborough, but on reaching Lincoln on 11 September received some very disturbing news. The southern counties had risen against him, and one of the rebels was the Duke of Buckingham, who had helped him to the throne only three months earlier. No one knows why Buckingham turned against Richard. The smooth-tongued Bishop Morton, who was his prisoner at Brecon Castle, may have had a hand in it, but what arguments of Morton's could have produced such a dramatic change of allegiance? It has been suggested that although Buckingham had been well rewarded he had still not received everything he wanted, that he had been alienated by the fate of the Princes (whatever that was), and even that he wanted to be king himself. Each of these explanations is possible, but perhaps he was first and foremost an opportunist whose main concern was to protect his own position. He may have thought that there was a strong likelihood that the uprising would prove successful, and he intended to finish on the winning side.[11]

The uprising has been called 'Buckingham's Rebellion' because the Duke was its most powerful adherent, but he was neither the instigator nor the effective leader. Its principal supporters were gentlemen who lived south of a line drawn from the Thames to the Severn, from Kent in the east to Cornwall in the west, some of them former members of Edward IV's household. They had been too shocked – and wrong-footed – to oppose Richard's seizure of power in June, but had now come together with the avowed aim of restoring Edward V to the throne. Members of the Queen-Dowager's family, her eldest son the Marquis of Dorset and her brothers Richard and Lionel, were also implicated, and so was Margaret Beaufort, who hoped that a change of government would allow her exiled son Henry Tudor to return to England. Polydore Vergil claimed that Margaret 'was commonly called the head of that conspiracy',[12] and she may have encountered Buckingham (by chance or design?) as he rode back to Wales.

Margaret would never have lost sight of the fact that Henry had a distant claim to the throne through her decent from John of Gaunt and the Beauforts, and it may be no coincidence that, shortly afterwards, 'a rumour was spread that the sons of King Edward had died a violent death, but it was uncertain how. Accordingly, all those who had set on foot this insurrection, seeing that if they could find no one to take the lead in their designs, the ruin of all would speedily ensue, turned their thoughts to Henry',[13] and Buckingham wrote to him on or before 24 September urging him to join them. Meanwhile, Margaret proposed to Elizabeth Woodville that Henry should marry her eldest daughter, Elizabeth of York, when he had deposed Richard. She knew that a distant Lancastrian claimant would find it difficult to command the loyalty of mainstream Yorkists, but was sure they would support Henry for the girl's sake.

Buckingham concurred – or appeared to concur – with this new plan to crown Henry, but he was himself descended from Edward III's youngest son, Thomas of Woodstock. John of Gaunt's illegitimate Beaufort children had been legitimated in Parliament after he married their mother Katherine Swynford, but with the subsequent proviso that the extirpation of their bastardy did not make them candidates for the kingship. The legality of this was debatable – the victor would clearly interpret or amend the legislation to suit his purpose – but Buckingham could argue, quite reasonably, that his claim took precedence over Henry's. It had been a simple matter to remove Edward V a few months earlier, and he may have thought that Henry, who had few friends in England and who had not set foot in the country for twelve years, could be set aside when he had played his part.

There are hints in the sources that Richard was expecting trouble – he had asked for 2,000 Welsh bills (long staffs with hook-shaped blades) to be sent to him on 17 August and had seized the estates of Margaret Beaufort's half-brother John Welles and others – but Buckingham's defection was a body blow. He at once ordered a general mobilisation of his forces – those summoned were to meet him at Leicester on 21 October – and wrote to his Chancellor, Bishop Russell, concluding his letter with the bitter comment that he was 'truly determined to resist the malice of him that had best cause to be true, the Duke of Buckingham, the most untrue creature living'.[14] The uprising began in Kent – John Howard, Duke of Norfolk, was preparing to resist the rebels there by 10 October – and had spread to Wiltshire by the 17th and to Newbury and Salisbury by the 23rd. The West Country may not have become involved until early November, and Henry Tudor was only proclaimed at Bodmin on 3 November, a day after the captured Buckingham had been executed. It is unclear if some of the insurgents moved too soon or if others were simply unready, but their overall co-ordination was evidently poor.

Richard decided to leave the eastern rebels to Howard while he led his main army into the south, and ultimately the west, of the country, and found that luck was again with him. The localised groups of dissidents desperately needed leadership, but Buckingham proved unable to provide it. He seems to have been little loved by his tenants and neighbours, and no sooner had he left than one of them, Sir Thomas Vaughan of Tretower, attacked and plundered his castle at Brecon. A violent storm that broke over western England about 15 October prevented him from crossing the flooded River Severn, and with his wet and unenthusiastic army disintegrating he fled into Shropshire. He probably hoped that Thomas, Lord

Stanley, Henry Tudor's stepfather, would aid him, but the Stanleys feared his intrusion into their area of influence in north Wales and had decided to support Richard this time.

Henry Tudor left Brittany somewhat belatedly about 31 October, but foul weather scattered his flotilla and he arrived off Plymouth with only two ships. Too cautious to land personally, he sent a boat to reconnoitre, and soon learned that the rebellion was all but over. Buckingham had been betrayed into Richard's hands by the servant with whom he had sought refuge, and as the King advanced resolutely to Salisbury and then Exeter resistance collapsed before him. A few other rebels were captured and executed, the most notable being Richard's brother-in-law Sir Thomas St Leger, his sister Anne's widower, but more escaped to join Henry in his renewed exile.

Richard had won an almost bloodless victory, but the apparent ease of his triumph should not blind us to the fact that the situation had been – and remained – very serious. A letter that Francis Lovell sent to his 'cousin' and Oxfordshire neighbour Sir William Stonor, asking him to bring both his own and Lovell's retainers to Leicester, suggests that the King and his friends had failed to grasp of the extent of the opposition (Stonor had already joined the rebels), and any one of several factors – a change of heart on the part of the Stanleys, for example – could have produced a different outcome.[15] Richard had been careful to allow the majority of his late brother's officials to retain their positions, and had made as few new appointments as possible. Russell had replaced Rotherham as chancellor; Edmund Chaderton, a member of his ducal council, had been appointed treasurer of the chamber in place of Sir Thomas Vaughan (not to be confused with Sir Thomas of Tretower), who had been executed with Earl Rivers at Pontefract; his ducal chancellor Thomas Barowe had succeeded Bishop Morton's nephew Robert as master of the rolls of chancery; and he had retained the services of his own secretary, John Kendall, at the expense of Oliver King, who had served Edward IV in this capacity. The message was clearly that change was to be kept to a minimum, but many of the southern gentlemen who took up arms may have feared that, ultimately, they would be superseded by his trusted northerners. This is, of course, precisely what *did* happen, but only because (as we shall see), Richard *had* to rely increasingly on men he knew he could trust in the aftermath of the rebellion. It was a victory of sorts, but the damage inflicted would cast a long shadow over the rest of his reign.

10

REGAINING THE INITIATIVE, 1484

The successful suppression of an uprising usually made a king more, rather than less, secure on his throne, but in Richard's case the effect was precisely the opposite. All hope that the events of the summer would be quietly forgotten had been shattered, and he had to try to build a new power base on the ruins of the old. His first, and perhaps most pressing, worry was that although thirty-six of the sixty-two peers of the realm had attended his coronation, the attitude of some of them was decidedly questionable. Professor Colin Richmond has estimated that only twelve were Ricardian loyalists, and categorises the remainder as either 'query-Ricardians' (six), 'compliant, undecided or indifferent' (seventeen), or anti-Ricardian (one). The twenty-six who did not attend included five Ricardians who were prevented by age or other responsibilities, one query-Ricardian, six compliant, and as many as fourteen who either opposed him or were likely to do so. In other words, the King could count on the backing of just over a third of the peerage (the seventeen 'Ricardians' plus the seven 'query-Ricardians'), but a quarter were against him and the remaining twenty-three were 'don't knows'.[1]

Calculations of this sort are inevitably based on estimates and contain some errors; but the broad picture that emerges is clear enough. Some of the uncommitted were minors whose views (if they had any) could be disregarded, but there was no denying that two of the three greatest lords in the kingdom had not always been well disposed towards Richard. He could rely on John Howard, whom he had made Duke of Norfolk and who had proved his loyalty by his response to the Buckingham rebels; but Thomas, Lord Stanley, who had been arrested with Hastings, and Henry Percy, Earl of Northumberland, who had been his rival in the north in the early 1470s, were clearly less dependable. Removing them was not an option: they had to be given a vested interest in the new regime.

Richard began the process of developing better personal relations with both men by awarding them lands forfeited by the rebels. Stanley was granted estates worth £687 yearly and allowed to keep the profits of his wife Margaret Beaufort's former interests, while Northumberland received Buckingham's rich lordship of Holderness (valued at over £1,000 p.a.) and recovered properties in south-west England he claimed by inheritance. Stanley was made Constable of England, Northumberland became Steward, and the extension of Stanleyan influence into north Wales was matched by Northumberland's appointment as warden general of the Scottish March. He was not permitted to intrude into Richard's West March, but his family's main interests lay in the east.

Stanley and Northumberland were happy to accept whatever the King was prepared to grant them, but it is doubtful if either felt more obligated or committed to him. Stanley was still Henry Tudor's stepfather, and if Northumberland hoped that Richard's removal to Westminster would restore him to his former position of authority in the north he was soon disillusioned. Richard's ducal council and household in the region continued to function under the nominal authority of Prince Edward, and when Edward died suddenly in March 1484 the King turned not to Northumberland but to his nephew and likely heir apparent, John de la Pole, Earl of Lincoln. The north remained crucial to his interests, and he would not, could not, allow it to pass wholly into other hands.

Northumberland (who came of an old Lancastrian family) and Stanley both had conflicting claims on their loyalties, and they were not alone. One of the lords described by Professor Richmond as 'pro-Ricardian' was William Herbert, Earl of Huntingdon, son of William Herbert, Earl of Pembroke, who had been executed after the battle of Edgecote in 1469. William of Pembroke had become Henry Tudor's guardian in 1462 with the result that Henry and the younger William, who was two years his senior, had been brought up together: and although there is no evidence that a lasting friendship developed between them, they must have known one another very well. William of Huntingdon married Mary Woodville, the Queen's sister, and three years after her death in 1481 wed Katherine, King Richard's bastard daughter; but at one point during his exile Henry contemplated a marriage alliance with the Herberts, and William did not, apparently, fight at Bosworth. Perhaps the decision was too painful to make.

Richard could not diminish – and was obliged to augment – Stanley's and Northumberland's regional authority, but his overriding aim was to exercise power himself rather than bestow it on others. His closest supporters were also granted properties forfeited by the rebels, but they were denied the prestige and authority that Edward IV had allowed Richard, and Richard had so recently allowed Buckingham. Francis, Viscount Lovell and Sir

Richard Ratcliffe, two of his closest confidants, were given lands and offices in the Thames Valley and in Devonshire; but there is no evidence that they exercised quasi-regal powers there, nor were they created earls of Oxford and Devon. The northern knight Sir Marmaduke Constable was appointed steward and constable of the Duchy of Lancaster honours of Tutbury, Castle Donnington, and the High Peak, the offices from which William, Lord Hastings, had dominated the north midlands on behalf of King Edward; but unlike Hastings, Constable was not permitted to retain large numbers of the local gentry. On the contrary, he was required to administer an oath that all duchy tenants would be the loyal liegemen of the King and would be retained by no other person (himself included), and Richard did not enhance his influence in other ways, by granting him wardships for example. These men were the King's representatives in their areas, not substitutes for the royal authority itself.

Richard could seek to exert authority over national and regional matters, but he was bound to leave local affairs in the hands of a multitude of lesser individuals. In normal circumstances this would have posed no problem, but approximately a hundred southern knights and gentlemen had been indicted for their part in the rebellion and needed to be replaced by men whose loyalty was unimpeachable. He had little choice but to turn to his trusted northerners, although he must have known that many of them would be stigmatised as aliens and outsiders. In the words of the Croyland writer,

what immense estates and patrimonies were collected into this king's treasury in consequence of this measure [the act of attainder passed against the rebels], all of which he distributed among his northern adherents, whom he planted in every spot throughout his dominions, to the disgrace and lasting and loudly expressed sorrow of all the people in the south, who daily longed more and more for the hoped-for return of their ancient rulers, rather than the present tyranny of these people.[2]

The chronicler may have exaggerated – some members of Richard's northern affinity had southern interests, he had not lacked southern associates even when Duke of Gloucester, and some of Edward IV's household men came from northern backgrounds – but resentment was still widespread. People usually prefer the old and familiar to the new and uncertain, but in this case the fact that so many of the newcomers were northerners made the 'plantation' more threatening than it might have appeared otherwise. The idea that Englishmen who lived north of the River Trent were somehow 'different' and potentially more aggressive had probably existed for generations, but the campaign waged by Queen Margaret's large northern army at the beginning of 1461 brought it into sharp focus. Clement Paston, writing to his brother John on 23 January, refers to the 'people in the north [who] rob and steal and [have] been appointed to pillage … and give away men's goods and livelihoods in all the south country',[3] a threat John, who had already been told by Friar Brackley that Margaret and her men intended to kill all the friars minor in southern England, would readily have believed.[4] At Croyland Abbey, the monks listened anxiously to stories of churches being plundered, priests slaughtered, and the creation of a thirty-mile-wide path of pillage as the Lancastrian army advanced – a 'whirlwind', to borrow the author's own colourful phrase. Fortunately, Margaret's forces did not approach the abbey and he lived to conclude his story. 'Blessed be God', he writes, 'who did not give us for a prey into their teeth.'[5]

The fears expressed by Paston, the Croyland writer, and others were generated by the heat of the moment, but almost certainly owed something to the economic decline of the north of England and the relative prosperity of the south. Professor Pollard has estimated that 'at a very rough guess only 15 per cent of the population lived in the six northern counties of Cumberland, Northumberland, Westmoreland, Durham, Lancashire and Yorkshire' although they represented a quarter of the area of the kingdom. 'Recent work in urban history has indicated a profound shift in the balance of urban wealth away from the north and east towards the south and west' in the late fourteenth and fifteenth centuries, a decline that particularly affected York (after 1450) and towns on, or looking towards, the eastern seaboard. 'The cumulative evidence seems to be pointing to the conclusion that during the second half of the fifteenth century the contrast between the impoverished and declining north and the prosperous and growing south-east was becoming ever more striking', and it seems likely that it was an awareness of this which, in Professor Pollard's words, 'lay behind the ready credence given to the idea that northerners were itching for the chance to rob and pillage in the wealthier south'.

The men who Richard 'planted' in the south in the aftermath of Buckingham's rebellion were bound to be tainted by this fear of northerners, and he could only wonder how many of his southern subjects thought of him in the same context. He had spent many years in the north – as a youth in Warwick's household and, after 1471, serving as his brother's viceroy – and may have become increasingly out of touch with what was both the political and economic heart of the kingdom. There were no easy solutions

– he could only hope that sound government at the centre coupled with good lordship in the localities would eventually persuade the doubters to accept both him and the men he had placed over them. About a third of the rebels were afterwards pardoned, but very few were restored to their former positions. This may have been because Richard remained reluctant to trust them; but, equally, he would have found it all but impossible to dispossess his loyal northerners of the lands and offices they had received from him. He may not have realised it immediately, but his room for manoeuvre was decidedly limited: he was as committed to them as they were to him.

One consequence of setting northerners to rule the south, one which, again, Richard may not have appreciated at the outset, was that it made further campaigns against the Scots all but impossible. King James renewed the 'auld alliance' with France in March 1484 and a joint Franco-Scottish fleet inflicted losses on English shipping in the North Sea during the summer. Richard responded vigorously – the Croyland writer says that 'by means of his skill in naval warfare he gained a victory in a surprising manner over the Scots'[6] – but the major land campaign he had planned earlier in the year had to be abandoned. Instead, there were more peace talks, and the agreement reached in September provided for a three-year truce and the marriage of James's son to Richard's niece, Anne de la Pole. Richard may have thought that a breathing space of three years would allow him to deal with his southern difficulties and with Henry Tudor, and he could then return to his 'unfinished business' in the north.

With hindsight, it is evident that Richard could do nothing to retrieve the situation in which he found himself in the time available to him, and it is part of his tragedy that he was destined to spend the final twenty months of his life striving to attain the unattainable. One way in which he tried to win approval was by dealing firmly with local officials who abused their authority. Sir Marmaduke Constable, his Steward of Tutbury, was instructed to review and overhaul the day-to-day administration of the duchy estate, replacing incapable and corrupt officers with 'able and well disposed persons' who would 'be attending daily on their offices when they await not on his grace'.[7] Admittedly, the well-being of those who lived and worked at Tutbury was not the only consideration – Richard also wanted to maximise the Crown's income – but the message was that Henry VI's weakness and Edward IV's indolence were things of the past.

King Edward had left the treasury virtually empty at his death, and Richard had to find ways of funding his government without alienating large numbers of his subjects in the process. He decided against asking Parliament to grant taxation, and tried to improve the situation by insisting on greater efficiency and by ensuring that all who owed the Crown money met their obligations. Royal receivers were to submit their returns promptly, auditors were to be men learned in the law who would maximise income at minimum cost (by not 'taking great fines and rewards of the King's tenants'),[8] and clerks were set to comb dusty records looking for old feudal dues that could still be exploited. The Croyland continuator (who was presumably one of the victims) wrote that 'he [Richard] accordingly sent chosen men, children of this world, wiser in their generation than the children of light, who were by means of prayers and threats, by right or by wrong, to scrape up immense sums of money, after examining the archives of the realm, from persons of nearly all conditions'.[9] He again exaggerated of course, but his comments testify to Richard's ability to take stock of a situation and seize whatever opportunities came to hand.

The orders sent to deputies like Constable touched the lives of royal tenants and a few others, but were never going to be enough in themselves. Laws passed in Parliament, on the other hand, affected everyone, and Richard's appeal to his subjects through this medium earned the grudging admiration of the otherwise critical Lord Bacon. He was, in Bacon's words, 'a good law-maker, for the ease and solace of the common people', even if this and his other supposed virtues 'were conceived to be rather feigned and affected things to serve his ambition, than true qualities ingenerate in his judgement or nature'.[10] Bacon does not say which of the thirty-three Acts of Richard's only Parliament most impressed him, but there are several possibilities. Edward IV had partly financed his 1475 French expedition by 'benevolences', sums wrung from unwilling subjects that were supposed to be gifts but were really arbitrary, extra-parliamentary taxes. They had provoked considerable anger, and Richard's statute on the subject acknowledged that they were illegal and should be 'damned and annulled for ever'.[11] When monies did, finally, have to be raised from private individuals, he treated them as repayable loans.

An Act of this sort would clearly meet with widespread approval, and so would Richard's efforts to make the criminal justice system fairer. He acknowledged that the 'packing' of juries to obtain verdicts for or against an accused was unacceptable, and sought to combat it by introducing a minimum property qualification for jurors. Only men who owned freehold land worth at least 20s or copyhold worth 26s 8d (and who were assumed to be 'respectable') could thereafter serve on juries, and a bailiff or sheriff who admitted a juror without this qualification would be liable to a fine of 40s or 80s according to his rank. Other legislation laid down that a felon's goods were not to be seized until he had been convicted, gave every accused the right to be granted bail, and imposed restrictions on local officials who dealt with disputes arising at fairs and markets at courts of *piepowder* – from *pied* (foot), and *pouldre* (dusty), literally 'dusty feet'. This somewhat summary justice had given rise to abuses, and the perpetrators would henceforward be fined.

Richard was also concerned to reform the existing laws relating to land and property which had been shown to be susceptible to abuse and fraud. There was a limit to what could be done in the short term, but two particular areas of exploitation were identified. Lands that formed part of a trust were to be regarded as the property of the beneficiary – a change designed to prevent concealment and frustrate malicious challenges where the legal title was obscure – and another Act outlawed the practice of conveying property secretly by requiring that all such transactions should be made public and be legally binding. Anyone wanting to challenge an existing arrangement had to do so within five years.

Among the groups in society Richard was keenest to befriend were the commercially powerful merchants, and a number of his laws were passed for their benefit. No fewer than five statutes protected English traders against unfair foreign competition, and there was also legislation designed to prevent commercial dishonesty. Wine and oil were not to be sold until they had been 'gauged' by the King's gauger to ensure the buyer was not being charged too much or given short measure (the Act refers to the 'short' vessels imported before 1449 in the reign of Henry VI, 'late in deed and not of right King of England'), and a most detailed law regulated the sale of cloth. Some of its terms were:

(a) Broad cloth must be fully watered before it be put up for sale.

(b) Broad cloth, and whole woollen cloth, must be 24 yards long, 2 yards broad 'within the lifts'. Half cloth must be 12–16 yards long. If the statutory dimensions are exceeded, the buyer need pay only for the difference.

(c) The town of origin of cloths is to be identified by the deal. The aulnager (sealer) is to be appointed by the Treasurer, who must be assured that he is expert in making cloth, and worth £100.

(d) Cloth must not be drawn or 'tentored' (stretched) after watering, and tentors are not even to be kept in houses, but 'in open places'; mayors must see 'that all cloths, which shall be put upon tentors, shall not be drawn out in length or breadth otherwise than is before rehearsed etc.'[12]

The Act encouraged informers to report breaches of the law by giving them a third of the fine imposed on the individual responsible. The Exchequer and the relevant local authority received the remaining two-thirds.

H.G. Hanbury, Vinerian Professor of English Law at the University of Oxford, was most impressed by this last piece of legislation:

This statute may be said to provide a powerful index of Richard III's thoroughness, his insight into technical processes, and, above all, his appreciation of the necessity to keep in close touch and consultation with technical and commercial experts. He had a quality of manysidedness which recalls Henry II and Edward I.[13]

He may be right, of course, but in the final analysis we do not know the extent to which Richard personally initiated these laws or was responsible for their drafting. All we can say with certainty is that he undoubtedly approved of them.

Richard's concern that his subjects should enjoy the benefits and protection the law gave them was not confined solely to Acts of Parliament. One of his proclamations begins 'the king's grace willeth that for the love that he hath for the ministration and execution of justice for the common wealth of this realm, the which the most tendereth', and the members of his northern council were told that they must not allow 'favour, affection, hate, malice or meed [reward]' to influence their decisions, 'nor speak in the council otherwise than the king's laws and good conscience shall require, but be indifferent and no wise partial'.[14] There is also evidence that he promoted the concept of a separate council, or court, of requests, which heard petitions from those who could not afford to seek justice through the conventional legal system. John Harrington, who later became common clerk of the city of York, was appointed *clericus consili nostril requisicionum ac supplicacionum* in December 1483 (the Latin is ambiguous and could mean 'clerk of requests and supplications of the council' or 'clerk of the council of requests and supplications'), and two Colchester burgesses reported that a bill to *abolish* such a court or separate council had been introduced into Henry VII's first Parliament.[15] Nothing is known of its workings, but it seems likely that this was another of Richard's reforms which was revoked, at least temporarily. Petitions were again being made to the King in Council by 1493 – perhaps they had never ceased to be made – and Cardinal Wolsey gave 'the King's Council in his Court of Requests' a permanent home at Westminster in 1519.

The only criticism that can be levelled at Richard in this context is that after he became Protector and King he sometimes anticipated the legal processes before they had been completed. He seized and granted away lands held by Earl Rivers, the Marquis of Dorset and some of the Buckingham rebels before they had been formally attainted (without first taking inquisitions to establish the rights of widows and others who had legitimate interests in them), and transferred the estates and titles of the duchy of Norfolk to John Howard and William Berkeley, the natural heirs, without troubling to repeal the Act of Parliament that had settled them on his nephew Prince Richard. He did not, apparently, think that acting above the law on occasion risked undermining respect for it, and we are again confronted – and to some extent confounded – by the apparent contradictions in his character. Political necessity invariably, perhaps unavoidably, triumphed over 'right'.

59. The seals of Richard's parents, Richard, Duke of York (left), and Cecily Neville.

60. Henry VI in his youth, from a picture in King's College, Cambridge. Henry founded the college in 1441.

61. Edward IV, from a painting formerly at Southwick, Northampton.

62. Edward V, from a MS in the Archbishop of Canterbury's library at Lambeth.

Above: 63. Richard III, from a painting on glass belonging to Trinity College, Cambridge. Richard had close links with a number of Cambridge scholars.
Above right and right: 64. Edward, Prince of Wales, Richard and Anne's son, from the English version of *The Rous Roll*.

posite: 65. Richard III and Queen Anne Neville, from the English version of *The Rous Roll*.

ove: 66. George, Duke of Clarence, and his duchess, Isabel Neville, from the English version

The *Rous Roll*.

67. Richard Neville, Earl of Warwick, the 'Kingmaker', and his countess Anne Beauchamp, from the English version of *The Rous Roll*.

68. Barnard Castle (County Durham). The remains of a Norman and fourteenth-century castle granted to Richard in 1475 as part of the Neville inheritance. The Brackenbury Tower, named after Sir Robert Brackenbury, his Constable of the Tower of London, is in the north-east section of the curtain wall.

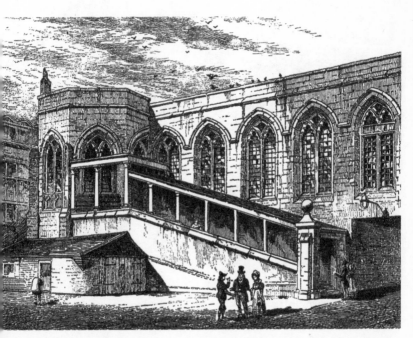

69. Crosby Hall, the Great Hall of Crosby Place built by Sir John Crosby in 1466. Richard rented the property as his town house when he resided in London in his brother's reign.

70. Pontefract Castle. A mainly Norman fortress which became Richard's official residence as Steward of the Duchy of Lancaster. Earl Rivers, Lord Richard Grey and others were executed here in June 1483.

71. Warwick Castle. Anne Neville's birthplace. Richard began the building of the Bear and Clarence towers, and spent a week here during his royal progress in 1483.

72. The interior of the Great Hall of Leicester Castle as it appeared before 1821. Richard
sealed letters here in the course of his royal progress in August 1483.

Left: 73. The cenotaph of Henry Stafford, Duke of Buckingham, is in the church at Britford in Wiltshire. Britford was one of his properties and is close to Salisbury, where he was executed.
Below: 74. Sheriff Hutton Castle from the north-west, as it appeared in 1824. It was one of the seats of Richard's Council of the North during his brief reign.

Above left: 75. The damaged cenotaph of Bishop (later Cardinal-Archbishop) John Morton in the crypt of Canterbury Cathedral.
Above right: 76. Engraving of the tomb effigy of Bishop James Goldwell in Norwich Cathedral.

Left: 77. Memorial brass to Bishop Richard Bell in Carlisle Cathedral.

Above: 78. Signatures of Elizabeth Woodville, from a receipt she gave for her annuity in 1491, and Elizabeth of York, from a letter sent to the Prior of Christ Church, Canterbury in 1499. Note the similarity.

79. Yorkist Suns and Roses livery collar with Richard's boar pendant. A drawing by C. Stothard from the now lost effigy of Ralph Neville, second Earl of Westmoreland, in Brancepeth church, Durham.

Above: 80. Nottingham Castle, where Richard received the news of his son's death and where he awaited Henry Tudor's invasion. A reconstruction based on archaeological evidence and analogous architecture elsewhere.

Right: 81. The Blue Boar Inn, Leicester. Richard is said to have stayed here for two nights on his way to Bosworth, and to have left his bedstead, containing his treasure, in an upper chamber. The building was demolished in 1836.

I I

CULTIVATING THE BISHOPS, 1484

A great deal has been written about Richard's relations with his principal noblemen, with John Howard, Duke of Norfolk; with Henry Percy, Earl of Northumberland; and with Thomas, Lord Stanley, who betrayed him at Bosworth,[1] but not much has been said about his dealings with members of the other powerful interest group in late medieval society, the episcopacy. Richard's bishops lacked the political influence of their fourteenth-century counterparts – they no longer enjoyed a monopoly of learning and literacy, and laymen (and women) were increasingly adopting the 'mixed life' and becoming devoutly religious. But they were still a force to be reckoned with, and could give powerful moral backing to a king whose hold on power was threatened from both within and without.

There were two archdioceses – Canterbury and York – and fifteen dioceses in late fifteenth-century England: Bath & Wells, Carlisle, Chichester, Durham, Ely, Exeter, Hereford, Coventry & Lichfield, Lincoln, London, Norwich, Rochester, Salisbury, Winchester and Worcester, together with four in Wales, Bangor, Llandaff, St Asaph and St David's. The two archbishops were

Thomas Bourchier and Thomas Rotherham, and the bishops John Alcock (Worcester), Edmund Audley (Rochester), Richard Bell (Carlisle), Peter Courtenay (Exeter), William Dudley (Durham), Richard Edenham (Bangor), James Goldwell (Norwich), John Hales (Coventry & Lichfield), Thomas Kempe (London), Thomas Langton (St David's), John Marshall (Llandaff), Thomas Milling (Hereford), John Morton (Ely), Richard Redman (St Asaph), John Russell (Lincoln), Robert Stillington (Bath & Wells), Edward Story (Chichester), William Waynflete (Winchester), and Lionel Woodville (Salisbury). William Dudley died on 29 November 1483 and was replaced by John Shirwood, and when Thomas Langton took Lionel Woodville's place at Salisbury in February 1485 he was succeeded at St David's by Hugh Pavy.[2]

Personal details of some of these men are inevitably lacking, but the general impression is that, with one notable exception, they were elderly even by medieval standards. The seventy-two-year-old Archbishop of Canterbury, Thomas Bourchier, had been in post since 1454, while his northern counterpart Thomas Rotherham, who had disgraced himself by giving the Great Seal to Elizabeth Woodville, was aged sixty. Edmund Audley was forty-four, Peter Courtenay fifty-one, and John Alcock, Thomas Langton and John Russell, who had been born in or around 1430, were all fifty-three. But Richard Bell and Robert Stillington were about seventy-three, John Hales seventy-six, and William Waynflete eighty-six. The exception was Lionel Woodville, the Queen-Dowager's younger brother, who had been born *c.* 1454 and who was therefore a comparatively youthful twenty-nine in 1483.

Almost inevitably, some of them had firm, discernible political allegiances (whether pro- or anti-Ricardian or 'Yorkist' or 'Lancastrian'), while others were apolitical or kept their opinions to themselves. The bishop most opposed to Richard was John Morton of Ely, who (as we saw) had helped foment Buckingham's rebellion, and who escaped to join Henry Tudor when it became apparent that the uprising had failed. He had shared Margaret of Anjou's exile in France in the 1460s and had been chancellor to her son Edward; but after the Lancastrian cause had been destroyed at Tewkesbury he bowed to the inevitable and accepted a pardon from King Edward. Edward appointed him Master of the Rolls, employed him on diplomatic missions, named him an executor of his will, and in October 1478 asked the Pope to 'provide' him to the bishopric of Ely. He had every reason to remain part of the Yorkist establishment, but he was not prepared to countenance the boy-king's removal and his arrest with Hastings shows that he was already identified with the opposition. Richard pardoned him in December 1484 in the hope of winning him over, but he rejected the overture and went to Rome to seek papal permission for Henry Tudor to marry King Edward's daughter, Elizabeth of York.

Richard had alienated the entire Woodville family by his treatment of young Edward, and it is hardly surprising that Bishop Lionel of Salisbury joined his brothers and nephew Dorset in rebellion. His appointment to a commission of the peace in Dorset and Wiltshire soon after Richard's accession may indicate that the King hoped he would accept the new situation, but he was in trouble by late September when his temporalities (his properties and revenues) were seized and he became the second of Buckingham's clerical prisoners.[3] After the failure of the uprising he sought sanctuary in Beaulieu Abbey, where his life ended before 1 December. There is no evidence to support the belief that he joined Morton and Henry Tudor in exile and died abroad.

A less likely opponent was Peter Courtenay of Exeter, a member of the staunchly Yorkist Courtenay family of Powderham who did not always see eye to eye with their Lancastrian cousins, the Courtenay earls of Devon. He supported the Duke of Clarence in the troubles of 1469–71, but subsequently became King Edward's secretary and was described as a royal counsellor in 1477–8. Richard initially regarded him as an ally and intended to make use of his services;[4] but Courtenay reconsidered his position during the late summer and joined the rebellion. He escaped to join Henry Tudor in Brittany, and returned with him to England in August 1485.

These men were all unequivocally hostile to Richard, and he would have expected little of four others who did not oppose him openly but who were all closely associated with the Queen-Dowager and the Prince of Wales. Thomas Milling had been Abbot of Westminster when Elizabeth Woodville sought sanctuary there in 1470, and had stood godfather to the newborn Prince Edward. He became the Prince's chancellor after King Edward's restoration, and his promotion to Hereford made it easier for him to spend time with the boy at Ludlow. John Alcock's career also advanced markedly after 1471, and it is likely that he too had been of particular assistance to the royal family. Appointed Bishop of Rochester in 1472, he became Prince Edward's tutor and the president of his council before being translated to Worcester in 1476. He may have been something of a Vicar of Bray character since he actively negotiated with the Scots on behalf of Richard, but this did not prevent Henry Tudor from appointing him Chancellor of England in October 1485. Edward Story, who was provided to Carlisle in 1468 and translated to Chichester ten years later, was the Queen's confessor from the late 1460s, and Edmund Audley of

Rochester officiated at her markedly low-key funeral in 1492. His previous service is uncertain, but few wished to be associated with her after she fell under suspicion in her last years.

The two archbishops, Thomas Bourchier of Canterbury and Thomas Rotherham of York, were both ardent Yorkists, but both had their difficulties with Richard. Bourchier had led the notables who persuaded Queen Elizabeth to release her younger son from sanctuary, but Mancini says that he did so only 'to mitigate the fierce resolve of the duke [Richard]' while Croyland used the word *compelled*.[5] It was apparently only with reluctance that he crowned Richard (he absented himself from the coronation banquet on account of his great age), and he may have taken the view that he had been misled or tricked into abetting King Edward's sons' downfall. He was on such openly bad terms with Richard in the latter half of 1483 that some of his tenants withheld their rents from him, and it was perhaps this that persuaded him to bow to what must have seemed the inevitable. He was formally pardoned on 8 December, and the King ordered his tenants to pay him their dues 'forasmuch as we have accepted and received our said cousin [Bourchier] into the good favour of our grace … ascertaining you [that] we be unto him perfect and very good sovereign lord'.[6] The cracks were papered over, but there is no evidence that he attended meetings of the Council after 1483.

Thomas Rotherham had served the House of York as Keeper of the Privy Seal and Chancellor of England, combining these posts with his bishoprics and archbishopric. He had demonstrated his loyalty to the royal family by taking sanctuary when Henry VI was restored in 1470–1, and Richard would have expected him to oppose his deposition of young Edward. He was dismissed as Chancellor after briefly surrendering the Great Seal to Elizabeth

Woodville, and then arrested with Hastings and Morton in the Council chamber in June. The Croyland writer says that he was imprisoned in a Welsh castle and he was not among those who welcomed Richard to York in August; but he seems to have accepted the situation soon afterwards and began to co-operate with the new government. Richard ordered his tenants to pay him their dues in September (he had apparently suffered the same fate as Bourchier), and he served as a trier of petitions in the January Parliament. He was twice the King's age, and may have concluded that continued resistance would damage his own prospects without improving those of Edward V.

John Russell, who succeeded Rotherham as Keeper of the Privy Seal, as Bishop of Lincoln, and finally as Chancellor in the summer of 1483, was also a career civil servant but a far more cautious man than his predecessor. He had not taken sides in 1470–1 (he negotiated a truce with France on behalf of Henry VI's government in February), and continued to be employed as an envoy after Edward IV regained power. Richard may have adjudged that he would serve any king whatever the circumstances, and this may be why he dispossessed him of the Great Seal at two moments of crisis – during Buckingham's rebellion and on 9 July 1485, six weeks before the battle of Bosworth. One source says that Russell was dismissed on 29 July, but why, or in what circumstances, is uncertain. The best that can be said of him is that he was a capable, hard-working royal administrator, but never a Ricardian partisan.

The same is true of four other bishops who did not actively oppose Richard, but who kept their heads well below the parapet. James Goldwell of Norwich had been Edward IV's proctor at the papal curia between 1467 and 1471, and had officiated at the marriage of the infant Prince Richard to the equally youthful Anne

Mowbray in 1478. He had helped facilitate the marriage of George of Clarence to Isabel Neville (in defiance of King Edward's wishes) in 1469, and his 'guilty knowledge' was shared by the Bishop of London, Thomas Kempe. Kempe, John Hales of Coventry, and William Waynflete of Winchester, had all been raised to the episcopacy in Henry VI's reign and were all former royal servants. Waynflete had been appointed to Henry's collegiate foundation at Eton in 1441, Kempe was a King's clerk and chaplain by 1443, and Hales became a chaplain to Queen Margaret when he was provost of Oriel College between 1446 and 1449. They accepted the change of dynasty in 1461, but when Henry was restored nine years later Waynflete escorted the liberated King from the Tower to the Bishop of London's palace, and Hales was appointed Keeper of the Privy Seal. King Edward subsequently pardoned them and they seem to have been on good terms with him in the 1470s; but only Kempe and Goldwell are known to have attended Richard's coronation in 1483. Waynflete afterwards welcomed the King to Magdalen College much as he had welcomed Edward IV in 1481; but if he wanted his great project to continue to enjoy royal approval he arguably had little choice.

The attitude of these men towards Richard ranged from grudging acceptance to outright opposition, but there were, nevertheless, a few members of the episcopacy who gave him their unqualified backing. Bishop Langton's ringing tribute to the King was noted in the prologue, and his fellow northerners, Richard Bell of Carlisle, Richard Redman of St Asaph, and William Dudley of Durham, all joined him on the royal 'progress'. They had all been associated with Richard when he was Duke of Gloucester, and it is likely that three of them, Langton, Bell and Redman, had been promoted to the episcopacy with his help. The fourth, William Dudley, had been an extremely pliant Bishop of Durham, who, in the words of his biographer, fell 'completely under the sway of the King's brother'[7] in the late 1470s. He granted Richard the Forest of Weardale and Stanhope Park for life (the equivalent of an annuity of £100), appointed ducal servants to senior positions in the palatinate, and in 1480 and 1482 allowed men nominally under his authority to join the war against Scotland. His sudden death on 29 November 1483 created a vacancy that could not easily be filled on a like-for-like basis, and it may be no coincidence that his successor, John Shirwood, the King's proctor at the curia, was permanently absent from England in Richard's lifetime. Richard, in fact, kept the temporalities of the see in his own hands until as late as 16 August 1485.

The Welsh bishops were little concerned with politics in England – Richard Redman, who remained Abbot of Shap, in Westmoreland, after his elevation to the impoverished see of St Asaph, is the exception – but the same cannot be said for the last of these men we have to deal with, Robert Stillington of Bath and Wells. He served Edward IV as Keeper of the Privy Seal (1461–7) and as Chancellor (1467–73), taking sanctuary during the King's exile and helping to persuade George of Clarence to return to his Yorkist allegiance. He was arrested shortly after George was tried and executed in 1478, and spent a week in the Tower of London. It is usually assumed that he was in some way implicated in whatever had caused the Duke's downfall, but precisely what he had done is a matter of speculation. All that can be said is that he was able to convince the King and Council that he had acted properly, and he was formally pardoned in June.

We have already noted that it was Stillington who allegedly informed Richard of Edward IV's precontract with Eleanor

Butler, but surprisingly the story is found only in the *Memoirs* of the Franco-Burgundian writer Philippe de Commynes. It is possible that Commynes, who was close to Louis XI, had learned something that was not widely known even in England, but it is hard to credit his claim that Richard meant to marry the Bishop's bastard son to Princess Elizabeth of York. Still, a yearbook of 1488 does say that it was Stillington who drew up the petition inviting Richard to assume the kingship, and the overriding impression is that contemporaries associated him with the events of that summer and thought he had been active on Richard's behalf.

Richard, then, could rely on a few of the bishops just as he could count of the support of some members of the greater nobility; but the reality was that the majority of both groups were unreliably tolerant or openly hostile. Time would work in his favour of course, but in the meantime – and it was likely to be a long meantime – he had to make the best of what was available to him. With the possible exception of Redman they were all university-trained scholars, and although William Dudley had joined Edward IV at Doncaster with 160 men when he returned from exile in 1471 the days of fighting bishops like Odo of Bayeux and Henry Despenser of Norwich were long over. Their support, and inclinations, were more likely to be moral than military, and Richard tried to capitalise on this by uniting them in a war against immorality. In a circular letter sent to them on 10 March 1484 he declared that 'our principal intent and fervent desire is to see virtue and cleanness of living to be advanced, increased and multiplied, and vices and all other things repugnant to virtue provoking the high indignation and fearful displeasure of God to be repressed and annulled'. It was, he said, known that in every jurisdiction as well in your pastoral cure as other, there be many, as well of the spiritual party as of the temporal, delyring [deviating] from the true way of virtue and good living to the pernicious example of other[s] and [to the] loathsomeness of every well disposed person. We therefore will and desire you and on God's behalf inwardly exhort and require you that according to the charge of your profession you will see within the authority of your jurisdiction [that] all such persons as set apart virtue and promote the damnable execution of sin and vices, be reformed, repressed and punished condignly after their demerits, not sparing for any love, favour, dread or affection whether the offenders be spiritual or temporal. Wherein ye may be assured we shall give unto you our favour, aid and assistance if the case shall so require, and see to the sharp punishment of the repugnators and interruptors hereof if any such be ...[8]

We could suppose that Richard was simply trying to 'make a good impression' and was really no more moral or upstanding than the next man: but there is evidence that this was a matter which genuinely concerned him. The letter castigating the Buckingham rebels he despatched from Leicester on 23 October 1483 was headed 'Proclamation for the reform of Morals', and it expressed his disappointment that 'all oppressors of his subjects, horrible adulterers and bawds' had not been reconciled 'to the way of truth and virtue'. The Marquis of Dorset, the Queen's eldest son by her first marriage, could have been upbraided for his disloyalty, but his principal offence, according to Richard, was that 'not fearing God, nor the peril of his soul, [he] hath many and sundry maids, widows and wives damnably and without shame devoured, deflowered, and defiled'. The King's friends were urged to resist 'the malicious intent of the said traitors' and see to the 'punishing of the great and damnable vices of the said traitors, adulterers and bawds, so that by their true and faithful assistance virtue may be lifted up and praised in the realm to the honour and pleasure of God, and vice utterly rebuked and damned to the surety and comfort of all the true and good commons of this realme'.[9]

The idea that because Richard was virtuous (at least in his own eyes) his enemies must *ipso facto* be immoral, is a strange one, but it is a theme that runs through all his propaganda. One of his reasons for arresting Lord Rivers, Richard Grey and the others at Northampton and Stony Stratford was that 'they were accounted the companions and servants of his [King Edward's] vices and had ruined his health';[10] and his criticisms of his late brother's government in *Titulus Regius*, the Act of Parliament that confirmed his right to the kingship, included the assertion that 'this land was ruled by self-will and pleasure ... so that no man was sure of his life, land, or livelihood, or of his wife, daughter, or servant, with every virtuous maiden and woman standing in dread of being ravished and defiled'.[11] Henry Tudor's supporters were described as 'murderers, adulterers, and extortioners [who] against all truth, honour and nature, have forsaken their natural country', while Henry himself was 'descended of bastard blood both of father side and of mother side ... whereby it evidently appeareth that no title can or may [rest] in him'.[12] It is not entirely clear how a man who had fathered at least two illegitimate children in his youth could justifiably rail against the immorality of others. Perhaps the explanation is that Richard had not always been so self-righteous, but became increasingly austere and puritanical as the years passed.

The bishops should have been mightily impressed by all this, but there is no evidence of how they responded or if Richard's pronouncements boosted his 'approval ratings' among them. As far as can be ascertained they were all highly moral men themselves – Commynes's reference to Stillington's bastard son is the only slight evidence for an illicit liaison – but this is not to say that they would have been scandalised by the behaviour of courtiers like the Marquis of Dorset and Lord Hastings. The Church condemned adultery and fornication, and illegitimate children had no right of inheritance; but there was a grudging recognition that rules governing sex were always likely to be broken, and that bastards were the inevitable consequence of human frailty. A moral king was a 'good' thing, but an immoral ruler who brought peace and prosperity could still enjoy great popularity. Edward IV had proved that.

We might suppose that the bishops who had served or admired Richard would have been dismissed from the Court and refused promotion in the Church in Henry VII's reign, but the opposite proved to be the case. Henry was as insecure as Richard had been, and was prepared to favour anyone willing to make a seamless transition from one king to another. Thomas Langton, arguably Richard's greatest admirer, forfeited his temporalities in the aftermath of Bosworth, but was pardoned and restored on 6 November. He was excluded from Henry's first Parliament, but he attended regularly thereafter and in 1493 was translated to Winchester, then England's richest see. He would have become Archbishop of Canterbury in succession to John Morton, but died (of plague) only five days after being elected on 22 January 1501.

Of the others who had been close to Richard, Richard Redman was suspected of complicity in Lambert Simnel's Yorkist rebellion against Henry in 1487 – the Pope afterwards accused him of conduct contrary to the tranquillity and peace of the realm – but he was able to clear himself and resume his career in royal service. He treated with the Scots on a number of occasions between 1488 and 1494, and was translated to the wealthier sees of Exeter (1495), and Ely (1501). Richard Bell was by now very elderly and, unusually, resigned his see in 1495; while John Shirwood served intermittently as the King's proctor in Rome until his death in January 1493. His biographer suggests that his allegiance was possibly to the Crown rather than to the individual who wore it at any moment in time.[13]

The one loyalist whose career did not prosper under the new government was Robert Stillington. Henry ordered his arrest on 22 August 1485 – within a few hours of winning the battle of Bosworth – and five days later the King's agents imprisoned him at York 'sore crazed by reason of his trouble'. He was allowed to 'continue still within the said city for four or five days for his ease and rest' at the request of the mayor, Nicholas Lanchester, and he pleaded 'his great age, long infirmity and feebleness' when he petitioned for a pardon in November.[14] Old and feeble he may have been, but his loyalty was again tested when the Simnel rebels sought to crown as king Edward, Earl of Warwick, the son of his old friend George of Clarence. He was accused of complicity in March 1487, but took refuge in Oxford University and refused to surrender. The masters tried to protect him by arguing that they could not, in conscience, compel him to yield to the King's agents – but the threat of force and the loss of their franchises persuaded them to change their minds.[15] He was taken to Windsor, where he was presumably interrogated and spent some time in confinement before dying in April or May 1491. He was perhaps the only member of the Ricardian episcopacy to put his principles before his comfort and the furtherance of his career.

12

THE TWO ELIZABETHS,
FEBRUARY–MARCH 1485

Edward IV's queen Elizabeth Woodville had been implicated, either directly or indirectly, in no fewer than three conspiracies against Richard, and they had all failed. Lord Hastings, her once bitter rival and belated ally, had been beheaded in June 1483; four men who had caused disturbances in London with the intention of liberating her sons from the Tower and perhaps smuggling her daughters abroad had been executed in July or August; and she had agreed that her eldest daughter Princess Elizabeth should marry Henry Tudor if Buckingham's rebellion succeeded. She had remained in the Westminster sanctuary with her five girls throughout this period, constantly believing that their situation was about to change for the better. But months of planning and hoping had all come to nothing, and the future looked decidedly bleak.

In normal circumstances, sanctuary men (and women) had forty days to decide between surrendering to justice and leaving England forever, and although this choice was clearly not going to be imposed on Elizabeth she had many other worries. She and her daughters must have found the confines of the room(s) in which they were housed increasingly uncomfortable; the Church authorities would, almost certainly, have regarded their continued presence as detrimental to their own good relations with the new monarch; and there was the fear that Richard would lose patience and remove them by force. With hindsight, he had probably decided not to incur the opprobrium such a step would have brought upon him, but his sister-in-law's intransigence, and the rebuke implied by it, risked damaging his reputation while the situation remained unresolved.

Elizabeth's feelings towards Richard have not been recorded, but they must have been a mixture of fear and loathing. We do not know what he had done – or what she thought he had done – with her boys Edward and Richard, but he had indisputably seized the throne; ordered the executions of her brother Earl Rivers and Richard Grey, the younger son of her first marriage; bastardised all her royal children; and accused her of witchcraft. Her natural reaction would have been to despise and to refuse to have anything more to do with him, but he was king and seemed likely to remain so. She had the future of her five girls to consider, and decided, reluctantly, that if dealing with him would secure their interests, she had no other choice.

Richard spent the months after Buckingham's rebellion using what the Croyland writer described as a mixture of 'threats and entreaties'[1] to persuade Elizabeth to leave the sanctuary, and may have been pleasantly surprised when she indicated that she was at last willing to negotiate. Their discussions cannot have been easy – Richard would have been reluctant to admit that he could not dictate to Elizabeth while she would have tried to wring every last concession from him – but agreement was reached eventually. 'Dame Elizabeth Grey', as she was now termed, undertook to surrender her daughters in return for a pledge that Richard would treat then as his own kinswomen, putting them 'in honest places of good name and fame', and marrying them to 'gentlemen born' with appropriate dowries. She was to receive 700 marks (£466 13s 4d) annually for her own maintenance, and was assured that the King would not imprison or believe any ill report of them without first hearing their side of the story.[2] In Charles Ross's opinion, the arrangement was guaranteed 'by the most solemn and public promise Richard could contrive' and 'reeked of the queen-dowager's suspicions'.[3] Perhaps it did, but both parties wanted to bring their uncomfortable stand-off to an end.

Elizabeth may still have had her misgivings, but there is every indication that Richard would have been as good as his word. He arranged for Cecily, who at fifteen was the second eldest of the girls, to marry Ralph Scrope, a younger brother of Thomas, Lord Scrope of Masham (Yorks.), and invited her elder sister Elizabeth to join the Court for Christmas. The Croyland writer remarked sourly that 'far too much attention was given to dancing and gaiety', and raised his clerkly eyebrows at how 'vain changes of apparel ... of similar colour and shape' were presented to Elizabeth and Queen Anne.[4] The younger woman clearly enjoyed royal favour, and there were suspicions that Richard intended to marry her when his sickly wife died.

Elizabeth Woodville had 'supped with the devil' (as she saw it) in order to salvage something from a bad situation, but there are indications that relations between the new King and the ex-Queen improved markedly after she left sanctuary. At some point in the winter of 1484/85 she wrote to Thomas, Marquis Dorset, the elder son of her first marriage, urging him to make his peace with King Richard and return to England. Thomas, who had joined Henry

Tudor in exile after the failure of Buckingham's rebellion, would have been deeply suspicious of any approach instigated by the man who had executed his brother Richard and his uncle Anthony; but whatever his mother told him, it was enough to convince him that the King could be trusted. He tried to slip away quietly, but was pursued by some of Henry's supporters and 'persuaded' to rejoin the Tudor 'court' in Paris.

The question, of course, is what lay behind this apparent thawing of relations between these two once bitter enemies? One possible explanation is that Elizabeth had learned that her royal sons had not been killed as she had once feared, but another is that Richard had confirmed to her that he wanted to marry her eldest daughter. Vergil says that he complained to a number of courtiers that Queen Anne was unable to give him the heir he needed, and Croyland was in no doubt that that he meant to be rid of her 'for it appeared that in no other way could his kingly power be established'. Anne's health had deteriorated rapidly since Christmas, and there were rumours that her end was being hastened by sorrow (because Richard no longer slept with her), and even by poison. This last story could be dismissed as another Tudor slur on the King's reputation, but if Anne was being treated with inappropriate and highly toxic substances such as mercury and arsenic she may well have shown symptoms of poisoning in the last weeks of her life. According to Vergil she heard what was being whispered and tearfully confronted Richard who 'kissing her, made answer lovingly, and comforting her, bade her be of good cheer'. His enemies thought him guilty of hypocrisy, but there is no reason to doubt that he genuinely sympathised with her predicament and regretted the course of action he felt obliged to take.

Henry Tudor had promised to wed the younger Elizabeth to secure the backing of disaffected Yorkists, but if Richard thought he could use the same tactic he was to be disappointed. Sir Richard Ratcliffe and William Catesby, two members of his 'kitchen cabinet', told him bluntly, 'to his face' as Croyland has it, that 'if he did not abandon his intended purpose ... all the people of the north, in whom he placed the greatest reliance, would rise in rebellion against him'.[5] Their real fear was that a new Woodville queen would seek to punish them for their part in the executions of the men arrested at Stony Stratford; and Richard was so beholden to them that, a few weeks later, he denied publicly that he had ever considered the idea.

We might suppose that the younger Elizabeth would have recoiled from the prospect of marrying an uncle who was responsible for the deaths of several members of her family, but, on the contrary, she seems to have embraced it with enthusiasm. Sir George Buck, Richard's earliest apologist, saw, 'in the cabinet of the Earl of Arundel', a letter she had written to Arundel's ancestor, the Duke of Norfolk, towards the end of February 1485 asking Norfolk to do all he could to hasten the matter. The letter has disappeared and Buck did not provide a full transcript, but in his words she 'prayed him [Norfolk] as before to be a mediator for her in the cause of her marriage to the king, who, as she wrote, was her only joy and maker in [this] world, and that she was his in heart and in thoughts, in [body] and in all'.[6] It is difficult to imagine her taking this stance without her mother's encouragement and approval, and Elizabeth Woodville surely saw it as a way of recovering much of what she and her family had lost.

The Croyland writer tells us that Ratcliffe and Catesby 'brought to him [Richard] more than twelve doctors of divinity who asserted that the pope could grant no dispensation [i.e. a relaxation of the law] in the case of such a degree of consanguinity',[7] but their opinion would not have been shared by everyone. The Old Testament Book of Leviticus specifically prohibited a marriage between an aunt and her nephew, but did not say that an uncle could not wed his niece. Some theologians thought that this meant that a union between uncle and niece was permissible, while others took the view that the relationships mentioned by Leviticus were only examples and that, logically, if an aunt could not wed her nephew, an uncle could not marry his niece either. Then there was the question of whether or not the Pope had the power to dispense a relationship banned by divine law in any circumstances. Some thought that he could not permit anything that was contrary to Leviticus unless specifically authorised to do so, while others argued that he could dispense in all matters unless the power was expressly denied to him. There were also those who believed that a dispensation might become possible if there was 'a great and pressing reason' (if the marriage would settle an international dispute, for example), although it is likely that most suppliants thought their reasons 'great and pressing' at the time.

It is therefore distinctly possibly that if Richard had sought Rome's permission to marry Princess Elizabeth, he would have been allowed to do so. John Shirwood, his representative at the papal court, would have presented his case learnedly and sympathetically – although his arguments would doubtless have been refuted by Bishop Morton, who was trying to persuade Pope Innocent to back Henry Tudor. It is instructive that a decade later Rodrigo Borgia (Pope Alexander VI) permitted Ferrante, King of Naples, to marry his aunt Joanna (who was seven years his junior), although their relationship was specifically prohibited by Leviticus. Perhaps nothing was unattainable if the Pope was obliging and the parties could pay.

Securing the consent of the Church would have overcome a major obstacle, but would not have solved all Richard's problems. The reality was that the girl he now wanted to marry had been declared a bastard in his own Parliament only twelve months previously, and he could not 're-legitimate' her without admitting that the allegation that his brother and Elizabeth Woodville had not been legally married had been spurious. His own claim to the throne would have become inferior to that of Edward V or Prince Richard and this proves, in the opinion of some commentators, that both boys must have been dead by this time. They could have been, but a king, once crowned, could not be 'unmade' whatever the circumstances. Richard might have contrived to rule both in his own right and as the husband of Edward IV's eldest child.

A marriage between Richard and Elizabeth would have prevented Henry Tudor from wedding her and dealt a serious blow to Henry's bid to replace him. Vergil says Henry was 'pinched by the very stomach' when he heard what was intended, because 'he thought it was to be feared lest his friends should forsake him' if he was unable to keep the promise he had made to them.[8] He considered marrying a daughter of his former guardian William Herbert, Earl of Pembroke, as an alternative, hoping, perhaps, to influence the Earl of Northumberland, who had also wed one of Pembroke's offspring; but Herbert influence in Wales had declined since the Earl's death at Edgecote, and his eldest son, William, Earl of Huntingdon, was the husband of Richard's illegitimate daughter Katherine. Such a girl would have been a poor substitute for the Princess even if the proposal had somehow been accepted, and Henry must have been mightily relieved to learn that Richard had been forced to abandon his plan.

Richard still needed a wife and Elizabeth a husband, not least because a marriage between the Princess and someone acceptable to him would still deny her to his rival. His thoughts turned towards seeking an alliance with a foreign royal family descended from the rival House of Lancaster, one that (he hoped) would make him acceptable to Lancastrian dissidents in England and at the same time fulfil his pledge to Elizabeth Woodville. The direct

male Lancastrian line had ended with the death of Henry VI in
1471, but there were a number of alternative claimants:

- Philippa, daughter of John of Gaunt and his first wife Blanche of Lancaster
  and Henry IV's sister had married King John I of Portugal. Their immediate
  descendants in 1485 were their great-grandchildren King John II and his
  sister Joanna.
- John I and Philippa's daughter Isabel had become the third wife of Philip the
  Good, Duke of Burgundy, giving their son Charles the Bold (d. 1477) and
  granddaughter Mary (d. 1482) a 'Lancastrian' claim to the throne. Their heir
  in 1485 was Mary's seven-year-old son Philip.
- Catherine, John of Gaunt's daughter by his second wife Constance, had
  married King Henry III of Castile. Their descendants in 1485 were their
  granddaughter Isabella (who had married Ferdinand of Aragon) and great-
  granddaughter, the Infanta Isabella.

Arguably, all these families had a better claim to the throne of England
than Henry Tudor who was of the line of John of Gaunt and his mistress
(later third wife), Katherine Swynford. Henry's only advantages were
that he was English (more or less) and the man on the spot.

The Infanta Isabella was a nubile fourteen-year-old, ideal for a
king seeking to found a dynasty, but Richard decided to seek the
hand of Joanna of Portugal, who was some eight months his senior.
At thirty-three she might, or might not, give him the son he needed,
but she was the principal heir of Lancaster after her brother and
his children. Queen Anne died on 16 March 1485, and six days
later Sir Edward Brampton was sent to Portugal to propose a union
between Richard and Joanna, and between Elizabeth of York and
John's cousin, Manuel, Duke of Beja.[9] John welcomed the embassy
which may have included the promise of English support against
dissidents in his own country, but Joanna was a deeply pious lady
who spent most of her time in a convent. She had already refused
to marry the Emperor's son and the King of France's brother and,
presumably, did not want to marry Richard either; but she agreed
to consider the matter after coming under intense pressure from
her brother and other family members. She had a dream, or vision,

in which a 'beautiful young man' informed her that Richard 'had gone from among the living', and told King John that if he was still alive she would go to England to marry him, but that if he was dead she was not to be given to another suitor.[10] News of the battle of Bosworth reached Portugal a few days later, and the 'Holy Princess' died in her convent, still unmarried, five years after her intended spouse.

It has recently been claimed that Richard never intended to marry Elizabeth of York, and that the marriage she wanted the Duke of Norfolk to hasten was her proposed union with the Duke of Beja.[11] This is highly unlikely, however. Elizabeth's letter was written towards the end of February, almost a month before Queen Anne died, and cannot be read in this context without accusing Richard of planning to seek Joanna's hand some time before he became a widower. This, arguably, is as reprehensible as the allegation that he privately contemplated marrying his niece (the charge the author is attempting to refute); and it is significant that he does not mention either Elizabeth's fulsome statement that her uncle 'was her only joy and maker in [this] world, that she was his in heart and in thoughts, in [body] and in all', or the Croyland writer's wry comment that when Richard publicly denied that he wanted to marry her 'there were some persons present … who very well knew the contrary'.[12] It is possible to argue that Buck's précis of her letter is unreliable, but this is the only logical conclusion that can be drawn from the evidence we have.

Medieval widows and widowers traditionally spent a year in formal mourning before remarrying, but Richard knew only too well that time was working against him. Even if he was able to wed within the next few months and have a son almost immediately (an even bigger 'if'), he would still have to live to be fifty to ensure his by then sixteen-year-old heir would succeed him and reign securely. This does not sound particularly problematic, but Edward IV had died at the early age of forty, Henry IV at forty-seven, and Henry V at only thirty-five. The contemporary Portuguese commentator Gomes dos Santos was in no doubt that 'it suits the King of England to marry straight away'.[13]

It is difficult, and perhaps even dangerous, to attempt to penetrate the thoughts and feelings of a medieval personage, but Richard had every reason to feel depressed as the months lengthened. The deaths of his wife and only legitimate son, the threat posed by Henry Tudor, and the failure of his plan to marry Princess Elizabeth must all have weighed heavily upon him, and the latter had exposed how beholden he was to relatively humble acolytes like Ratcliffe and Catesby. Like most of his contemporaries, he would have believed in the notion of divine punishment, and would have interpreted these blows as signs that God disapproved of his actions. And if God had rejected him, he could not hope to prosper or reign for long.

Elizabeth of York subsequently married Henry Tudor (Henry VII) and became the mother of Henry VIII. We tend to picture her as a rather benign lady who led what was, by medieval standards, a relatively humdrum existence, but she had experienced changes of fortune as dramatic as any of her contemporaries. At Christmas 1482 she had been a royal princess; a year later she was a bastard in sanctuary; by the end of 1484 she was at Richard's court enjoying Queen Anne's friendship; and twelve months later Richard and Anne were both dead and she was Queen of England. The battle of Bosworth not only sealed Richard's fate: it sealed Elizabeth's too.

13

THE GATHERING STORM, APRIL–JUNE 1485

We have already noted that the defeat of Buckingham's rebellion was only a limited success for Richard, and that it presented him with new challenges which, for the time being, were insurmountable. Men who thought they would not be pardoned their part in the uprising (or who chose to remain in opposition), gravitated towards Henry Tudor, and this gave Henry a credibility he had not enjoyed previously. On Christmas Day 1483 he and his companions went to Rennes Cathedral, where he solemnly promised to marry Princess Elizabeth when he had gained England, and they knelt before him as though he was king already. Before the rebellion he had been a possible, somewhat unlikely, candidate for the Crown: after it he was *the* alternative to Richard III.

Henry had enjoyed the protection of Duke Francis of Brittany during his years of exile, and Edward IV's attempts to persuade the Duke to return him to England had all ended in failure. There had been one occasion when Edward had convinced Francis that he only wanted to marry the fugitive to one of his own daughters, but Henry, who had no doubt that he was being sent to his death, feigned sickness until his friends interceded for him. The most Francis would promise was that he would not allow him to trouble Edward, and even this undertaking was abandoned when Edward died and Richard succeeded. We saw in chapter nine that Dr Thomas Hutton was not specifically charged to discuss Henry's future when he travelled Brittany in July 1483, but Francis hinted that he would be obliged to surrender his 'guest' to the French unless Richard sent 4,000 English archers to help defend the duchy against King Louis. Louis's death on 30 August removed the immediate threat to Brittany, but mercantile disputes and the assistance given to Henry when he sailed for England in October only made relations with Richard worse.

Richard's official line was to treat Henry's claim to the throne as derisory, but the enhanced threat from the pretender after the failure of Buckingham's rebellion obliged him to approach Brittany again in 1484. By now Duke Francis was sinking into his dotage, and his treasurer Peter Landois, who was effectively running the duchy, agreed to surrender Henry in return for the services of a thousand English archers. It seemed that Richard was about to get his hands on his arch-enemy, but Bishop Morton heard of the plan in Flanders and warned Henry to escape to France as quickly as possible. Henry sent his most senior followers to Duke Francis, who was then residing near the French border, ostensibly to plead his cause but with instructions to cross into Anjou at the first opportunity. He himself left his base at Vannes a day or two later on the pretext of visiting a friend at a nearby manor, but after travelling about five miles he withdrew into a wood, disguised himself as a serving man, and rode hard to join his advance party. Landois sent troops in pursuit when he realised that something was afoot, but was too late to catch him. Henry crossed the border with barely an hour to spare.

Henry's flight placed the three hundred or so English exiles left behind in Vannes in some jeopardy, but Duke Francis fortunately roused himself at this moment and allowed them to join their master in France. The French regency government welcomed them and provided them with money; but Henry knew only too well that aid for his greater enterprise would depend on how relations between France, Brittany and England stood at any given moment. It was no secret that France wanted to absorb Brittany, the last great semi-independent duchy, at the earliest opportunity, and Henry's pitch was that an invasion of England would prevent Richard from assisting the Bretons. But he recognised that the situation was fluid, and feared that his new friends would lose interest in his enterprise if Brittany happened to fall into their hands sooner. In the event, Henry landed at Milford Haven on 7 August 1485, ten months after he had first arrived in France but only two days before the Treaty of Bourges ended Franco-Breton hostilities. Charles Ross has observed that if Henry had not sailed when he did, 'the Tudor dynasty might never have been born'.[1]

Trying to capture Henry or at least prevent him from making mischief was central to Richard's strategy, but he also took a number of other measures designed to counter an invasion. At the end of 1483 commissions of array were issued for most counties, a fleet commanded by Sir Thomas Wentworth was stationed in the Channel, and sheriffs and other officers were told to ensure that those residing in their jurisdictions wore only the King's livery or cognisance, to make every effort to arrest rebel sympathisers, and to administer oaths of allegiance.[2] In February, Richard oversaw what was for him the most important of all oaths when the leading notables formally recognised his son as his successor. The Croyland writer describes how nearly all the lords of the realm, both spiritual and temporal, together with the higher knights and esquires of the king's household ... met together at the special command of the king, in a certain lower room, near the passage which leads to the queen's apartments, and here, each subscribed his name to a kind of new oath, drawn up by some persons to me unknown, of adherence to Edward, the king's only son, as their supreme lord, in case anything should happen to his father.[3]

The boy's death only two months later struck at the heart of all Richard's hopes for the future, but preparations to resist Henry continued. The commissions of array were reissued in December, the commissioners being instructed to see that their men were 'well horsed and harnessed and no rascals'. They were to check that funds earmarked for the campaign had not been used for other purposes, and were to tell all 'lords, noblemen and captains' to abandon their private 'quarrels grudges, rancours and unkindness' and to be 'loving and assisting' to one another in promoting the King's interests. Officials in the Home Counties were asked to ascertain how many men they could raise at 'half a day warning' if Henry and his followers happened to arrive unexpectedly.[4] This was most unlikely in practice – Richard's spies would have kept him informed of Henry's activities and movements – but the order testifies to the thoroughness of his plans.

It was during this period – while Henry was seeking French help and Richard busied himself with countermeasures – that both men engaged in what may be described as a 'phoney war' based on character assassination. A letter written by Henry to those he called his 'right trusty and honourable friends and allies' described Richard as 'that homicide and unnatural tyrant which now unjustly bears dominion over you', and promised to 'be most forward to remember and wholly to requite this your great and most loving kindness in my just quarrel' if they gave him their support.[5] Richard responded by complaining to the mayor of Windsor (and no doubt to others) that his enemies were 'tending writings ... to provoke and stir discord', and ordered him to 'search and enquire of the first shewers and utterers thereof ... and proceed to their sharp punishment in example and fear of all other'.[6] The following day, 7 December 1484, he instructed the Chancellor to prepare a formal proclamation which described the leading rebels as a gang of

> open murderers, adulterers and extortioners contrary to truth, honour and nature ... who have chosen to be their captain one Harry late calling himself Earl of Richmond which of his ambitious and insatiable covetousness ... encroaches upon him the name and title of royal estate of this realm of England whereunto he hath no manner interest, right or colour as every man well knoweth.

Henry, it was claimed, would abandon Calais along with the English claim to the crown of France (an obvious appeal to patriotism), and 'do the most cruel murders, slaughters, robberies and disinheritances that ever were seen in any Christian realm'.[7]

The letter from Henry quoted above is the only example of his propaganda to have come down to us, but Richard's further responses imply that there were others. At the beginning of April 1485 he wrote to York and probably other towns to advise them that

> divers seditious and evil disposed persons both in our city of London and elsewhere within this our realm, enforce themselves

> daily to sow seed of noise and dissension against our person ...
> to abuse the multitude of our subjects and avert their minds from
> us ... some by setting up of bills, some by messages and sending
> forth of false and abominable language and lies, some by bold and
> presumptuous open speech and communication one with another.

He goes on to describe how he had summoned the leading citizens
of London together with many lords spiritual and temporal and
members of his household 'to whom we largely shewed our true
intent and mind in all such things as the said noise and dissension
rein upon in such wise as we doubt not [that] all well-disposed
persons were and be therewith right well content'.[8] The meeting
was probably the occasion of his denial that he intended to marry
Elizabeth of York, and it is tempting to speculate that Henry (who
desperately wanted to marry her himself) was behind some of the
defamatory notices and whisperings that contributed to his rival's
disappointment. Anyone finding such a bill was told to take it to
the authorities without reading or showing it to anyone else.

In June Richard revised the proclamation he had first issued the
previous December, this time omitting the name of the Marquis of
Dorset (who he undoubtedly knew had tried to desert the exiles),
but adding to the opprobrium heaped upon Henry, 'son of Edmund
Tydder, son of Owen Tydder', personally. He was

> descended of bastard blood both of father side and of mother side,
> for the said Owen the grandfather was bastard born, and his mother
> [Margaret Beaufort] was daughter unto John, Duke of Somerset, son
> unto John, Earl of Somerset, son unto Dame Katherine Swynford,
> and of her in double adultery begotten, whereby it evidently
> appeareth that no title can nor may [rest] in him.[9]

We noted in chapter nine that John of Gaunt's children by Katherine had been born before their marriage, but had been subsequently legitimated by a patent and Act of Richard II. Henry IV had confirmed the patent but had added the limiting phrase *excepta dignitate regali*, effectively barring any claim they might have to the throne. It is unclear if he was legally entitled to do this, but the provision only added to the uncertainty and Richard was happy to make use of it. Arguments based on allegations of bastardy had served him well two years earlier and might do so again.

It would be fascinating to know if any of these assertions actually influenced or affected the loyalties of those who mattered politically, but as time passed it became ever more apparent that some of those Richard trusted or had hoped to mollify were working against him. Towards the end of 1484, William Colyngbourne, a Wiltshire gentleman who had been a servant of his mother, was arrested and charged with secretly urging Henry Tudor to invade that autumn and of fastening a rhyme lampooning Catesby, Ratcliffe, Francis Lovell (whose heraldic crest was a wolf), and Richard the 'hog', to the door of St Paul's Cathedral:

The Cat, the Rat and Lovell our dog,
Rule all England under a Hog.

Richard decided to make an example of him, and he was sentenced to be hung, drawn and quartered after a 'show' trial at the Guildhall held in the presence of two dukes, seven other noblemen, and five justices. The chronicler Robert Fabyan described how he was half-hanged then:

cut down, being alive, and his bowels ripped out of his belly and cast into the fire there by him, and lived till the butcher put his hand into the bulk of his body, insomuch that he said in the same instant 'O Lord Jesus, yet more trouble,' and so died to the great compassion of much people.[10]

It was meant to be a salutary warning, but may have elicited more sympathy (and even revulsion) than fear.

Colyngbourne was a relatively minor figure, but the defection of James Blount, the governor of Hammes Castle, one of the fortresses defending Calais, could not be brushed aside so easily. Blount went over to Henry Tudor at the beginning of November, taking with him his prisoner, the battle-hardened Lancastrian Earl of Oxford, and others. Blount was a former retainer of Lord Hastings and may have resented his late master's brutal treatment; but he had also become involved in a long and apparently fruitless struggle to acquire a share in the lands forfeited by his wife's attainted kinsman, Sir John Delves. Perhaps Oxford convinced him that his claims would be satisfied by a grateful King Henry, and he decided to take the risk.

Richard ordered the Calais garrison to take possession of Hammes, but those left behind, who included Blount's wife, refused to surrender and sent to Henry for assistance. Part of Oxford's relieving force gained access to the castle, and the confrontation ended only when the besiegers allowed the defenders to leave unmolested and join their leader in Paris. Vergil says that Henry was 'ravished with joy'[11] by Oxford's liberation, and the whole episode boosted his standing with his French paymasters. Blount was a key office-holder in the Ricardian government, and his defection proved there was disillusionment at the heart of the regime.

Colyngbourne and Blount had made little secret of their opposition to Richard, but there were others who paid him lip service who he suspected had little love for him. In the summer of 1485 Lord Stanley, who had remained impeccably loyal since Richard's accession, sought permission to visit his family at Lathom in Lancashire. It was the sort of request that would have been granted with hardly a second thought in normal circumstances, but Richard acquiesced only on condition that Stanley's eldest son, George, Lord Strange, take his father's place at court. The ostensible reason was that someone had to deputise for Lord Thomas during his absence, but few can have doubted that George was effectively a hostage. The King suspected that his stepmother Margaret Beaufort might still persuade the Stanleys to back her own son; and he would have been still more concerned had he known that Sir John Savage, their nephew, had already committed himself to Henry, and that Margaret's man Reginald Bray had raised a large sum of money to pay troops.[12]

Lord Stanley's political acumen had allowed him to successfully negotiate the pitfalls of the Wars of the Roses, and there were others lower down the social scale whose loyalty was always at a premium. One such individual was Henry Vernon of Haddon in Derbyshire, whose instinct for self-preservation had become apparent when King Edward returned from exile in 1471. The Earl of Warwick and the Duke of Clarence expected Vernon, whom Clarence had appointed steward of his lordship of the High Peak, to support them in the coming conflict, and on 15 March the Duke wrote from Bristol commanding him to ensure that 'as well all your tenants and servants as ours in those parts be ready upon an hour's warning to wait upon us in defensible array whensoever we send for you and them'. News of Edward's landing reached Clarence at Wells on 23 March, and he immediately ordered Vernon to join him with all his forces and 'to send surely unto us all the money that ye have received and can get of our livelihood in your receipt'. The letter expressed the Duke's 'special trust' in his deputy's loyalty; but there is a clear note of uncertainty in a second summons that Warwick despatched to Haddon two days later concluding with the impassioned postscript, 'Henry I pray you fail not now as ever I may do for you.' Clarence was still urging Vernon to join him 'with more speed and greater haste' at the beginning of April, but he still failed to appear at the battle of Barnet. There is no record of how, precisely, he excused himself, but when the Duke, who had himself changed sides in the meantime, wrote to him shortly after the battle of Tewkesbury he professed himself satisfied with his conduct and again asked him to wait upon him, 'the matters and causes of the let and impediment of your coming now ceased'.[13] The two points that arise from this are that Vernon had contrived to emerge unscathed from a period of great political upheaval, and that Clarence preferred to remain on good terms with his slippery but capable lieutenant rather than punish what amounted to a betrayal. He could not have fared better if he had become involved in the conflict, and might, very possibly, have fared worse.

Richard had to deal with Vernon himself in 1485, and can have had few illusions. The summons he despatched to him when Henry Tudor landed was couched in the formal language of the day, but the closing threat was not, perhaps, one that a king would have sent to a supporter who enjoyed his full confidence:

Trusty and well beloved we greet you well. And forasmuch as our rebels and traitors accompanied with our ancient enemies of France and other strange [foreign] nations departed out of the water of Seine the first day of the present month making their course westwards been landed at Nangle [Angle] besides Milford Haven in Wales on Sunday last passed, as we be credibly informed, intending our utter destruction, the extreme subversion of this our realm and disinheriting of our true subjects of the same, towards whose *recountring*, God being our guide, we be utterly determined in our own person to remove in all haste goodly that we can or may. Wherefore we will and straitly charge you that ye in your person with such number [of soldiers] as ye have promised unto us sufficiently horsed and harnessed be with us in all haste to you possible, *to give unto us your attendance without failing, all manner excuses set apart, upon pain of forfeiture unto us of all that you may forfeit and lose* [my italics]. Given under our signet at our lodge of Beskwood, the xi day of August.[14]

The King could only guess how many others might, or might not, make good their promises, and it seems that in each of these cases he was doomed to disappointment. Both Lord Stanley and Henry Vernon failed to support him, and both prospered under the new Tudor government. Stanley was created Earl of Derby and died in his bed in 1504, while Vernon, who lived eleven years longer, became governor to King Henry's eldest son and a knight of the Body. They had served – or failed to serve – all the monarchs of the Wars of the Roses, and if caution was their watchword it had profited them more than an unswerving commitment to Lancaster or York.

14

BOSWORTH FIELD, AUGUST 1485

The force that accompanied Henry Tudor to England in 1485 was
by no means overwhelming, but was perhaps the best he could
have hoped for. In addition to his 300–400 English followers he
is said to have recruited some 1,800 soldiers discharged from the
military base at Pont de l'Arche in Normandy, a body of Scots then
serving in the King of France's army, and an unknown number
of freebooters. The Frenchmen were described by the chronicler
Commynes as 'Normans, the loosest and most profligate persons
in all that country',[1] but they were presumably happy to find
employment and none doubted their ability to fulfil their new
master's expectations. King Charles's government also provided
Henry with the necessary shipping, some pieces of ordnance, and
that most essential of all commodities, cash.

Henry's Welsh ancestry and his uncle Jasper's tenure of the
earldom of Pembroke meant that he would probably choose
to land somewhere in the principality, but Richard could not
afford to take chances. Francis Lovell was sent to Southampton
with orders to repel any descent on the south coast, and a small
fleet commanded by Sir George Neville was set to patrol the

Channel. The rebels may, or may not, have been forewarned of these countermeasures, but they gave their enemies the slip and reached Milford Haven on 7 August. Their landing was unopposed and they advanced northwards via Haverfordwest, Cardigan, Aberystwyth and Machynlleth, hugging the coast and in constant fear of attack from Ricardian forces. At Haverfordwest they heard that Rhys ap Thomas, a local chieftain, was preparing to move against them, and were mightily relieved when a rumour that Walter Herbert, the Earl of Huntingdon's brother, was assembling an army at Cardigan proved unfounded. Machynlleth was reached on 14 August, and here they turned inland towards Welshpool, Shrewsbury, and Stanleyan Cheshire. Rhys ap Thomas, whose allegiance had been bought with lavish promises, joined them at Welshpool, and after more negotiations they were allowed to enter Shrewsbury. Other recruits awaited them in England, and Henry may have had more than 4,000 men at his disposal by the time he reached Stafford on 19 August.

Richard was aware of Henry's arrival by 11 August (the day he wrote to Henry Vernon), and immediately summoned his supporters to meet him at Nottingham, where he had been based since mid-June. Lord Stanley was ordered to bring his forces, but sent word that he was suffering from the 'sweating sickness', and could not come for the present. Any excuse from Stanley would have fuelled Richard's suspicions, and these were not eased when Lord Strange tried to slip away without permission. Strange confessed that his uncle William (Lord Stanley's younger brother) and Sir John Savage meant to aid Henry, but insisted that his father would remain loyal. He decided, or was 'advised', to write to Lord Thomas emphasising the threat to his own safety and urging him to join Richard without delay.

Richard apparently intended to leave Nottingham on 16 August, but changed his mind.[2] Some of his more distant followers had not yet arrived, and he may have wanted to see which route Henry followed before deciding where to intercept him. One of the most intriguing – and difficult to answer – questions that can be asked about any medieval battle is why it occurs where and when it does. On Friday 19 August Richard at Nottingham and Henry at Stafford were separated by only just over fifty miles or little more than a day's journey, but neither, it seems, wanted to fight at this moment. Richard had arranged to meet his southern and East Anglian contingents at Leicester, while Henry was still trying to persuade the ambivalent Stanleys to declare for him. Lord Thomas and Sir William were in the field with substantial forces which appeared to fall back before Henry as he advanced. The pretender held meetings with one or both of them at Stafford and later at Atherstone, where, according to Vergil, they took one another by the hand and 'all their minds were moved to great joy';[3] but neither – not even the avowed traitor William – would wholly commit himself. Their excuse was almost certainly that Lord Strange would be killed if they did so, but Henry was left with the nagging suspicion that if things went badly for him they could still join the battle on Richard's side.

With hindsight, it is clear that the Stanleys – and Lord Thomas in particular – were simply doing what they nearly always did in these circumstances, and it is likely that they were looking to a future beyond the coming battle. We know now that Richard was killed at Bosworth and that Henry founded a dynasty that was to last for more than a century, but neither Lord Thomas nor his brother would have expected this outcome. No English king had been killed in battle since 1066, and the vast probability was that even if Richard was defeated he would escape and try to recover his throne at the first opportunity. The Stanleys, it is reasonable to suppose, had one eye on the *next* change of ruler, and Richard's death was a bonus they could not have foreseen.

Richard finally left Nottingham on Friday 19 August, reaching Leicester just before sunset and remaining there for two nights. Henry meanwhile turned onto the Watling Street and advanced via Lichfield and Tamworth to Atherstone in Warwickshire. He may have hoped to slip past the royal forces and enter London, but Atherstone is less than twenty-five miles from Leicester and both commanders must have realised that a battle was now inevitable. Richard accordingly left Leicester on Sunday the 21st and marched directly west towards his adversary, while Henry, many of whose troops had been on the road for a fortnight, snatched some welcome rest in the vicinity of Merevale Abbey. It is likely that they both knew the whereabouts of the Stanley forces, but not, of course, how they intended to behave.

There have been many attempts to estimate the strength of the rival armies, but reliable evidence is hard to come by. Some desertions from Richard's camp had added to Henry's power and he may – at a guess – have had approximately 5,000 men available to him. Richard probably had twice this number, but his superiority would be seriously eroded if the Stanleys turned their several thousand men against him. It is likely that Henry's force disposed a higher proportion of 'professional' soldiers, and included many Englishmen who had betrayed their King and who had no hope of pardon if they were defeated. Richard's army consisted largely of manorial tenants who had been required to answer the royal summons by their landlords, but whose main concern (we may assume) would have been to return safe to their families. They would do what was required of them for as long as necessary, but lacked the motivation, desperation even, of some of those on the other side.

It would be surprising if Richard or Henry slept long or easily this night, although we should not over emphasise the Croyland writer's statement that '*as it is generally stated* [my italics], in the morning he [Richard] declared that during the night he had seen dreadful visions, and imagined himself surrounded by a multitude of demons'. There is, however, some evidence of disarray in the royal camp the following morning. Croyland adds that 'at day-break ... there were no chaplains present to perform Divine service on behalf of King Richard, nor any breakfast prepared to refresh his flagging spirits'.[4] It must be thought highly improbable that Richard would have gone into battle without breaking his fast or first hearing mass, and the episode could be dismissed as a later elaboration if Sir Ralph Bigod had not also remarked upon it. Lord Morley recalled that Bigod often spoke of the confusion in the King's household that prevented him from hearing mass before he met Henry Tudor in battle, and how that when the chaplains 'had one thing ready, evermore they wanted another, when they had wine they lacked bread, and ever one thing was missing'.[5] In this version the clergy are disorganised rather than entirely absent, but it is difficult to avoid the conclusion that *something* was amiss.

There is no surviving eyewitness account of the battle of Bosworth, and confusion arising from Victorian and earlier attempts to locate and interpret the action has prevailed until very recently. A detailed survey undertaken during the last few years has pinpointed the site of the conflict, but we still have to rely on writers like Polydore Vergil – who might have talked with some of the participants – to tell us how the commanders deployed their forces and how the fighting developed. Both leaders formally summoned Lord Stanley to join them, but to no avail. The negative or evasive answer he returned to Richard was enough to prompt the King to order Lord Strange's execution, while Henry was 'no little vexed, and began to be somewhat appalled'[6] when Lord Thomas declined to join him either. It is possible that he almost abandoned hope at this moment, but he was now too close to his enemy to avoid a fight.

Richard drew up his army on a wide front 'so full replenished both with footmen and horsemen that to the beholders afar off it gave a terror for the multitude', while Henry 'made a slender vanward for the small number of his people'. Richard's forward division attacked expecting, perhaps, an easy victory; but the Earl of Oxford, who commanded Henry's main force, held his men together and the royalists failed to break them. A lull in the fighting gave Oxford the opportunity to reorganise his troops 'in array triangle' and his renewed assault forced Richard to try to regain the initiative. With what Vergil describes as 'a choice force of soldiers',[7] probably his household knights and squires, he launched a direct attack upon Henry who was stationed some distance from his main force and protected only by a small bodyguard. The momentum of the charge brought him almost face to face with Henry – William Brandon, who carried Henry's standard, was among those who perished – but the pretender was rescued by Sir William Stanley, who brought his men into action at this crucial moment. Richard was killed, his remaining forces disintegrated, and Henry Tudor found himself king.

Vergil notes that a hundred rebels and a thousand members of the royal army died in the fighting, but his figures may be both under- and over-estimates unless the routing of the royalists added substantially to their casualties. With Richard fell John Howard, Duke of Norfolk, Sir Richard Ratcliffe, his secretary John Kendall and other intimates, while William Catesby was captured and executed three days later. William Brandon was the only fatality of note on Henry's side, and even Lord Strange lived to be of further service. Croyland says that 'the persons to whom this duty [i.e. his execution] was entrusted, seeing that the issue was doubtful in the extreme, and that matters of more importance than the destruction of one individual were about to be decided, delayed the performance of this cruel order of the King'.[8]

Vergil heard that Richard's 'crown', the circlet he had worn on his helmet, had been found among the 'spoil', and that Henry 'replenished with joy incredible ... got himself unto the next hill' (presumably Crown Hill in Stoke Golding), where Lord Stanley placed it upon his head. He ordered those about him to 'cure the wounded and to bury them that were slain', before making his way to Leicester, taking with him Richard's body 'naked of all clothing, and laid upon an horse back with the arms and legs hanging down on both sides'.[9] The corpse was put on public display for two days – not because Henry was particularly vindictive but because kings who had not died visibly enough had a nasty habit of returning to trouble their supplanters. Henry IV was plagued by rumours that Richard II was still alive and would one day reappear to claim his kingdom, and the uncertainty surrounding the fate of Edward V and his brother troubled Henry Tudor for many years.

The events of Richard's life were much criticised by the Tudors, but no one belittled the manner of his dying. Both Vergil and Juan de Salazar, a Spanish soldier of fortune who fought for Richard, state that he was urged to escape when the battle began to go against him, but replied, according to Salazar, 'God forbid I yield one step. This day I will die as a King or win.'[10] Richard then 'began to fight with much vigour, putting heart into those that remained loyal, so that by his sole effort he upheld the battle for a long time';[11] and Croyland adds, 'while fighting, *and not in the act of flight* [my italics], the said King Richard was pierced with numerous deadly wounds, and fell in the field like a brave and most valiant prince'.[12] Even Vergil admitted that 'King Richard alone was killed fighting manfully in the thickest press of his enemies'.[13] Cowardice was never one of his sins.

But why did Richard, an experienced commander leading a numerically superior army, lose the battle of Bosworth? One reason, apparent even from the limited evidence available to us, was that his enemies were better disciplined. The conventional army of his brother-in-law, Charles, Duke of Burgundy, described as 'flabby' by the latter's biographer Richard Vaughan, had been defeated on no fewer than three occasions by a better organised, densely packed force of part-time Swiss soldiers in the mid-1470s. Professor Vaughan writes that Charles's

> cavalry contingents were on a *de luxe*, heavily armoured basis, needing a numerous and complicated support organisation. It [his army] was full of non-combatants. Worst of all it had with it the duke and his extravagant court, with its non-military paraphernalia. All this made it something less than a fighting machine. It was slow-moving and spread out. It could offer no concentration of power comparable to the phalanxes of civic halberds the League [of Constance] could send into the attack.[14]

Richard may not have been handicapped to quite this extent, but the Earl of Oxford's instruction to his men not to 'go above ten foot from the standards'[15] makes it clear that they were drawn up in close formation and were accustomed to obeying orders. The King must have known the reason for his brother-in-law's downfall, but could not change the mindset of his aristocratic supporters or turn their tenant farmers into professional fighters. John Howard, his principal commander, was an experienced soldier who had fought at Towton in 1461, but there had been no pitched battle in England since Tewkesbury fourteen years earlier. Desultory raids into France and Scotland had not taught many the arts of war.

It is, however, unlikely that discipline and tactics would have prevailed against odds of approximately two to one if all Richard's men had been committed to him. Vergil wrote that some 'fought faintly' and that 'many more forbear to fight, who came to the field with king Richard for awe, and for no goodwill, and departed without any danger, as men who desired not the safety but the destruction of that prince [Richard] whom they hated'.[16] Their main concern, as we noted earlier, was probably to save their own skins rather than to deliver the crown to Henry, but it seems likely that if all Richard's available forces had joined the initial assault Henry would have been overwhelmed and the Stanleys would have remained neutral. The Croyland writer observed that 'in the part [of the battlefield] where the earl of Northumberland was posted, with a large and well-provided body of troops, there was no opposition made, as not a blow was given or received during the battle'.[17] He implies that Northumberland was not asked to intervene or was prevented from bringing his men into action by his situation or by the abrupt way the battle ended, but one is bound to wonder if that was quite the whole story. Northumberland was not in league with Henry because he was imprisoned for a time afterwards, but his old dispute with Richard, and the reduction of his power in northern England, may have made him a less than reliable ally. Kendall suggests that he was placed in the rear to guard against an attack from Lord Stanley – if so, it might have suited him very well.[18]

15

LEGACY & LEGEND

A king who reigned for only two years and two months would not normally be expected to leave much in the way of a permanent legacy, but Richard's short time in power was profoundly significant. It is impossible to speculate what might have happened if he had won the battle of Bosworth or even allowed Edward V to succeed his father; but what is clear is that without him there would (almost certainly) have been no Henry VIII and no Queen Elizabeth, and England would have remained part of the Roman Catholic communion for far longer, if not indefinitely. It may not be immediately apparent that the ruins of England's great abbeys are mute testimony to the dramatic events that flowed directly from his seizure of power, but the fact remains that without Richard, Henry Tudor would have remained an exile with few prospects and would not have married Edward IV's daughter. Henry might, possibly, have made his peace and been recognised as Earl of Richmond, but he would not have become the founder of a royal line.

It is also apparent that Henry would have faced a very different situation if he had somehow managed to seize Edward V's throne and the dramatic events of the summer of 1483 had never happened. Between then and 1485 five great noblemen who exercised wide regional authority all perished – Anthony Woodville, Earl Rivers; William, Lord Hastings; Henry Stafford, Duke of Buckingham; John Howard, Duke of Norfolk; and Richard himself. The result was that when Henry became king he was able to keep their lands in his own hands or replace them with less powerful men he could dominate – something he could not have done if they had remained entrenched in their localities. The principal survivors, Lord Stanley and the Earl of Northumberland, retained some of their local power, but neither was as influential in the new reign as in the old. It was largely thanks to Richard that there were no more 'kingmakers' after 1485.

All these were changes that Richard could not have anticipated and was powerless to prevent anyway, but there were others that proceeded directly from his reforms and policies and proved equally enduring. Some of his legislation, like *Titulus Regius*, the statute that confirmed his right to the throne, was bound to be repealed by his supplanter, but other Acts of his only Parliament remained on the statute book and affected the lives of Englishmen far into the future. Laws that regulated trade and the transfer of land or prevented the seizure of goods before conviction were clearly seen as progressive, and his enemies shared his desire 'to see due administration of justice throughout this his realm, and to reform, punish and subdue all extortions and oppressions in the same' and to allow his subjects to 'live in rest and quiet and peaceably enjoy their lands, livelihoods and goods ... which they be naturally born to inherit'.[1] If some of the 'evil' he did lived after him, not all the good was 'interred with his bones'.

The Tudors did their best to blacken Richard's reputation, but they failed to convince everyone. When, in 1525, Cardinal Wolsey asked the mayor and corporation of London to give Henry VIII money (a 'benevolence'), one of the citizens was bold enough to tell him that a statute of Richard III had made such extra-parliamentary exactions illegal. Wolsey retorted, 'I marvel that you speak of Richard the third, which was a usurper and murderer of his own nephews. Then of so evil a man, how can the acts be good? Make no such allegations; his acts be not honourable': to which the citizen replied, 'And it please your Grace, although he did evil, yet in his time were many good acts made, not by him only, but by the consent of the body of the whole realm, which is the Parliament.'[2] Richard was not above criticism, but was still held in esteem in some quarters forty years after his death.

Wolsey could be dismissive of Richard when it suited his purpose, but there was at least one occasion when he held him up as an example. The Scottish border was then commanded by Sir Thomas Dacre, second Lord Dacre of Gilsland, who not infrequently wrote to the Cardinal complaining that he was a 'man of much less substance' than the Duke of Gloucester [Richard] and the Earl of Northumberland, and could not be expected to secure the region without additional resources. He argued that Richard and Northumberland, whose status and wealth far exceeded his own, had only enjoyed limited success as wardens of the Marches, but Wolsey told him bluntly that this was no excuse. Quoting such examples would not help him because Richard (and others) 'took effectual means to punish and repress offenders'. He hoped that Dacre would 'obey his wholesome and friendly admonitions, and acquire as good a character as they did'.[3] No mention of murder here – just a recognition that Richard had been an effective lord of the north.

Two other innovations that were destined to survive Richard were his foundation of the College of Arms in 1484, and his re-establishment of the system of posts introduced by King Edward to speed the transmission of news. The royal heralds had used a common seal and acted in some ways like a corporation since 1420; but it was Richard who gave them a charter of incorporation and a house in Coldharbour in Upper Thames Street, London, in which to keep their records. When Henry Tudor became king he gave Coldharbour to his mother, Margaret Beaufort, and the heralds had to wait until the reign of Queen Mary and her husband Philip of Spain to receive the charter under which they now operate together with new headquarters in what was then Derby Place. This building was destroyed in the Great Fire of London in 1666, and the present College of Arms constructed on the site.

When Richard was waging war in Scotland in 1482 King Edward had arranged for horsemen to be stationed every twenty miles between the border and London so that, in the words of the Croyland writer, 'news was always able to be carried by letter from hand to hand two hundred miles within two days'.[4] This was very fast – a single horseman would not have been able to cover much more than fifty miles in a day – and it is hardly surprising that Richard revived the system when invasion threatened in 1485. He must have extended it since he had no way of knowing where Henry Tudor would make landfall, and the fact that he knew that Henry had landed 210 miles away within four days of his arrival indicates that it had served him well.[5] It was not until 1635 that Charles I opened his Royal Mail to the public and another two centuries before Rowland Hill devised the first stamps, but there would be no oaks without acorns. People who download their emails of a morning may not think they have anything in common with Richard, but they share his desire to receive information in the fastest possible way.

Richard's achievements are arguably greater than those of some kings who reigned for longer, and there are indications that they would have been greater still if he had been allowed more time. A document entitled 'a remembrance made, as well for hasty levy of the king's revenues growing of all his possessions and hereditaments as for the profitable estate and governance of the same possessions', preserved among his signet papers, highlights his determination to reform the administration and maximise the Crown's income.[6] Debts owed to the Exchequer were to be pursued vigorously, and those appointed to Crown office were to be suitable persons who had received proper training. The King's auditors were instructed to 'make a book ... so that his grace may be ascertained yearly of the whole revenues of all his livelihood and what thereof is paid and what is owing', and receivers were to notify cases where woods had been wasted or where deductions allowed for the repair of castles and manors had been spent inappropriately. Stewards who had demanded 'great fines and rewards of the king's tenants ... to the king's hurt and impoverishment of the said tenants' were to be replaced, and men responsible for the collection of money were not to be appointed to positions that would allow them to personally certify that their accounts were accurate. It was both an attack on corruption and an attempt to make the system work more efficiently, although, clearly, it would not find favour with all.

The lives of individuals who have acquired notoriety are often embellished with legendary or apocryphal stories, and Richard is no exception. Sir Richard Baker recorded in his *Chronicle of the Kings of England* that:

upon this bridge [Bow Bridge in Leicester] stood a stone of some height; against which King Richard, as he passed toward Bosworth, by chance struck his spur: and against the same stone, as he was brought back, hanging by the horse-side, his head was dashed and broken: as a wise woman (forsooth) had foretold: who before his going to battle, being asked of his success, said, that where his spur struck, his head should be broken.[7]

Baker makes it clear that he was only reporting hearsay, and the same stricture must be applied to a tale printed in a work entitled *Ten Strange Prophecies* in 1644. According to this,

as King Richard the Third, before the battle of Bosworth, rode through the south [*sic*] gate of Leicester; a poor old blind man (by profession a wheelwright) sat begging, and, hearing his approach, said, that if the Moon changed twice that day, having by her ordinary course changed in the morning, King Richard should lose his crown, and be slain. And a nobleman that carried the Moon for his colours revolted; thereby he lost his life and kingdom.[8]

The moon – and the nobleman in question – are not readily identifiable, but Lord Stanley's arms included three gold roundels – or plates – which could have been taken for full moons, while those of his brother Sir William were differenced by a crescent (moon) indicating that he was a second son.

The circlet from Richard's helmet which was used to 'crown' Henry on the battlefield was said by later writers to have been found in a thorn (i.e. hawthorn) bush, a detail which may have been invented afterwards but which could be genuine. The thorn bush was a badge used by members of the House of Lancaster, but it was apparently Henry who added a crown and used it to adorn his tomb and the east windows of his chapel at Westminster. No contemporary authority tells us in so many words why he chose to do this and his reasons may have had nothing to do with Bosworth; but we cannot exclude the possibility he associated it with what was undoubtedly the greatest day of his life.

Then there is the strange story of what happened to Richard's body after it was brought back to Leicester and put on public display. It was given to the Franciscan friars – presumably they asked for it – and Polydore Vergil records that it was buried in their church (in the choir according to Rous) two days later. In July 1495 King Henry commissioned a memorial, probably a table tomb, which was placed over the grave and which incorporated the late King's image, but no detailed description of its appearance has come down to us. The local antiquary William Burton noted that Henry 'erected for him a fair alabaster monument with his picture cut out, and made thereon',[9] suggesting, perhaps, that the portrayal took the form of an incised slab.

The friary was suppressed in November 1538, and the building and its monuments were quarried and destroyed in the years that followed. John Leland, who visited Leicester in 1543, remarked that 'there was buried King Richard 3 and a knight called Mutton, sometime mayor of Leicester',[10] but his words do not confirm that the tomb was still standing or that he actually saw it. The popular legend is that the King's remains were dug up and carried jeeringly through the streets before being thrown into the river or buried under the end of Bow Bridge; but curiously, no one mentioned the story until John Speed included it in his *Historie of Great Britaine* seventy years later. Evidence that Leicester's citizens wanted to 'punish' their former ruler is entirely lacking (on the contrary, events such as the 'Pilgrimage of Grace' had seriously tested Henry VIII's popularity), and Speed's story was flatly contradicted by his contemporary, Christopher Wren.

Wren, the future Dean of Windsor and father of the famous architect, was at this time (1612) tutor to the son of Sir William Herrick of Beaumanor (Leics.) whose brother Robert, an alderman and former mayor of Leicester, had built a large house on the site of the former friary. One day, as Wren walked with Robert Herrick in his garden, the alderman showed him a 'handsome stone pillar, three foot high' which he had caused to be erected and on which was inscribed the legend 'here lies the body of Richard III, some time King of England'.[11] The original superstructure of the tomb must have disappeared by this time or there would have been no need for a substitute memorial; but it seems that the place where it had stood was still remembered locally. Speed, who may have visited the wrong friary, had described it as being 'overgrown with weeds and nettles ... very obscure and not to be found',[12] but Herrick either knew its location or found someone who could show it to him. It is unlikely that he would have risked ridicule by claiming that Richard's remains were buried in his garden when everyone else knew they had been thrown into the river (he had been born about the time of the alleged desecration), and he clearly believed the grave had not been disturbed.

There is no indication of how long Alderman Herrick's stone pillar survived him, but it is quite possible that, as one authority has suggested, it was destroyed in the English Civil War.[13] Later visitors to Leicester failed to mention it, and instead turned their attention to a stone coffin in which Richard's body was said to have lain. The story that it had become a drinking trough for horses at a 'common inn' in the city was known to Speed in 1611;[14]

and in mid-century the diarist John Evelyn described Leicester as 'famous' for this receptacle 'which is now converted to a cistern at which (I think), cattle drink'.[15] Another traveller, Celia Fiennes, noted that it was 'cut out in exact form for his [Richard's] body to lie in', and identified the inn as the 'Greyhound', meaning, perhaps, the Talbot in Talbot Lane.[16] But by the time Miss Fiennes saw the coffin in about 1700 it was already broken; and twenty years later, the Revd Samuel Carte, vicar of St Martin's, Leicester, noticed what he believed was a fragment of it 'in which one may observe some appearance of the hollow, fitted for retaining the head and the shoulders'[17] preserved at another tavern, the 'White Horse'. John Throsby, the historian of Leicester, claimed that in his boyhood, in the 1740s, the 'end of it that then remained' stood as part of a heap of rubbish in the same inn yard, but his words imply that it had disappeared fifty years later.[18] Indeed, when the Birmingham businessman William Hutton tried to locate it in 1758 he was told that 'it was destroyed about the latter end of the reign of George the First, and some of the pieces placed as steps in a cellar, at the same inn where it had served as a trough'.[19]

A stone coffin bearing a resemblance to the one described above is now displayed at the Bosworth Battlefield Visitor Centre, but it cannot be the *same* one of course, nor the first time that the story has been appropriated. A number of such sarcophagi must have been unearthed as Leicester's former religious buildings were demolished and excavated, and more than one innkeeper may have tried to attract custom by claiming that *his* was the genuine article. What they did not know was that coffins of this type were little used after the end of the fourteenth century, and King Richard would not have been buried in one unless, in the unexpected aftermath of Bosworth, he was placed in anything that happened to be available. Naturally, they assumed that his grave had been desecrated and the coffin was all that was left of it; but the likelihood was that it remained – and still remains – somewhere beneath the site of the old friary. Throsby records that skeletons were found when the friary site was bisected by New Street in the 1740s,[20] and future reconstruction may bring more to light.

Another popular legend concerns the fate of what was allegedly the King's bed. According to tradition, Richard spent the nights of 19 and 20 August 1485 at the White Boar Inn in what was then Leicester's High Street (now Highcross Street), and brought his own portable bedstead with him. He left it there when he marched to Bosworth next day, and since he never returned to reclaim it, it became part of the furniture of what had prudently been renamed the *Blue* Boar (a badge of the Earl of Oxford), in the aftermath of the battle. The inn passed into the hands of a Mr and Mrs Clark in Queen Elizabeth's reign, and one day, as Mrs Clark was making the bed, a piece of gold fell from a concealed compartment. Further investigation revealed a false bottom containing a hoard of coins worth 'about £300 of our present money, but then worth many times that sum ... part of it coined by Richard III and the rest in earlier times'. The Clarks' new-found wealth attracted unwelcome attention, and some years after Mr Clark's death Alice Grimbold, a maid-servant at the inn, became involved in a conspiracy to rob his widow. The girl's male accomplices, Thomas Harrison and Edward Bradshaw, gained access to the property by taking lodgings, and when Mrs Clark discovered them loading her valuables onto their horses she 'endeavoured to cry out for help upon which her maid thrust her fingers down her throat and choked her'. All three were apprehended, tried and sentenced to death, the men by hanging and the girl by being burnt at the stake.[20]

The execution of the three miscreants is a matter of record, but was this really King Richard's bedstead and was he literally sleeping on his treasure? He might have been expected to stay at Leicester Castle, where he had passed several nights in the course of his 1483 progress (it seems unlikely that, as some have suggested, it was too dilapidated to receive him), and it may be no coincidence that William Hutton sold some of his books through public houses. Both Richard's stay at the Blue Boar and Henry Tudor's alleged sojourn at the Three Tuns in Atherstone may have been concerned more with boosting profits than with strict historical accuracy, and significantly, perhaps, the bed was not mentioned at the murderers' trial. The superstructure of the bed now displayed at Donnington le Heath manor house (Leics.) is undeniably Tudor or Jacobean, but the base, or stock, is older and could have been in existence in the late fifteenth century. A connection with Richard is not particularly likely therefore, but nor can it be entirely ruled out.

A bedstead of this sort would have been a cumbersome item to take on campaign; and since later visitors observed it in a large upstairs room at the inn, we cannot discount the possibility that this had always been its home. It would not therefore have contained Richard's treasure – whether or not he slept on it – and there is no reason to suppose that it was the source of the Clarks' wealth. Later generations may have supposed that because Clark was a publican he was a rather ordinary sort of fellow, but he had been elected one of the borough chamberlains as early as 1568, and served as mayor on two occasions, in 1583–4 and again in 1598–9. He was always one of the most prominent – and presumably wealthiest – men in local society, not someone who needed a remarkable piece of luck to make his fortune. His widow was certainly murdered for her money, but there is no evidence it came from King Richard's bed!

Another story associated with Richard is the so-called 'Prophecy of G' which foretold that after E, that is, Edward IV, G would reign. Edward's son and heir was another Edward, and John Rous claimed that the King thought that G was his brother George of Clarence, whom he had perhaps never fully trusted after 1470. George was executed to prevent him from seizing the throne in the event of Edward's death, leaving Richard of *Gloucester* to fulfil the prediction, but was Rous just being wise after the event? A retrospective prophecy could easily have come into being by the time he wrote his *History* in about 1490, and no one has suggested that Edward was suffering from paranoid schizophrenia. Nor, logically, would he have been blind to the fact that Richard's name – or at least the name of his title – began with G too.[22]

Still more improbable is the allegation that Richard was unusually interested in fashion and finery, and was something of a dandy, or fop. The idea seems to have originated with the words Shakespeare put into his mouth after he had persuaded Anne Neville to marry him:

I'll be at charges for a looking-glass,
And entertain a score or two of tailors,
To study fashions to adorn my body:
Since I am crept in favour with myself,
I will maintain it at some little cost.[23]

Sharon Turner, writing at the beginning of the nineteenth century, believed he had found evidence of this in a letter preserved in British Library Harleian Manuscript 433, the record of Richard's signet office, and in certain Great Wardrobe accounts for the period 9 April 1483 to 2 February 1484;[24] but do fine clothes bought by or on behalf of a king really tell us anything about his personality? The garments mentioned were all to be worn when Richard's son Edward was created Prince of Wales in York Minster, a moment when splendour and *gravitas* would have been deemed essential; and Turner was taken to task by his contemporary Sir Nicholas Harris Nicolas, who recognised that the King's supposed 'love of splendid clothes ... belonged to the age and not to the individual'.[25] Nicolas was firmly of the opinion that 'there is not a single circumstance ... which justifies the opinion that he [Richard] was more fond of splendour and parade than his predecessors', but the willingness of some later writers to take Turner at face value has given the myth a life of its own. It was easy to suppose that foppishness was another flaw in Richard's already much-flawed character; but all that can be said with certainty is that he wore clothes appropriate to his station. He may have enjoyed flaunting the best that money could buy him, but we simply do not know.

The 'fop' story was born of misunderstanding on the part of a nineteenth-century 'amateur' historian, but we would be wrong if we supposed that a similar legend could not arise today. Richard's Book of Hours lacks a folio which contained most of a prayer of intercession to St Julian which had always been part of the volume (only the first few words of the rubric, or heading, survives), and the first three or four lines of the personal prayer he added himself. The best known St Julian was Julian 'the Hospitaller', patron of innkeepers, ferrymen and travellers, who accidentally killed his own father and mother and obtained forgiveness by giving shelter to travellers and ferrying them across a dangerous river. There can be no direct link between the two entries, one written for the original owner of the book in about 1420 and the other added more than sixty years later, but in 1973 Dr Pamela Tudor-Craig joined them with a few conjectural words and printed them as one text.[26] This allowed a later writer, Desmond Seward, to make a 'connection' between Julian, who killed his parents, and Richard, who murdered his nephews,[27] and to explain why Richard sought Julian's help in obtaining forgiveness of his sins. Richard's prayer was *not* addressed to Julian, of course, and even if it had been, Julian would have been unable to assist him. No saint venerated by the medieval church specialised in interceding for murderers, but the story 'proved' that Richard had a guilty conscience and was another nail in his reputation's coffin.[28]

It was perhaps inevitable that a king who both gained and lost his throne in such dramatic circumstances would become the stuff of legend, and these myths and half-truths tell us nothing about him personally. But what they do make clear is that he has never lost – and will never lose – his fascination for both historians and the general reading public. This book has tried to tell the story of his life within the context of his times – there has been no conscious attempt either to accuse or to exonerate him – and the man who emerges from its pages is both principled and unprincipled, a flawed diamond. He has attracted sympathy partly because later generations have been unkind to him and because the English always feel sorry for a loser; but another reason is that somewhere in his complex and ultimately unfathomable character we may all recognise something of ourselves.

16

EPILOGUE
The Discovery of King Richard's Grave

On Saturday 25 August 2012 a team of University of Leicester archaeologists led by Richard Buckley began to excavate a car park which overlaid part of the site of the medieval Grey Friary. The Richard III Society, who, with the University of Leicester and Leicester City Council had jointly sponsored the dig, hoped that it would be possible to locate the King's grave and remains, but the aims of the professionals involved were more modest. They thought it would be possible to learn something about the precise layout of part of the friary, but felt there was little prospect of finding an intact royal burial. Human bones might well be unearthed, but how could Richard's be distinguished from those of the innumerable friars who had also been buried there over several hundred years?

Preliminary investigations undertaken in the months and years before the excavation began offered only slight encouragement. A small part of the site was examined when a single-story extension to the National Westminster Bank adjoining the modern street named after the Grey Friars was demolished in 2007, but the only evidence that a church might have stood in the vicinity was a fragment of a stone coffin lid found in a post-medieval drain.[1] Attention subsequently switched to a car park owned by Leicester City Council located further to the west, where a ground-penetrating radar survey was completed in August 2011. This identified three possible burial sites, but was hampered by the presence of approximately a metre of rubble immediately beneath the tarmac.

The radar could not readily distinguish between medieval – or, for that matter, Roman – foundations and the accumulated debris of later years.

The main difficulty facing the archaeologists was that they had only a limited area to work in, but comparison with the ground plans of other friaries suggested that the religious – as opposed to the domestic – buildings could have stood in the vicinity. The Friars' church would have been constructed on an east–west axis, so the team decided to sink two trenches running from north to south in the hope of discovering traces of its foundations at some point. Trench one revealed the remains of a building 5 metres wide with large blocks of stone (seats) against each of the wall lines, while the second, more westerly, excavation exposed two parallel walls about 2 metres apart separated by a mortar floor which had clearly once been tiled. The former was almost certainly the Chapter House where the friars met to transact their daily business, and the latter, which would have abutted it, the eastern side of the cloister walk. Comparative architecture suggested that that the remains of a building with walls 1.5 metres thick found further north in trench one could be part of the ruined church, a view reinforced by the discovery of fragments of carved masonry and a scatter of glazed ridge tiles of the sort used to roof important medieval buildings. The ornamental stones included some large pieces of window tracery and a decorated block that could have formed part of a frieze.

The next step was to sink a third trench to the north-east, which revealed more walls together with a floor marked with tile prints and fragments of a monumental arched window. The tiles had been laid both longitudinally and diagonally, indicating that this was where two adjoining parts of the building had met, and was tentatively identified as the place where the choir joined the presbytery, the setting for the high altar. The more northerly foundations uncovered in trench one must also have formed part of the choir where John Rous says that Richard was buried, but the archaeology here was in a generally poor state of preservation. All the floor levels had been destroyed and the construction of an outhouse in Victorian times had caused further damage; but in the space between the walls, and remarkably on the first day of the dig, the team found bones in a grave cut which had fortuitously survived the nineteenth-century building works. The roughly hewn pit was too small for the person who had been buried in it – the legs were straight but the torso was twisted with the head propped up against the side of the cutting – and contained no trace of a coffin or shroud, an unusual circumstance given that the individual was presumably someone of high status. Both factors could imply that the interment was hurried, or unexpected, and haste would have been necessary if the body was already decomposing – if, for example, it had been exposed to public view for several days in high summer. The University applied to the Ministry of Justice for permission to exhume the remains under the 1857 Burials Act on Friday 31 August, and the delicate task began on Tuesday 4 September.

The body was clearly in the 'right' place and when examined displayed a number of most interesting features. It was clearly that of an adult male whose wisdom teeth had erupted and whose clavicle was fully fused. The former normally occurs between the ages of seventeen and twenty-five and the latter, which is one of the last bones to fuse, between twenty-two and thirty. The teeth showed some signs of wear, but the absence of any degenerative disease suggested that the individual had not yet entered 'old' age at say, forty-five. Richard was almost thirty-three when he was killed at Bosworth, so there was no obvious reason why the bones could not be his.

So far, so good, but the most exciting discovery was that here was a man who had suffered from scoliosis (curvature of the spine forcing the right shoulder blade higher than the left), and who had evidently been killed in battle. A corroded lump of iron found lodged high in his spinal column, between the second and third thoracic vertebrae, was not, as was first thought, part of a barbed arrow-head, but it was apparent that he had suffered a number of head wounds, two of which would have proved fatal. A bladed weapon had sliced away a significant part of the base of the skull (although without actually 'beheading' him), while a smaller wound in the same area had penetrated to the inner surface opposite the entry point. The individual had almost certainly lost his helmet by the time he died, and there was evidence of other, lesser, wounds including one to the pelvis caused by a dagger thrust into the right buttock, perhaps a 'humiliation' or 'insult' injury inflicted after death. His feet were missing, destroyed, presumably, during earlier building works, and the position of his arms suggested that his hands could have been tied; but there was no sign of the kyphosis that would have made him a hunchback or the bone wasting associated with a withered arm.[2]

A set of disarticulated female bones were found near the first body, but it is unlikely that they are in any way related. The female skeleton had been disturbed at some point in the intervening centuries, and reburied at a level higher than the floor of the church. Only one woman is known to have been buried in the Friars' church, Ellen Luenor, a possible founder and benefactor with her husband Gilbert, who died about 1250. The remains could be hers, but it is impossible to be sure.

In one sense it is fortunate that the bones were found in 2012 rather than a generation or more ago, because the scientific tests that can now be applied to them were either unknown then or have improved greatly since. Today, high-precision radiocarbon dating can pinpoint the age of remains to within seventy years, stable isotope analysis can help establish the individual's lifestyle, environment and diet (by identifying the geological origin of the minerals his teeth had absorbed from his food and drink during their formation), and genetic fingerprinting can match his DNA (an abbreviation for 'deoxyribonucleic acid') to another member of his family. Mitochondrial DNA, found in the mitochondria or energy-producing powerhouse of a cell, is often the only form of DNA that can be extracted from ancient remains, and has the drawback that it can only be handed down from mothers to children. In other words, a woman must produce at least one daughter in each generation for the sequence to be passed on to the next. Strictly speaking it cannot prove the identity of a person – only that the owners of the two samples being compared are related to each other.

In Richard's case the chances of finding a mtDNA match were not good. His mother Cecily Neville's remains had been moved to a new grave at Fotheringhay (Northamptonshire) in Elizabethan times while those of his sister Elizabeth, Duchess of Suffolk still rest beneath her effigy in Wingfield church in Suffolk. His grandmother Joan Beaufort and great-grandmother Katherine Swynford are both buried in Lincoln Cathedral, and mtDNA which could be extracted from the remains of any of their numerous offspring would also match Richard's:[3] but it is very difficult to obtain permission to disturb graves on the grounds of historical curiosity. The alternative was to look for a living, modern-day descendant of one of the women who shared his mtDNA and whose ancestry could be traced exclusively through females. The King's youngest sister, Margaret, Duchess of Burgundy, was childless, and although Elizabeth of Suffolk produced many children (including several daughters), she had only one grandchild and no great-grandchildren. Anne, Duchess of Exeter, his eldest sister, had two daughters, both named Anne, one by her first husband Henry Holand, Duke of Exeter, who died young, and another by her second spouse, Sir Thomas St Leger. At first, Anne St Leger did not look particularly promising, but her descent in an unbroken female line was traced to a lady named Joy Ibsen who died in 2008 and who would have been Richard's sixteenth-generation niece.[4] Her son Michael (who with his brother and childless sister is the last of the line), provided samples for comparison with the bones recovered from the Grey Friars site.

One question which is inevitably asked is 'would proving that the skeleton is King Richard's help us to confirm whether or not the remains preserved in an urn in Westminster Abbey are those of his nephews, the "Princes in the Tower"?' Renewed access to the bones of the 'Princes' would be required of course, something the authorities have been unwilling to grant in recent times, but it is just possible that more could be learned if they were subjected to modern scientific investigation. Mitochondrial DNA would be useless here because the Princes would carry the mtDNA of their mother Queen Elizabeth Woodville, while Richard possessed that of his mother Cecily Neville, but there is another element, the Y chromosome (the male sex chromosome), which all males inherit from their father. Richard, the Princes, and the entire Plantagenet male line would share the same Y chromosome, and if this could be extracted from both sets of bones it would strengthen the argument for a close relationship between them. But it would not, unfortunately, tell us how or when the boys died.

Newspaper reporting of the find was generally accurate, but there was one 'fact', reported in The Times and subsequently repeated in Current Archaeology, which seemed decidedly questionable. The Burgundian chronicler Jean Molinet heard that at Bosworth, Richard's horse 'leapt into a marsh from which it could not retrieve itself. One of the Welshmen [fighting for Henry Tudor] then came after him, and struck him dead with a halberd.' Ben Macintyre, writing in The Times, named the assailant as Wyllyam Gardynyr, who 'stove in Richard's head with a poleaxe', a detail previously unknown to most students of the period.[5] William Gardiner was presumably one of the Welsh soldiers who followed Rhys ap Thomas to Bosworth, but his identification as the man who killed Richard relied on an entry in Wikipedia based on Gardiner Generations and Relations, vol. 1, by Richard Thomas Gardiner, published in 1991. William was allegedly a cloth merchant turned mercenary who had been born in Oxfordshire in 1451. Henry Tudor is said to have knighted him for his good service at Bosworth, and allowed him to marry his uncle Jasper's illegitimate daughter Helen, who bore him a son, Stephen, the future Bishop of

Winchester. This last detail is almost certainly inaccurate – Stephen Gardiner's parents were most probably John and Agnes Gardiner of Bury St Edmunds – and more particulars of the 'Welsh accounts' which underpin the rest of the story are needed before it can be accepted as fact.

At a press conference held on Monday 4 February 2013, the University of Leicester revealed that scientific tests carried out over the preceding months confirmed beyond all reasonable doubt that the skeleton was that of King Richard. The principal conclusions were:

- He was a white male, of slender, gracile (almost feminine) build. His natural height was 5 feet 8 inches (1.72m), a little taller than average, but scoliosis, which it was thought developed only after he reached the age of ten, could have reduced this by up to a foot (0.3m). The scoliosis may also have placed additional strain on his heart and lungs and caused him pain.
- He had enjoyed a high-protein, upper-class diet including significant quantities of seafood, and had died from wounds to the head at some time between 1455 and 1540. Experts from the East Midlands Forensic Pathology Unit and the University's Department of Engineering concluded that he was aged between thirty and thirty-three.
- mtDNA samples taken from Michael Ibsen matched those of another donor whose ancestry had been traced (but who wished to remain anonymous), and both matched mtDNA extracted from the skeleton. 'All three individuals shared the same relatively rare mitochondrial DNA sequence.'[6]

Additionally, the Richard III Society commissioned Caroline Wilkinson, Professor of Craniofacial Identification at the University of Dundee, to reconstruct the King's features, and the image she produced confirmed the scientific evidence. This Richard is younger and less careworn than he appears in the more traditional portraits, calm and thoughtful but also determined – a man who would not hesitate to stand up for himself.

So what more have we learned about Richard? The tests have clearly added to our knowledge of his height and physical appearance, and have demonstrated that although he was not the hunchback portrayed by generations of Shakespearian actors his deformity was more than a Tudor legend. The numerous injuries he sustained confirm the words of contemporary writers who said he died fighting bravely, and there is evidence that his body was stripped and mistreated after death. What his remains do not tell us (unfortunately) is any more about what he was like as a person or whether he was guilty of any of the crimes attributed to him. The best hope is that the interest and enthusiasm generated by the excavation will encourage others to continue the search for new evidence, and that future discoveries will shed further light on his character and actions as the years pass.

Finally, there was the thorny question of where Richard's remains should be re-buried. Leicester Cathedral, adjacent to the car park, was an obvious candidate, but so too was York Minster which lay in his northern heartland and where he had planned to establish a college of 100 priests. Other possibilities were Westminster Abbey, the church of St Mary and St Alkelda near Middleham Castle (where his collegiate foundation had come into being), Barnard Castle in Durham (where the proposed foundation had, again, not materialised), Fotheringhay in Northamptonshire (where his parents, brother and ancestors were buried), and even Worksop in Nottinghamshire, suggested, perhaps rather tongue in cheek, on the grounds that it lay midway between York and Leicester. However, much of the debate could have been avoided if the fact that the formal permission to exhume the bones stated that they were to be reinterred at the discretion of the licence holder, the University of Leicester, had been made clear at the outset. So unless there are any last-minute challenges or rethinks, Leicester Cathedral it will be.

APPENDIX
Fees & Annuities Charged to the Receiver of Middleham 1473–4 (National Archives, Duchy of Lancaster, 29/648/10485)

During the year in question, Richard Conyers, the principal accountant of the estate, made payments to at least forty-nine men and one woman who were employed or retained by Richard of Gloucester between 20 August 1471 and 16 October 1473. The terms of the retainers' contracts are usually abbreviated, although in five cases (those of Richard Knaresborough, Roger Conyers, Thomas Blakeston, Robert Wycliffe and Alice Burgh) much fuller details are given. The formal agreement, the indenture, was separated by an indented cut so that each party had a record of the undertaking, and Richard would then issue an open (patent) letter granting the annuity. It was usually paid in two instalments at Easter and Michaelmas (29 September).

Those retained for life, the dates their contracts were signed (where stated), and the annuities granted were:

John Conyers, knight		£20 0s 0d
Thomas Markenfield, knight	11/12/71	£10 0s 0d
ThomasTunstall, esquire	20/11/71	£33 6s 8d
William Burgh	04/10/71	£6 13s 4d
Thomas Metcalfe, esquire	20/08/71	£6 13s 4d
Brian Metcalfe, esquire	06/10/71	£2 0s 0d
Roland Pudsay, esquire	26/10/71	£5 0s 0d
Thomas Talbot, esquire	11/11/71	£6 13s 4d
Richard Conyers junior	12/12/71	£6 13s 4d
Robert Clifford, esquire	08/10/71	£6 13s 4d
Richard Conyers (the accountant)		£6 13s 4d
Lionel Claxton, esquire		£2 13s 4d
John Redman, esquire	20/03/73	£5 0s 0d
Richard Knaresbrough	27/04/73	£6 0s 0d
Robert Danby, knight		£6 13s 4d
Roger Conyers, knight	03/09/73	£6 13s 4d
Thomas Blakeston, esquire	03/09/73	£6 13s 4d
Robert Wycliffe, esquire	04/10/73	£13 6s 8d
Alice Burgh, gentlewoman	01/03/73	£6 13s 4d
William Clerionet, esquire	03/07/73	£6 13s 4d
Thomas Otter	12/05/73	£3 6s 8d
Richard Hardwyk	16/05/73	£1 6s 8d

Alice Burgh was William Burgh's sister, and was perhaps related to Henry and Isabel Burgh who were granted an annuity in recognition of their good service to the King and Queen in 1484. Isabel had been Prince Edward's nurse, but we do not know why Alice was retained.

William Burgh's contract is typical of many others. Abbreviated words are given in full and spelling and punctuation has been modernised:

> R. GLOUCESTER. This indenture made between the right high and mighty prince Richard Duke of Gloucester, Great Chamberlain, Constable, Admiral and Warden of the West Marches of England against Scotland on that one party, and William Burgh, Squire, on that other party, witnesseth that the same William is withholden and belast [bound] for term of his life with and toward the said Duke against all persons, his allegiance [to the King] excepted. And the same William well and covenably [appropriately] horsed and harnessed shall be ready to ride, come and go with, toward and for the said Duke, as well in time of peace as of war, at all times and into all places upon reasonable warning to be given unto him on behalf of the said Duke, at his cost or reasonable reward; the said William taking yearly for his fee ten marks sterling [£6 13s 4d] of the issues, profits and revenues coming and growing as well of the farm of the vicarage of Sleightholme as of the farms and revenues of the Lordship of Middleham by the hands of the receivers, farmers, bailiffs [or] of other occupiers thereof for the time being at the terms of Martinmas [11 November] and Whitsuntide by even portions. And the same Duke shall have the thirds of all winnings of war won or gotton by the said William, and the third of thirds of all his servants that he shall have at the wages or costs of the said Duke. And if any captain or man of estate by the said William or any of his servants be taken, the said Duke shall have him [for ransom] giving to the taker reasonable reward for him. In witness whereof as well the said Duke as the said William to these indentures interchangeably set their seals. Given the fourth day of October, the eleventh year of the reign of the King our sovereign lord Edward the Fourth.

The division of the profits of war are a significant feature of the contract. Clearly, Richard expected to be involved in conflict, and was not above demanding a third of Burgh's third share of any booty seized by his men.

NOTES & REFERENCES

Prologue: Conflicting Opinions

1. *Christ Church Letters*, ed. J.B. Sheppard (Camden Society, 1877), pp. 45–6.

2. *British Library Harleian Manuscript 433*, ed. R. Horrox & P.W. Hammond, 4 vols. (1979–83), iii, pp. 123–4.

3. Dominic Mancini, *The Usurpation of Richard III*, ed. C.A.J. Armstrong (Gloucester, 1984), p. 93.

4. *Ibid.*, pp. 93, 63–4, 83.

5. *York House Books 1461–1490*, ed. L.C. Attreed, 2 vols. (Stroud, 1991), i, pp. 368–9. *York Civic Records*, vol. 1, ed. A. Raine (Yorkshire Archaeological Society Record Series, lxxxxviii, 1939), p. 126.

6. *York House Books*, p. 696. For the riots see A. Hanham, *Richard III and his early historians 1483–1535* (Oxford, 1975), pp. 61–2.

7. *Extracts from the Municipal Records of the City of York during the reigns of Edward, IV, Edward V and Richard III*, ed. R. Davies (1843), p. 221.

8. The most popular candidate is John Russell, Bishop of Lincoln, who held the posts of privy seal under Edward IV and chancellor under Richard III. Others are Henry Sharp, protonotary of chancery (proposed by Nicholas Pronay and John Cox), Richard Lavender, archdeacon of Leicester (H.A. Kelly), Piers Curtis, keeper of the great wardrobe (Daniel Williams), Richard's privy seal John Gunthorpe (the present author), and Richard Langport, clerk of the council from 1462 until the beginning of Richard's reign (Michael Hicks).

9. *Ingulph's Chronicle of the Abbey of Croyland*, ed. H.T. Riley (1854), pp. 488, 490, 496, 501, 503. Pronay and Cox say that *dire* threats were made against Elizabeth Woodville. *The Crowland Chronicle Continuations 1459–1486*, ed. N. Pronay & J. Cox (1986), p. 171.

10. *Ingulph's Chronicle*, pp. 491, 497, 504. The continuator refers to 'a rumour that the sons of King Edward had died a violent death', but does not say if he knew, or thought, it was true.

11. See *The Rous Roll*, ed. C. Ross (Gloucester, 1980).

12. Hanham, *Early Historians*, pp. 106, 120, 123. Richard was actually born under the sign of Libra.

13. *Ibid.*, pp. 121, 123.

14. R. M. Warnicke, 'Lord Morley's Statements about Richard III', *Albion*, xv (1983), p. 176.

15. *The Great Chronicle of London*, ed. A.H. Thomas & I.D. Thornley (Gloucester, 1983), p. 238.

1. 'Richard Liveth Yet', 1452–1461

1. See A.F. Sutton & L. Visser-Fuchs, '"Richard Liveth Yet": an Old Myth', *The Ricardian*, ix, no. 117 (1992), pp. 266–9. The writer also states that Richard Duke of York 'liveth yet', meaning

not that he was seriously ill but merely that he was alive – unlike earlier members of the Clare family who were dead.

2. Paul Murray Kendall's suggestion that Cecily and her boys awaited their enemies on the steps of the market cross in Ludlow is often repeated as a fact nowadays (*Richard III* [Folio Society, 2005], p. 23), but it is unlikely that she would have risked being abused by soldiers who did not recognise her. It is surely more probable that she remained in the safety of the castle until she could surrender to senior figures she knew.

3. Although Parliament did subsequently allow her a thousand marks a year from her husband's forfeited properties with which to maintain herself and her family.

4. *An English Chronicle of the Reigns of Richard II, Henry IV, Henry V, and Henry VI written before the year 1470*, ed. J.S. Davies (Camden Society, 1856), p. 83. Charles Ross suggests that Cecily remained behind because she was still at Fotheringhay (*Richard III* [1981], p. 4), but it is surely more probable that York did not take his wife and younger children with him because he could escape more quickly without them.

5. *The Paston Letters 1422–1509*, ed. J. Gairdner, 6 vols. (1904), iii, p. 233.

6. These particulars have been collected by Martha Carlin, 'Sir John Fastolf's Place, Southwark: The home of the Duke of York's family 1460', *The Ricardian*, v, no. 72 (1981), pp. 311–14, from documents now preserved at Magdalen College, Oxford.

7. Quoted by A.J. Pollard, 'North, South and Richard III', *The Ricardian*, v, no. 74 (1981), p. 384.

8. *Ingulph's Chronicle*, p. 422.

9. See H. Klieneke, 'Alice Martyn, Widow of London: An Episode from Richard's Youth', *The Ricardian*, xiv (2004), pp. 32–6.

10. *Calendar of State Papers and Manuscripts Existing in the Archives and Collections of Milan, I, 1385–1618*, ed. A.B. Hinds (1913), pp. 67–8. Quoted by L. Visser-Fuchs, 'Richard in Holland, 1461', *The Ricardian*, vi, no. 81 (1983), p. 188.

2. The King's Brother, 1461–1469

1. Kendall, *Richard III*, pp. 40–2.

2. This paragraph is based on Ross, *Richard III*, pp. 9–10, and R. Horrox, *Richard III. A Study in Service* (Cambridge, 1991), p. 29.

3. These figures are taken from A.F. Sutton, '*And to be delivered to the Lord Richard Duke of Gloucester, the other brother …*', *The Ricardian*, viii, no. 100 (1988), pp. 20–5.

4. Elizabeth is said to have had a sister named Martha who married Sir John Bromley of Hextall (Shropshire), but the earliest mention of her is apparently in an unreliable heralds' visitation pedigree of 1623.

5. Kendall has Richard entering Warwick's household at Middleham in Yorkshire as early as November 1461 and leaving in 1465 after the Earl and Edward began to have their differences (*Richard III*, pp. 34–43), but all references to Richard during this period place him in locations south of the River Trent.

6. *Calendar of the Patent Rolls, Edward IV, 1467–1477* (1900), p. 296, 10 December 1471. For Kendall's argument see *Richard III*, pp. 468–9 (note 21).

7. The phrase is Chaucer's, from the Prologue to *The Canterbury Tales*.

8. On this point see C. Ross, *Edward IV* (1974), appendix 2, p. 436.

9. *The Rous Roll*, no. 56.

10. John Leland, *De Rebus Britannicis Collectanea*, ed. T. Hearne, 6 vols. (Oxford, 1770), vi, pp. 3–4.

11. *The Paston Letters*, iv, p. 217. CPR 1467–1477, p. 51.

12. C. Ross, 'Some "Servants and Lovers" of Richard in his Youth', *The Ricardian*, iv, no. 55 (1976), pp. 2–4.

13. *CSP Milan*, pp. 118–20. The plan was that Richard would wed Louis's second daughter Jeanne, who would receive Holland, Zealand and Brabant as her dowry after Burgundy had been dismembered. But it only existed in the minds of Warwick and the French king.

14. *Ingulph's Chronicle*, p. 457.

15. Jehan de Waurin, *Recueil des Croniques et Anchiennes Istories de la Grant Bretaigne, a present*

nomme Engleterre, ed. W. & E.L.C.P. Hardy, 5 vols. (Rolls Series, 1864–91), v, pp. 458–9.

16. Kendall's assertion that Richard was also on bad terms with the Queen's family is entirely without foundation. There is no evidence that on his return to London he thought the court 'alive with Woodvilles', or that Elizabeth, 'beautiful and rapacious, would know how to show her haughtiness to the undersized lad from Yorkshire with the awkward torso and solemn face'. *Richard III*, pp. 44 & 52.

17. Historical Manuscripts Commission, 78. *Report on the Manuscripts of the late R.R. Hastings*, 4 vols. (1928–47), i, pp. 290–1.

18. These particulars are taken from P.W. Hammond, 'The Illegitimate Children of Richard III', *The Ricardian*, v, no. 66 (1979), pp. 92–96 revised in *Richard III. Crown and People*, ed. J. Petre (Gloucester, 1985), pp. 18–23. Richard is sometimes said to have had a second bastard son, Richard of Eastwell, who, I have argued elsewhere, could have been Richard, Duke of York, one of the missing 'Princes in the Tower'. See D. Baldwin, *The Lost Prince. The Survival of Richard of York* (Stroud, 2007). Dr Horrox has suggested that Katherine's mother could have been Katherine Haute, the Queen's kinswoman – Richard gave her an annuity of £5 (the only annuity so recorded) from his estates in East Anglia. See *Richard III. A Study in Service*, p. 81.

3. The Years of Crisis, 1469–1471

1. Edward and Richard's visit to Walsingham has been imaginatively reconstructed in J. Ashdown-Hill's article 'Walsingham in 1469: The Pilgrimage of Edward IV and Richard, Duke of Gloucester', *The Ricardian*, xi, no. 136 (1997), pp. 2–16.

2. *Original Letters Illustrative of English History*, ed. H. Ellis, 2nd series, vol. 1 (1827), pp. 143–4. See also P. Tudor-Craig, *National Portrait Gallery Exhibition Catalogue* (1973), pp. 65–6.

3. *The Paston Letters*, v, p. 35.

4. John Warkworth, *A Chronicle of the First Thirteen Years of King Edward the Fourth*, ed. J.O. Halliwell (Camden Society, 1839), pp. 46–7.

5. *Chronicle of the Rebellion in Lincolnshire, in 1470*, ed. J.G. Nichols, Camden Miscellany, vol. 1 (1847), p. 22.

6. This tradition, which is several centuries old, has recently been challenged by D. Santiuste, *Edward IV and the Wars of the Roses* (Barnsley, 2010), p. 97 and footnote p. 169, citing P. Morgan, 'The Naming of Battlefields' in *War and Society in Medieval and Early Modern Britain*, ed. D. Dunn (Liverpool, 2000), p. 41. 'Losecoat', the name of a local field, is said to derive from the Old English *hlose-cot*, meaning 'pigsty cottage'.

7. See L. Visser-Fuchs, 'Richard was Late', *The Ricardian*, xi, no. 147 (1999), pp. 616–9.

8. Quoted by L. Visser-Fuchs in 'Richard in Holland 1471–2', *The Ricardian*, vi, no. 82 (1983), p. 24.

9. See R. Horrox, 'Preparations for Edward IV's Return from Exile', *The Ricardian*, vi, no. 79 (1982). The chronicler Waurin claims that Richard threatened to kill the Recorder of York and another burgess when they appeared reluctant to aid his brother (*Chroniques*, v, p. 647), but no English source mentions this. They were desperate times, however.

10. See chapter 2, note 12 above.

11. *Historie of the Arrivall of Edward IV. in England and the Finall Recoverye of his Kingdomes from Henry VI. A.D. M.CCCC.LXXI*, ed. J. Bruce (Camden Society, 1838), p. 30. *Warkworth's Chronicle*, p. 18.

12. *The Arrivall*, p. 38. *Warkworth's Chronicle*, p. 21.

13. *More's History of King Richard III*, ed. J.R. Lumby, (Cambridge, 1883), p. 6. Henry's death was so convenient that writers were bound to assume that he had been murdered, but he was forty-nine (already eight years older than Edward IV would be at *his* death), and 'natural causes' cannot be ruled out.

14. The fullest discussion of Henry's death, burials, and cult is W.J. White, 'The Death and Burial of Henry VI., A Review of the Facts and Theories', *The Ricardian*, vi, nos. 78, pp. 70–80, & 79, pp. 106–17 (1982).

4. Warwick's Heir, 1471–1475

1. See the study by R. Britnell, 'Richard, Duke of Gloucester and the Death of Thomas

Fauconberg', *The Ricardian*, x, no. 128 (1995), pp. 174–84, on which these paragraphs are based.

2. Quoted in P.W. Hammond & A.F. Sutton, *Richard III. The Road to Bosworth Field* (1985), p. 62.

3. National Archives, Duchy of Lancaster, 29/648/10485. I have added the payments made to the cook, Thomas Bulnas; the brewer, Thomas Hoton; and Thomas Louther, who were 'retained by letters of warrant' rather than for life to the fees and wages paid to the estate officials.

4. C. Given-Wilson and others (eds.), *The Parliament Rolls of Medieval England (P.R.O.M.E.)*, National Archives/Scholarly Digital Editions 2005, 1472 Parliament, 1st Roll, 38–39.

5. A.J. Pollard, 'Richard Clervaux of Croft: A North Riding Squire in the 15th Century', *Yorkshire Archaeological Journal*, vol. 50 (1978), p. 162, & E.E. Barker (ed.), *Register of Archbishop Rotherham* (Canterbury and York Society 1974–5), pp. 194–5, quoted in Hammond & Sutton, *Road to Bosworth Field*, pp. 73–4.

6. Washington DC, Library of Congress, Thatcher, 1004. Transcribed by A.J. Pollard in *Richard III and the Princes in the Tower* (Stroud, 1991), p. 237.

7. *The Paston Letters*, v, p. 135. *Ingulph's Chronicle*, p. 470.

8. *The Paston Letters*, v, pp. 188–9.

9. *Ibid.*, p. 195

10. *Ibid.*, p. 199

11. *P.R.O.M.E.*, 1472 Parliament, 2nd Roll, 100–101.

12. See M. Barnfield, 'Diriment Impediments, Dispensations and Divorce: Richard III and Matrimony', *The Ricardian*, xvii (2007). Ms Barnfield suggests that the blood relationships between Richard and Anne may have been dispensed when Warwick obtained papal consent for Isabel to marry George, but if Richard already had a dispensation in his pocket it is difficult to see what all the fuss was about.

13. Professor Hicks has argued that the Countess's lands would have passed automatically to Richard as the royal patentee 'unless something was done to prevent this outcome' (M.A. Hicks, 'The Last Days of Elizabeth Countess of Oxford', *English Historical Review*, ciii [1988], p. 81), but the grant of Oxford's paternal lands made no mention of his mother's properties or of others that would had fallen to him had he remained loyal. Oxford's estates were seized in 1471 but he was not attainted until 1475, so he could in theory have inherited his mother's lands when she died in 1473. They were worth some £600–700 annually, so the settlement was comparatively generous. I am grateful to James Ross and Marie Barnfield for their advice.

14. *Ibid.*, p. 82.

15. One deponent, William Paston, said that Stillington had been favourably disposed towards the Countess, but he was close to the Duke of Clarence and this was the time when the quarrel over the Warwick inheritance was reaching its height.

16. M.K. Jones, 'Richard, Duke of Gloucester and the Scropes of Masham', *The Ricardian*, x, no. 134 (1996), on which this paragraph is based.

17. M.A. Hicks, *Richard III as Duke of Gloucester: A Study in Character*, University of York Borthwick Paper no. 70 (1986).

18. K.B. McFarlane, *The Nobility of Later Medieval England* (Oxford, 1973), p. 53.

5. War & Peace, 1475–1482

1. F.P. Barnard, *Edward IV's French Expedition of 1475. The Leaders and their Badges* (Gloucester, 1975), pp. 9–10. The other figures are given by Ross, *Edward IV*, p. 220.

2. *Philippe de Commynes. Memoirs*, trans. M. Jones (Harmondsworth, 1972), p. 259.

3. Quoted in P.W. Hammond, *Edward of Middleham, Prince of Wales* (Cliftonville, 1973), p. 12. There is a suggestion they may have had a second son named George, but the evidence is inconclusive. See M.A. Hicks, 'One Prince or Two? The Family of Richard III', *The Ricardian*, ix, no. 122 (1993), pp. 467–8.

4. This description is based on A.F. Sutton and L. Visser-Fuchs with P.W. Hammond, *The Reburial of Richard Duke of York 21–30 July 1476* (1996).

5. Henry I, not the gentlest of kings, had imprisoned his brother Robert, Duke of Normandy, for some twenty-eight years.

6. Mancini, *Usurpation*, p. 63.

7. *York House Books*, i, p. 255.

8. Davies, *York Records*, pp. 140–1.

9. Ross, *Richard III*, p. 53.

10. Kendall, *Richard III*, p. 108.

11. 'Narrative of the Marriage of Richard Duke of York with Anne of Norfolk: the Matrimonial Feast and the Grand Jousting', *Illustrations of Ancient State and Chivalry from manuscripts preserved in the Ashmolean Museum*, ed. W.H. Black (Roxburghe Club, 1840), pp. 28–31.

12. *Great Chronicle*, p. 207.

13. National Archives Duchy of Lancaster, DL 29/637/10360A, transcribed in R. Horrox & A.F. Sutton, 'Some Expenses of Richard Duke of Gloucester, 1475–7', *The Ricardian*, vi, no. 83 (1983), pp. 266–9.

14. Richard's books have been discussed in detail by A. F. Sutton & L. Visser-Fuchs in a series of articles in *The Ricardian*, vols. vii–ix, nos. 94–119 (1986–92), and subsequently in their *Richard III's Books: Ideals and Reality in the Life of a Medieval Prince* (1997). This summary is based mainly on their 'Richard III's Books Observed', ix, no. 120, pp. 374–88, & 'Richard III's Books: Ancestry and True Nobility', ix, no. 119 (1992).

15. J. Raine (ed.), *Testamenta Eboracensia*, Surtees Society (1864), vol. iii, pp. 238–41, quoted in Hammond & Sutton, *Road to Bosworth Field*, p. 76.

16. See R. Horrox, 'Richard III and Allhallows Barking by the Tower', *The Ricardian*, vi, no. 77 (1982), pp. 38–40, on which this paragraph is based. The Tudor antiquarian John Stow said that Richard also rebuilt the chapel, but there would have been little time for this between the granting of royal free chapel status in March 1485 and his death in August of the same year.

17. Hicks, *Richard III as Duke of Gloucester: A Study in Character*, pp. 24–5. Professor Hicks suggests that Richard later obtained a grant of any territory he could conquer in Scotland in the hope of solving his financial problems, but it is possible to argue that the cost of defending such an enclave would have outweighed the potential benefits. Berwick is a case in point.

18. Richard's letter is preserved in the Bibliothéque Nationale, Paris, and has been transcribed and translated in A.F. Sutton & L. Visser-Fuchs, 'Richard of Gloucester and *la grosse bombarde*', *The Ricardian*, x, no. 134 (1996), pp. 461–4, on which this paragraph is based. I am grateful to Dr Glenn Foard for confirming that there is no evidence that this weapon, or one like it, was used at the battle of Bosworth.

19. *Ingulph's Chronicle*, p. 481.

20. Mancini, *Usurpation*, p. 65.

21. M.K. Jones, 'Richard III as a Soldier', in *Richard III. A Medieval Kingship*, ed. J. Gillingham (1993), p. 100. The evidence is derived from the Stanley ballads.

6. 'The King is Dead', April–June 1483

1. Mancini, *Usurpation*, p. 59. *Three Books of Polydore Vergil's English History*, ed. H. Ellis (Camden Society, 1844), p. 172. Peter Stride has recently suggested that Edward may have suffered from type two diabetes, an illness unrecognised at the time. *Ricardian Register*, vol. 42, no. 3 (2011).

2. *Ingulph's Chronicle*, p. 486.

3. Mancini, *Usurpation*, p. 71.

4. *Ingulph's Chronicle*, p. 485.

5. The sources differ in detail – for example, Mancini says that Rivers and Grey were not allowed to leave their lodgings the next morning, while Croyland's version is that they were arrested near Stony Stratford – but the result was the same.

6. Mancini, *Usurpation*, p. 77.

7. *Ibid.*, p. 83.

8. *More's Richard III*, pp. 19–20.

9. Mancini, *Usurpation*, p. 83.

10. *York House Books*, ii, pp. 713–14. The letter to Lord Neville is preserved in *The Paston Letters*, vi, pp. 71–2.

11. Mancini, *Usurpation*, p. 91.

12. *More's Richard III*, p. 51.

13. Cecily herself may have been partly responsible for this story, since Mancini claims that when Edward told her he had secretly married Elizabeth Woodville she 'fell into such a frenzy, that … she asserted that Edward was not the offspring of her husband the Duke of York but was conceived in adultery'. However, it is hard to imagine a noble and pious lady like Cecily having a fling with a French archer, and more recent claims that her husband was away on campaign when Edward was conceived rest upon questionable estimates and the assumption that she herself remained at home.

14. This is explained fully in R.H. Hemholz, 'The Sons of Edward IV: A canonical assessment of the claim that they were illegitimate', in *Richard III: Loyalty, Lordship and Law*, ed. P.W. Hammond (1986).

15. Henry VIII had been of the opinion that he had never been legally and bindingly married to Catherine of Aragon (Mary's mother) or to Anne Boleyn (Elizabeth's mother), and their legitimacy was therefore as doubtful as Edward V's.

16. See M.A. Hicks, 'Richard Lord Latimer, Richard III and the Warwick Inheritance', *The Ricardian*, xii, no. 154 (2001).

17. *More's Richard III*, p. 45.

7. 'Long Live the King!' July 1483

1. This summary is based on A.F. Sutton & P. W. Hammond (eds.), *The Coronation of Richard III. The Extant Documents* (Gloucester, 1983). Full particulars of the precise ordering of the several processions and a complete list of participants can be found there.

2. *Great Chronicle*, p. 234.

3. Mancini, *Usurpation*, p. 93.

4. The substitute bodies were allegedly those of the gatekeeper at Berkeley, killed by Edward II as he escaped, and Richard II's chaplain Maudelyn. The St Albans annalist says that the melancholic Richard 'sank into such great sadness that he wished to destroy himself by fasting. He is said to have abstained from eating to such an extent that, the orifice of his stomach having been closed, when he later wished to satisfy nature by eating, upon the advice of his friends, he was unable to eat, his desire for food having been altogether shut off …'

5. This reconstruction is based upon the accounts of the Elizabethan writer John Stow and the French chronicler Thomas Basin together with an order from Richard dated 29 July instructing the Chancellor to appoint a commission to try unnamed men for an 'enterprise'. See R. Horrox, *Richard III. A Study in Service*, p. 149. Professor Hicks wonders, quite reasonably, why the London chronicles do not report either the rescue attempt or the executions, and why legal records make no mention of a trial. 'Unweaving the Web: The Plot of July 1483 against Richard III and its Wider Significance', *The Ricardian*, ix, no. 114 (1991), pp. 106–9.

6. These contemporary comments have been conveniently brought together by K. Dockray in *Richard III. A Source Book* (Stroud, 1997), pp. 76–9. The Ashmolean reference is from Kendall, *Richard III*, p. 439.

7. *Ibid.*, p. 78.

8. *More's Richard III*, p. 84.

9. These problems are discussed more fully by P.W Hammond & W.J White, 'The Sons of Edward IV: A Re-examination of the Evidence on their Deaths and on the Bones in Westminster Abbey' in *Richard III: Loyalty, Lordship and Law* (1986), pp. 104–47. See also Bill White's last comments in 'The Remains in the Urn – Who were they?', *Ricardian Bulletin*, Spring 2009, pp. 23–26.

10. L. Visser-Fuchs, 'What Niclas von Popplau really wrote about Richard III', *The Ricardian*, xi, no. 145 (1999), pp. 529–30.

8. Richard 'Crookback'?

1. W. Shakespeare, *The Third Part of King Henry VI*, Act 3, Scene 2. *More's Richard III*, pp. 5–6. Hanham, *Early Historians*, pp. 120–1.

2. See, for example, Dr Pamela Tudor-Craig, who is clear that the shoulder-line in Richard's portraits has been exaggerated after the original or originals were painted, but who still concludes that 'the chances are that he did have some malformation' (*National Portrait Gallery Exhibition*

Catalogue [1973], p. 80).

3. These paragraphs are based on the following articles: P.J. Accardo, 'Deformity and Character: Dr Little's Diagnosis of Richard III', *Journal of the American Medical Association*, ccxxxxiv (1980); E.W. Jones, 'Richard III's Disfigurement: A Medical Postscript', *Folklore*, lxxxxi (1980); P. Rhodes, 'The Physical Deformity of Richard III', *British Medical Journal*, no. 6103 (24–31 December, 1977); and D. Unwin, 'A Werish Withered Arm', *Diagnostica*, ix (1968).

4. See Prologue.

5. L. Visser-Fuchs, 'What Niclas von Popplau really wrote about Richard III', p. 529. Von Popplau says elsewhere that Richard also gave him a 'dead boar', and Dr Visser-Fuchs wonders if this was to eat (perhaps at the farewell party he gave at his inn), or a jocular reference to the King's White Boar badge which very possibly hung from the gold collar.

6. Vergil (ed. Ellis), p. 227.

7. Hammond & Sutton, *Road to Bosworth Field*, pp. 191–3.

8. See, for example, Polydore Vergil, who says that Richard 'now repented of his evil deeds [and] began afterward to take on hand a certain new form of life, and to give the show and countenance of a good man, whereby he might be accounted more righteous, more mild, better affected to the commonalty, and more liberal especially toward the poor; and so first might merit pardon for his offences at God's hand'. Vergil, ed. Ellis, p. 192.

9. A. Fraser, *Cromwell. Our Chief of Men* (1993), p. 338.

10. J. Hughes, *The Religious Life of Richard III* (1997), p. 42.

11. L. Visser-Fuchs, 'What Niclas von Popplau really wrote about Richard III', p. 528.

12. Vergil (ed. Ellis), pp. 184–5.

13. *B.L. Harleian MSS 433*, i, p. 3.

14. N. H. Nicolas, *Testamenta Vetusta*, ii (1826), pp. 422–3.

15. *Ingulph's Chronicle*, pp. 496–7.

16. *More's Richard III*, pp. 54–5.

17. *Calendar of the Patent Rolls, Edward IV – Edward V – Richard III 1476–1485* (1901), p. 371

18. *Great Chronicle*, p. 233.

19. *More's Richard III*, pp. 53–4.

20. *B.L. Harleian MSS 433*, iii, p. 259.

9. Conspiracy & Rebellion, July–November 1483

1. Richard's journey has been reconstructed by Rhoda Edwards, *The Itinerary of King Richard III 1483–1485* (1983).

2. *B.L. Harleian MSS 433*, ii, p. 7. Hanham, *Early Historians*, p. 122. *York House Books*, ii, p. 713.

3. Hammond & Sutton, *Road to Bosworth Field*, p. 125.

4. *B.L. Harleian MSS 433*, iii, pp. 24–5.

5. Richard's exchange of letters with King Louis has been translated in Hammond & Sutton, *Road to Bosworth Field*, pp. 128–9.

6. *B.L. Harleian MSS 433*, iii, pp. 47–8. Langton's comment is in *Christchurch Letters*, p. 46.

7. Quoted in G. Waters, 'Richard III and Ireland', *The Ricardian*, vi, no. 87 (1984), p. 404, on which this paragraph is based.

8. The letters to Ireland have been printed in *B.L. Harleian MSS 433*, iii, pp. 36 & pp 108–9. Rather amusingly, Richard asked Desmond not to wear traditional Irish clothing (perhaps because he feared that he was becoming too 'native') and sent him English 'gowns, doublets, hose and bonnets'. He promised to send more 'as the case or change of the said fashion shall require'.

9. These details are taken from *York Records*, ed. Davies, pp. 159–67, and from p. 48 of the Bedern Statute Book preserved in York Minster Library and transcribed in Hammond & Sutton, *Road to Bosworth Field*, pp. 140–1.

10. Vergil (ed. Ellis), p. 190. At some point in the day Edward was knighted, and Richard also bestowed the accolade on his nephew Edward, Earl of Warwick, his bastard son John of Gloucester, and the Spanish ambassador, Galfridus de Sasiola, placing a gold collar about the

latter's neck. See A.C. Reeves, 'King Richard III at York in Late Summer 1483', *The Ricardian*, xii, no. 159 (2002).

11. Suggested by Rosemary Horrox in *Richard III. A Study in Service*, pp. 165–6.

12. Vergil (ed. Ellis), p. 204.

13. *Ingulph's Chronicle*, p. 491.

14. Hammond & Sutton, *Road to Bosworth Field*, p. 145.

15. *The Stonor Letters and Papers 1290–1483*, ed. C.L. Kingsford, 2 vols. (Camden Society, 1919), ii, pp. 162–3.

10. Regaining the Initiative, 1484

1. C. Richmond, 'The Nobility and the Coronation of Richard III', *The Ricardian*, xii, no. 148 (2000), pp. 653–9. The Ricardian xi, no. 147 (1999), pp. 590–615.

2. *Ingulph's Chronicle*, p. 496.

3. *The Paston Letters*, iii, p. 250.

4. These paragraphs are based on A.J. Pollard in 'North, South and Richard III'. *The Ricardian*, v, no. 74 (1981), p. 384, and B.M. Cron, 'Margaret of Anjou and the Lancastrian March on London 1461'. *The Ricardian* xi, no. 147 (1999), pp. 590–615.

5. *Ingulph's Chronicle*, pp. 422–3. These are the words of the monastery's own scribe, not those of the 'Yorkist civil servant' who contributed the knowledgeable 'continuation'.

6. *Ibid.*, p. 497.

7. *B.L. Harleian MSS 433*, iii, pp. 116–18.

8. *Ibid.*, p. 120.

9. *Ingulph's Chronicle*, p. 498.

10. Francis Bacon. *The History of the Reign of King Henry the Seventh*, ed. R. Lockyer (1971), p. 38.

11. H.G. Hanbury, 'The Legislation of Richard III', *American Journal of Legal History*, vi (1962), p. 104, on which these paragraphs are based.

12. *Ibid.*, p. 108.

13. *Ibid.*, p. 109.

14. *B.L. Harleian MSS 433*, iii, pp. 107 & 124.

15. For a fuller discussion of the problem see H. Klieneke, 'Richard III and the Court of Requests', *The Ricardian*, xvii (2007), pp. 22–32, on which this part of the paragraph is based.

11. Cultivating the Bishops, 1484

1. See, for example, J. Ashdown Hill, *Richard III's 'Beloved Cousyn'. John Howard and the House of York* (Stroud, 2009); M.A. Hicks, 'Dynastic Change and Northern Society: the career of the Fourth Earl of Northumberland 1470–89', *Northern History*, 14 (1978), and M. Jones, 'Richard III and the Stanleys' in *Richard III and the North*, ed. R. Horrox (1986).

2. This section is based on entries in the *Oxford Dictionary of National Biography*, ed. H.C.G. Matthew & B. Harrison, 60 vols. (Oxford, 2004), by R.B. Dobson (Bell), L. Clark (Bourchier), V. Davis (Waynflete), C. Harper-Bill (Morton), R.C.E. Hayes (Goldwell, Hales), M. Hicks (Stillington), R. Horrox (Courtenay, Rotherham), J. Hughes (Audley), A.J. Pollard (Dudley, Shirwood), R. K Rose (Redman), A Rhydderch (Milling), R.J. Schoeck (Alcock, Story), J.A.F Thomson (Russell, Woodville), and D.P. Wright (Langton). Particulars of the four bishops not included in the *Dictionary* (Edenham, Kempe, Marshall, and Pavy) may be found in A.B. Emden, *A Biographical Register of the University of Oxford to 1500*, 3 vols. (Oxford, 1959).

3. On 22 September he issued letters concerning the appropriation of a benefice from Buckingham's manor of Thornbury, and it seems likely that he had been committed to the Duke's custody. His temporalities were seized next day.

4. In May 1483 he was commissioned to deliver Richard's niece, Anne of Exeter, to the custody of the Duke of Buckingham, and was present when Richard gave the Great Seal to John Russell on 27 June.

5. Mancini, *Usurpation*, p. 89. *Ingulph's Chronicle*, p. 488.

6. *B.L. Harleian MSS 433*, i, p. 103 & ii, pp. 47. His favourite nephew, Sir Thomas Bourchier, had joined Buckingham's Rebellion, and this was probably an added source of friction between them.

7. A.J. Pollard, writing in the *Oxford DNB*.

8. *B.L. Harleian MSS 433*, iii, p. 139.

9. T. Rymer, *Foedera*, xii, p. 204, quoted in Hammond & Sutton, *Road to Bosworth Field*, pp. 146–7.

10. Mancini, *Usurpation*, p. 77.

11. *P.R.O.M.E.*, 1484 Parliament, 240.

12. *The Paston Letters*, vi, pp. 81–2.

13. A.J. Pollard, *Oxford DNB*.

14. *York House Books*, ii, p. 737. *Materials for a History of the Reign of Henry VII*, ed. W. Campbell, 2 vols. (1873–7), i, pp. 172–3.

15. The correspondence between the King and the masters has been printed in *Epistolae Academicae Oxon.*, ed. H Anstey, 2 vols. (Oxford, 1898), ii, pp. 513–23. The Universities also interceded for Archbishop Rotherham and Bishop Morton when they fell foul of Richard – see A.F. Sutton & L. Visser-Fuchs, 'Richard III, the Universities of Oxford and Cambridge, and Two Turbulent Priests', *The Ricardian*, xix (2009), pp. 95–109.

12. The Two Elizabeths, February–March 1485

1. *Ingulph's Chronicle*, p. 496.

2. *B.L. Harleian MSS 433*, iii, p. 190. The five girls were to surrender to Richard, but what was to become of Elizabeth herself is not specified. Her annuity was to be paid to John Nesfield, who had been responsible for guarding the sanctuary, and it seems likely that Nesfield continued to supervise her at one of his homes.

3. Ross, *Richard III*, p. 101.

4. *Ingulph's Chronicle*, p. 498. Nicholas Pronay and John Cox translate this passage as 'vain exchanges of clothing between Queen Anne and Lady Elizabeth ... who were alike in complexion and figure'. *The Croyland Chronicle Continuations*, p. 175.

5. *Ibid.*, p. 499.

6. Sir George Buck, *The History of the Reign of Richard the Third* (1619), ed. A.N. Kincaid (Gloucester, 1979), p. 191.

7. *Ingulph's Chronicle*, p. 499.

8. Vergil (ed. Ellis), p. 215.

9. It is worth noting that the Duke later became King of Portugal (as Manuel I, or 'The Fortunate'), and Elizabeth of York would have found herself queen of that country if her uncle's plans had come to fruition.

10. No opinion is offered as to the likely veracity of this story, of which the earliest account extant dates from 1621. Joanna is said by one source to have similarly anticipated the death of Charles VIII of France when he wanted to marry her, although he did not, in fact, die until years later. She was canonised as a saint in 1693.

11. J. Ashdown-Hill, *The Last Days of Richard III* (Stroud, 2010), pp. 32–3. Anne Crawford, *The Yorkists* (2007), p. 146, and Annette Carson, *Richard III. The Maligned King* (Stroud, 2008), p. 259, take a similar view.

12. Buck, *Richard III*, p. 191. *Ingulph's Chronicle*, p. 499.

13. D.M. Gomes dos Santos, *O Mosteiro de Jesus de Aveiro*, 3 vols. (Lisbon, 1963), i, p. 92 (from extracts translated by B. Williams in the Richard III Society Barton Library).

13. The Gathering Storm, April–June 1485

1. Ross, *Richard III*, p. 201. Richard's diplomacy has been much criticised – see, for example, Ross's comments on p. 203 and James Gairdner's *Letters and Papers Illustrative of the Reigns of Richard III and Henry VII*, 2 vols (1861–3), ii, pp. xiv–xv, but King Edward had been disappointed by both Brittany and Burgundy, and his success in France would not have been achieved without the threat of military force.

2. *B.L. Harleian MSS 433*, ii, pp. 44, 45, 48–9, 63, 69, 75–7, 90.

3. *Ingulph's Chronicle*, p. 496.

4. *B.L. Harleian MSS 433*, ii, p. 182, iii, pp. 125–6.

5. *Letters of the Kings of England*, ed. J.O. Halliwell, 2 vols. (1846), i, pp. 161–2.

6. Printed in W Hutton, *The Battle of Bosworth Field*, second edition with additions by J. Nichols (1813), pp. 190–1.

7. *B.L. Harleian MSS 433*, iii, pp. 124–5.

8. *York House Books*, i, pp. 359–60.

9. *The Paston Letters*, vi, p. 82.

10. R. Fabyan, *The New Chronicles of England and France*, ed. H. Ellis (1811), p. 672.

11. Vergil (ed. Ellis), p. 208.

12. *Ibid.*, pp. 215–16.

13. Historical Manuscripts Commission, 12th Report, Rutland Manuscripts, i (1888), pp. 2–6.

14. Hammond & Sutton, *Road to Bosworth Field*, pp. 212–13.

14. Bosworth Field, August 1485

1. *The Memoirs of Philip de Commines*, ed. A. R. Scoble, 2 vols. (1856), ii, p. 64.

2. *The Paston Letters*, vi, p. 85. The Duke of Norfolk was informed that the King would have marched on the 15th, but delayed because it was 'Our Lady Day', the feast of Assumption of Our Lady.

3. Vergil (ed. Ellis), p. 221.

4. *Ingulph's Chronicle*, p. 503. Polydore Vergil also reports that Richard had a bad dream which he attributes to a guilty conscience.

5. Warnicke, 'Lord Morley's Statements about Richard III', pp. 176–7.

6. Vergil (ed. Ellis), p. 223.

7. *Ibid.*, pp. 222–4.

8. *Ingulph's Chronicle*, p. 503.

9. Vergil (ed. Ellis), p. 226.

10. E.M. Nokes & G. Wheeler, 'A Spanish Account of the Battle of Bosworth', *The Ricardian*, no. 36 (1972), p. 2.

11. *Ibid.*

12. *Ingulph's Chronicle*, p. 504.

13. Vergil (ed. Ellis), p. 224.

14. R. Vaughan, *Valois Burgundy* (1973), p. 220. Michael Jones has suggested that Henry's army included a strong force of Continental pikemen and that Richard was wholly unprepared to deal with them (*Bosworth 1485: Psychology of a Battle* [2002]), but see L. Visser-Fuchs, 'Phantom Bastardy and Ghostly Pikemen', *The Ricardian*, xiv (2004), pp. 117–8.

15. Vergil (ed. Ellis), p. 223.

16. *Ibid.*, pp. 223–4.

17. *Ingulph's Chronicle*, p. 503.

18. Kendall, *Richard III*, p. 396. Northumberland had supported Richard's seizure of power, even presiding over the execution of Earl Rivers and the others arrested at Stony Stratford, but he had probably been disappointed by his subsequent failure to secure a free hand in the north.

15. Legacy & Legend

1. *B.L. Harleian MSS 433*, ii, p. 49.

2. Edward Halle, *The Union of the Two Noble Families of Lancaster and York* (1550, reprinted Menston 1970), 'The xvii year of King Henry the VIII', fol. cxl.

3. *Letters and Papers, Foreign and Domestic, of the Reign of Henry VIII 1509–47*, ed. J.S. Brewer, J. Gairdner, & R.H. Brodie, 21 vols. (1862–1910), i, pp 1054 & 1260, iv, p. 52.

4. *Ingulph's Chronicle*, p. 497.

5. This is the distance from Pembroke, near to where Henry landed, to Beskwood, just north of Nottingham, where Richard was then staying. Henry arrived on 7 August, and Richard knew this when he wrote to Henry Vernon on the 11th. O.D. Harris, 'The Transmission of the News of the Tudor Landing', *The Ricardian*, iv, no. 55 (1976), p. 10. Harris suggests that beacons may also have played a significant part.

6. *B.L. Harleian MSS 433*, iii, pp. 118–20.

7. R. Baker, *A Chronicle of the Kings of England* (1684, first published 1625), p. 235.

8. J. Nichols, *The History and Antiquities of the County of Leicester*, 4 vols. (1795–1811), iv, p. 553.

9. W. Burton, *The Description of Leicester Shire* (1622), p. 163. This section is based on my article 'King Richard's Grave in Leicester', *Transactions of the Leicestershire Archaeological and Historical Society*, lx (1986), pp. 21-4.

10. *The Itinerary of John Leland*, ed. L. Toulmin-Smith, 5 vols. (1906-10), i, p. 15.

11. C. Wren, *Parentalia, or Memoirs of the Family of the Wrens* (1750), p. 144.

12. J. Speed, *The Historie of Great Britaine* (1611), p. 725. Speed may, however, have been looking in the ruins of the Black rather than the Grey Friars.

13. Correspondence between S.H. Skillington, secretary of the Leicestershire Archaeological and Historical Society, and S. Saxon Barton, founder of the Richard III Society, in October 1935. I am indebted to Lorraine Pickering for this reference. There was heavy fighting in the vicinity in 1645.

14. Speed, *Historie*, p. 725.

15. *The Diary of John Evelyn*, ed. E.S. de Beer, 6 vols. (Oxford, 1955), iii, p. 122.

16. *The Journeys of Celia Fiennes*, ed. C. Morris (1947), p. 162. No 'Greyhound' is known to have existed in Leicester at this period.

17. Nichols, *History of Leicester*, i., p. 298.

18. J. Throsby, *The History and Antiquities of the Ancient Town of Leicester* (Leicester, 1791), p. 291, note b. Throsby noted in another part of his *History* that he remembered 'being shown some fragments of it about the year *1760*' (my italics), p. 64.

19. Hutton, *Bosworth Field*, p. 143.

20. Throsby, *Leicester*, p. 291.

21. The story is told in Charles Billson's *Medieval Leicester* (Leicester, 1920), pp. 187-99.

22. Quoted in A.F. Sutton & L. Visser-Fuchs, 'The Prophecy of G', *The Ricardian*, viii, no. 110 (1990). There is no independent evidence to support Thomas More's story that Sir Thomas Vaughan identified the 'G' as Gloucester before he was executed at Pontefract with Earl Rivers, but Lesley Coote and Tim Thornton are prepared to accept that the prophecy *could* have existed before Richard seized power. 'Richard, Son of Richard: Richard III and Political Prophecy', *Historical Research*, lxxiii, no. 182 (October, 2000).

23. *Richard III*, Act 1, Scene 3.

24. For the Harleian letter see *B.L. Harleian MSS 433*, ii, p. 42, and for the 1483-4 Great Wardrobe accounts *The Coronation of Richard III*, pp. 176-8.

25. Quoted in A.F. Sutton, 'Richard III as a Fop': A Foolish Myth', *The Ricardian*, xviii (2008), p. 62, on which this paragraph is based.

26. In the *National Portrait Gallery Exhibition Catalogue* (1973), pp. 26-7, 96-7.

27. *Richard III. England's Black Legend*, pp. 178-9. Seward remarks that 'A parricide was a fitting intercessor for an infanticide, let alone a man who had murdered another saint'.

28. See & A.F. Sutton & L Visser-Fuchs, 'Richard III and St Julian: A New Myth', *The Ricardian*, viii, no. 106 (1989), on which this paragraph is based.

16. Epilogue: The Discovery of King Richard's Grave

1. C. Wardle, 'Archaeological Excavations at Grey Friars, Leicester', *Ricardian Bulletin*, Summer 2008, pp. 34-37.

2. In Chapter 8 ('Richard "Crookback"?') I used the term kyphoscoloisis to allow for the possibility of either or both conditions, scoliosis (a sideward curvature of the spine) and kyphosis (an outward curvature) being present. But this individual suffered only from scoliosis. It is also worth noting that the bones displayed no evidence of old injuries which had healed, and there was nothing that would explain the curious appearance of the right hand in the 'standard' portrait of King Richard (see plate 3).

3. Katherine bore John of Gaunt four children, while Joan presented her husband the Earl of Westmoreland with no fewer than thirteen.

4. J. Ashdown-Hill, 'Alive and Well in Canada – The Mitochondrial DNA of Richard III', *The Ricardian*, xvi (2006), pp. 1-14.

5. *The Times*, 13 September 2012, p. 5. M. Bennett, *The Battle of Bosworth* (Gloucester, 1985), p. 161.

6. University of Leicester Press Pack, 4 February 2013.

BIBLIOGRAPHY

The place of publication is London unless otherwise stated. The dates given are those of the editions used.

Books

Attreed, L.C. (ed.), *York House Books 1461–1490*, 2 vols. (Stroud, 1991).

Bacon, Francis, *The History of the Reign of King Henry the Seventh*, ed. R. Lockyer (1971).

Baker, R., *A Chronicle of the Kings of England* (1684, first published 1625).

Barnard, F.P., *Edward IV's French Expedition of 1475. The Leaders and their Badges* (Gloucester, 1975).

Black, W.H. (ed.), 'Narrative of the Marriage of Richard Duke of York with Anne of Norfolk: the Matrimonial Feast and the Grand Jousting', *Illustrations of Ancient State and Chivalry from Manuscripts Preserved in the Ashmolean Museum* (Roxburghe Club, 1840).

Brewer, J.S., J. Gairdner, & R.H. Brodie (eds.), *Letters and Papers, Foreign and Domestic, of the Reign of Henry VIII 1509–47*, 21 vols. (1862–1910).

Bruce, J. (ed.), *Historie of the Arrivall of Edward IV. in England and the Finall Recoverye of his Kingdomes from Henry VI. A.D. M.CCCC.LXXI* (Camden Society, 1838).

Buck, Sir George, *The History of the Reign of Richard the Third* (1619), ed. A.N. Kincaid (Gloucester, 1979).

Burton, W., *The Description of Leicester Shire* (1622).

Calendar of the Patent Rolls, Edward IV, 1467–1477 (1900).

Calendar of the Patent Rolls, Edward IV – Edward V – Richard III 1476–1485 (1901).

Campbell, W. (ed.), *Materials for a History of the Reign of Henry VII*, 2 vols. (1873–7),

Carson, A., *Richard III. The Maligned King* (Stroud, 2008).

Davies, J.S. (ed.), *An English Chronicle of the Reigns of Richard II, Henry IV, Henry V, and Henry VI written before the year 1470*, (Camden Society, 1856).

Davies, R. (ed.), *Extracts from the Municipal Records of the City of York during the reigns of Edward, IV, Edward V and Richard III* (1843).

Dockray, K. (ed.), *Richard III. A Source Book* (Stroud, 1997).

Ellis, H. (ed.), *Original Letters Illustrative of English History*, 2nd series, vol. 1 (1827).

____, *Three Books of Polydore Vergil's English History* (Camden Society, 1844).

Emden, A.B., *A Biographical Register of the University of Oxford to 1500*, 3 vols. (Oxford, 1959).

Evelyn, John, *The Diary of John Evelyn*, ed. E.S. de Beer, 6 vols. (Oxford, 1955).

Fabyan, Robert, *The New Chronicles of England and France*, ed. H. Ellis (1811).

Fiennes, Celia, *The Journeys of Celia Fiennes*, ed. C. Morris (1947).

Gairdner, J. (ed.), *The Paston Letters 1422–1509*, 6 vols. (1904).

Gillingham, J., *The Wars of the Roses* (1981).

_____ (ed.), *Richard III. A Medieval Kingship* (1993).

Griffiths, R.A., & J. Sherborne (eds.), *Kings and Nobles in the Later Middle Ages* (1986).

Halle, Edward, *The Union of the Two Noble Families of Lancaster and York* (1550, reprinted Menston 1970).

Halliwell, J.O. (ed.), *Letters of the Kings of England*, 2 vols. (1846).

Hammond, P.W., *Edward of Middleham, Prince of Wales* (Cliftonville, 1973).

_____, *Richard III and the Bosworth Campaign* (Barnsley, 2010).

_____ (ed.), *Richard III: Loyalty, Lordship and Law* (1986).

_____ & A.F. Sutton, *Richard III. The Road to Bosworth Field* (1985).

Hanham, A., *Richard III and his Early Historians 1483–1485* (Oxford, 1975).

Hicks, M., *Richard III* (Stroud, 2000).

Hinds, A.B. (ed.), *Calendar of State Papers and Manuscripts Existing in the Archives and Collections of Milan, I, 1385–1618* (1913).

Hipshon, D., *Richard III* (2011).

Historical Manuscripts Commission, 12th Report, Rutland Manuscripts, i (1888).

_____, 78. *Report on the Manuscripts of the late R.R. Hastings*, i (1928).

Horrox, R. *Richard III. A Study in Service* (Cambridge, 1999).

_____ (ed.), *Richard III and the North* (1986).

Horrox, R., & P.W. Hammond, *British Library Harleian Manuscript 433*, 4 vols. (1979–83).

Hughes, J., *The Religious Life of Richard III* (1997).

Hutton, W., *The Battle of Bosworth Field*, second edition with additions by J. Nichols (1813).

Jones, M. (trans.), *Philippe de Commynes. Memoirs* (Harmondsworth, 1972).

Kendall, P.M., *Richard III* (Folio Society, 2005).

Kingsford, C.L. (ed.), *The Stonor Letters and Papers 1290–1483*, 2 vols. (Camden Society, 1919).

Leland, J., *De Rebus Britannicis Collectanea*, ed. T. Hearne, 6 vols. (Oxford, 1770).

_____, *The Itinerary of John Leland*, ed. L. Toulmin-Smith, 5 vols. (1906–10).

Lumby, J.R. (ed.), *More's History of King Richard III* (Cambridge, 1883).

McFarlane, K.B. *The Nobility of Later Medieval England* (Oxford, 1973).

Mancini, Dominic, *The Usurpation of Richard III*, ed. C.A.J. Armstrong (Gloucester, 1984).

Matthew H.C.G., & B. Harrison (eds.), *Oxford Dictionary of National Biography*, 60 vols. (Oxford, 2004).

Nichols, J.G. (ed.), *Chronicle of the Rebellion in Lincolnshire, in 1470*, Camden Miscellany, vol. 1 (1847).

Nicolas, N.H., *Testamenta Vetusta* (1826).

Petre, J. (ed.), *Richard III. Crown and People* (1985).

Pollard, A.J., *Richard III and the Princes in the Tower* (Stroud, 1991).

_____, *The Middleham Connection. Richard III and Richmondshire 1471–1485* (Middleham, 1983).

Pronay, N., & J. Cox (eds.), *The Crowland Coronicle Continuations 1459–1486* (1986).

Raine, A. (ed.), *York Civic Records*, vol. 1. (Yorkshire Archaeological Society Record Series, lxxxxviii (1939).

Riley, H.T. (ed.), *Ingulph's Chronicle of the Abbey of Croyland* (1854).

Ross, C., *Edward IV* (1974).

____, *Richard III* (1981).

Scoble, A.R. (ed.), *The Memoirs of Philip de Commines*, 2 vols. (1856).

Sheppard, J.B. (ed.), *Christ Church Letters* (Camden Society, 1877).

Seward, D. *Richard III. England's Black Legend* (1983).

Speed, J., *The Historie of Great Britaine* (1611).

Sutton, A.F., & P.W. Hammond, *The Coronation of Richard III. The Extant Documents* (Gloucester, 1983).

Sutton, A.F. & L. Visser-Fuchs, *The Hours of Richard III* (1990).

____, *The Reburial of Richard Duke of York 21–30 July 1476* (1996).

____, *Richard III's Books: Ideals and Reality in the Life of a Medieval Prince* (1997).

Thomas A.H. & I.D. Thornley (eds.), *The Great Chronicle of London* (Gloucester, 1983).

Throsby, J., *The History and Antiquities of the Ancient Town of Leicester* (Leicester, 1791).

Tudor-Craig, P., *National Portrait Gallery Exhibition Catalogue*, 1973.

Warkworth, John, *A Chronicle of the First Thirteen Years of King Edward the Fourth*, ed. J.O. Halliwell (Camden Society, 1839).

Waurin, Jehan de, *Recueil des Croniques et Anchiennes Istories de la Grant Bretaigne, a present nomme Engleterre*, ed. W. & E L.C.P. Hardy, 5 vols. (Rolls Series, 1864–91).

Wilkinson, J., *Richard, The Young King To Be* (Stroud, 2009).

Wren, C., *Parentalia, or Memoirs of the Family of the Wrens* (1750).

Articles and Booklets

Accardo, P.J., 'Deformity and Character: Dr Little's Diagnosis of Richard III', *Journal of the American Medical Association*, ccxxxxiv (1980).

Baldwin, D., 'King Richard's Grave in Leicester', *Transactions of the Leicestershire Archaeological and Historical Society*, lx (1986).

Coote, L., and Thornton, T., 'Richard, son of Richard: Richard III and Political Prophecy', *Historical Research*, lxxiii, no. 182 (October, 2000).

Davies, C.S.L., 'Bishop John Morton, the Holy See and the Accession of Henry VII', *English Historical Review*, vol. 112, no. 403 (January, 1987).

Davis, V. 'William Waynflete and the Wars of the Roses'. *Southern History*, vol. 11 (1989).

Dobson, B., 'Richard Bell, prior of Durham (1464–78) and bishop of Carlisle (1478–95)', *Transactions of the Cumberland and Westmoreland Antiquarian and Archaeological Society*, new series 65, pp. 182–221.

Dos Santos, D.M.G., *O Mosteiro de Jesus de Aveiro* (1963). Extracts translated by B. Williams.

Edwards, R., *The Itinerary of King Richard III 1483–1485* (1983).

Hanbury, H.G., 'The Legislation of Richard III', *American Journal of Legal History*, vi (1962).

Hicks, M.A., 'Descent, Partition and Extinction: the Warwick Inheritance', *Bulletin of the Institute of Historical Research*, lii, no. 126 (1979).

___, 'The Last Days of Elizabeth Countess of Oxford', *English Historical Review*, ciii (1988).

___, *Richard III as Duke of Gloucester: A Study in Character*, Borthwick Paper no. 70 (1986).

Jones, E.W., 'Richard III's Disfigurement: A Medical Postscript', *Folklore*, lxxxxi (1980).

Kelly, H.A., 'Canonical Implications of Richard III's Plan to Marry his Niece', *Traditio*, xxiii (1967).

Laynesmith, J., 'The King's Mother', *History Today* (March, 2006).

Mitchell, D., *Guide of Ricardian Yorkshire* (no date).

Myers, A.R., 'The Character of Richard III', *History Today* (August, 1954).

Pollard, A.J., 'Richard III and Richmondshire 1471–1485' (Text of public lecture given at York University, June 1983).

___, 'The Tyranny of Richard III', *Journal of Medieval History*, iii, no. 2 (1977).

Rhodes, P., 'The Physical Deformity of Richard III', *British Medical Journal*, no. 6103 (24–31 December, 1977).

Thomson, J.A.F., 'Bishop Lionel Woodville and Richard III', *Bulletin of the Institute of Historical Research*, lix (1986).

Unwin, David, 'A Werish Withered Arm', *Diagnostica*, ix (1968).

Visser-Fuchs, L., 'Edward IV's "memoir on paper" to Charles, Duke of Burgundy: the so-called "Short Version of the Arrivall"', *Nottingham Medieval Studies*, xxxvi (1992).

Warnicke, R.M., The Physical Deformities of Anne Boleyn and Richard III: Myth and Reality', *Parergon*, iv (1986).

___, 'Lord Morley's Statements about Richard III', *Albion*, xiv (1983).

Articles published in *The Ricardian*, the journal of the Richard III Society, edited by Anne F. Sutton

Ashdown-Hill, J., 'Walsingham in 1469: The Pilgrimage of Edward IV and Richard, Duke of Gloucester', xi, no. 136 (1997).

Barnfield, M., 'Diriment Impediments, Dispensations and Divorce: Richard III and Matrimony', xvii (2007).

Bolden, E.J., 'Richard III: Central Government and Administration', xii, no. 149 (2000).

Britnell, R., 'Richard, Duke of Gloucester and the Death of Thomas Fauconberg', x, no. 128 (1995).

Carlin, M., 'Sir John Fastolf's Place, Southwark: The Home of the Duke of York's Family 1460', v, no. 72 (1981).

Cron, B.M., 'Margaret of Anjou and the Lancastrian March on London, 1461', xi, no. 147 (1999).

Cunningham, S., '"More through fear than love". The Herefordshire Gentry, the Alien Subsidy of 1483 and Regional Responses to Richard III's Usurpation', xiii (2003).

Gribbin, J.A., 'Richard Redman: The Yorkist Years (*c.* 1461–88)', xii, no. 155 (2001).

Hammond, P.W., 'The Illegitimate Children of Richard III', v, no. 66 (1979).

Harris, O.D., 'The Transmission of the News of the Tudor Landing', iv, no 55 (1976).

Hepburn, F. 'Some Posthumous Representations of Richard III', vi, no. 82 (1983).

Hicks, M., 'Unweaving the Web: The Plot of July 1483 against Richard III and its Wider Significance', ix, no. 114 (1991).

___, 'One Prince or Two? The Family of Richard III', ix, no. 122 (1993).

___, 'Richard Lord Latimer, Richard III and the Warwick Inheritance', xii, no. 154 (2001).

____, 'Richard III, the Great Landowners, and the Results of the Wars of the Roses', xiii (2003).

Horrox, R., 'Richard III and Allhallows Barking by the Tower', vi, no. 77 (1982).

____, 'Preparations for Edward IV's Return from Exile', vi, no. 79 (1982)

____, 'Richard III and London', vi, no. 85 (1984).

____ & A.F. Sutton, 'Some Expenses of Richard Duke of Gloucester 1475–7', vi, no. 83 (1983).

Jones, M.K., 'Richard, Duke of Gloucester and the Scropes of Masham', x, no. 134 (1996).

Klieneke, H., 'Alice Martyn, Widow of London: An Episode from Richard's Youth' xiv (2004).

____, 'Richard III and the Court of Requests', xvii (2007).

Nokes, E.M. & G. Wheeler, 'A Spanish Account of the Battle of Bosworth', no. 36 (1972).

Petre, J., 'The Nevills of Brancepeth and Raby 1425–1499', v, no. 75 (1981) & vi, no. 76 (1982).

Pollard, A.J., 'North, South and Richard III', v, no. 74 (1981).

Reeves, A.C., 'King Richard III at York in Late Summer 1483', xii, no. 159 (2002).

Richmond, C., 'The Nobility and the Coronation of Richard III', xii, no. 148 (2000).

Ross, C., 'Some "Servants and Lovers" of Richard in his Youth', iv, no. 55 (1976).

Ross, J., 'Richard, Duke of Gloucester and the De Vere Estates', xv (2005).

Sutton, A.F., 'The Return to England of Richard of Gloucester after his First Exile', iii, no. 50 (1975).

____, '*And to be delivered to the Lord Richard Duke of Gloucester, the other brother* …', viii, no. 100 (1988).

____, 'Richard III as a Fop: A Foolish Myth', vxiii (2008).

____ & L. Visser-Fuchs, 'Richard III and St Julian: A New Myth', viii, no. 106 (1989).

____, 'Richard III's Books: Ancestry and True Nobility' ix, no. 119 (1992).

____, 'Richard III's Books Observed', ix, no. 120 (1993).

____, 'The Prophecy of G', viii, no. 110 (1990).

____, '*Richard Liveth Yet*: An Old Myth', ix, no. 117 (1992).

____, 'Richard of Gloucester and *la grosse bombarde*', x, no. 134 (1996).

____, 'Richard III, the Universities of Oxford and Cambridge, and Two Turbulent Priests', xix (2009).

Visser-Fuchs, L., 'Richard in Holland 1461', vi, no. 81 (1983).

____, 'Richard in Holland 1471–2', vi, no. 82 (1983).

____, 'Richard was Late', xi, no. 147 (1999).

____, 'What Niclas von Popplau really wrote about Richard III', xi, no. 145 (1999).

Waters, G., 'Richard III and Ireland', vi, no 87 (1984).

____, 'Richard III, Wales and the Charter to Llandovery', vii, no. 89 (1985).

White, W.J., 'The Death and Burial of Henry VI., A Review of the Facts and Theories', vi, nos. 78 & 79 (1982).

Williams, B., 'Richard III and the House of Dudley', viii, no. 108 (1990).

____, 'Richard III's Other Palatinate: John Shirwood, Bishop of Durham', ix, no. 115 (1991).

____, 'The Portuguese Connection and the Significance of "the Holy Princess"', vi, no. 80 (1983). Also communication and reply, nos. 81 & 82.

LIST OF ILLUSTRATIONS

All colour photographs are from the author's collection unless otherwise stated. The black and white pictures have been sourced from the following except where noted: *The Paston Letters*, ed. A Ramsay (1849), *The Rous Roll*, ed. W. Courthope (1859), J. Thompson, *Leicester Castle* (1859), *Christ Church Letters*, ed. J.B. Sheppard (1877), A.O. Legge, *The Unpopular King* (1885), W.H.H. Rogers, *The Strife of the Roses* and *Days of the Tudors in the West* (1890), C. Billson, *Medieval Leicester* (1920), and G. Brooks, *The Dukes of York* (1927).

1. © David Baldwin.
2. © David Baldwin.
3. © Ripon Cathedral.
4. © David Baldwin.
5. © David Baldwin.
6. © David Baldwin.
7. © Josephine Wilkinson and the Amberley Archive.
8. © G. Wheeler.
9. © David Baldwin.
10. © David Baldwin.
11. © Stephen Porter and the Amberley Archive.
12. © David Baldwin.
13. © David Baldwin.
14. © David Baldwin.
15. © David Baldwin.
16. © David Baldwin.
17. © Jonathan Reeve JR1561folio6 14001450.
18. © David Baldwin.
19. © David Baldwin.
20. © David Baldwin.
21. © David Baldwin.
22. © David Baldwin.
23. © David Baldwin.
24. © David Baldwin.
25. © David Baldwin.
26. © David Baldwin.
27. © David Baldwin.
28. © David Baldwin.
29. © David Baldwin.
30. © David Baldwin.
31. © David Baldwin.
32. © David Baldwin.
33. © David Baldwin.
34. © David Baldwin.
35. © David Baldwin.
36. © David Baldwin.
37. © Jonathan Reeve JR1569b13fp718 14501500.
38. © Jonathan Reeve JR1572b13p721 14501500.
39. © David Baldwin.
40. © David Baldwin.
41. © David Baldwin.
42. © G. Wheeler.
43. © David Baldwin.
44. © David Baldwin.
45. © Ripon Cathedral.
46. © Ripon Cathedral.
47. © David Baldwin.
48. © David Baldwin.
49. © David Baldwin.
50. © David Baldwin.
51. © David Baldwin.
52. © David Baldwin.
53. © David Baldwin.
54. © David Baldwin.
55. © David Baldwin.
56. © David Baldwin.
57. © David Baldwin.
58. © Jonathan Reeve JR1565b13p704 14501500.
59. © David Baldwin.
60. © David Baldwin.
61. © David Baldwin.
62. © David Baldwin.
63. © David Baldwin.
64. © David Baldwin.
65. © David Baldwin.
66. © David Baldwin.
67. © David Baldwin.
68. © David Baldwin.
69. © David Baldwin.
70. © David Baldwin.
71. © David Baldwin.
72. © David Baldwin.
73. © David Baldwin.
74. © P.W. Hammond.
75. © G. Wheeler.
76. © G. Wheeler.
77. © G. Wheeler.
78. © G. Wheeler and © David Baldwin.
79. © David Baldwin.
80. © Barry Vincent, after Nottingham Civic Society.
81. © David Baldwin.

Also available from Amberley Publishing

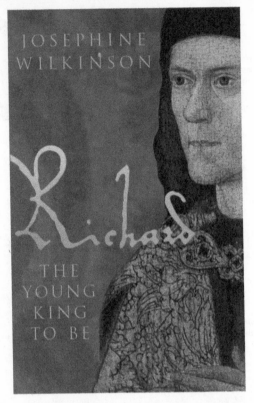

A major new biography of the young Richard III

Richard III is a paradox – the most hated of English kings, yet the most beloved, a deeply pious man,
yet materialistic to the point of obsession, puritan, yet the father of at least two illegitimate children.
This new biography concentrates on the much neglected early part of Richard's life – from his birth in
1452 as a cadet of the House of York to his marriage to the beautiful Anne Neville – and shows how his
experiences as the son of an ambitious duke, a prisoner of war, an exile, his knightly training and awe of
his elder brother, King Edward IV, shaped the character of England's most controversial monarch.

£9.99 Paperback
40 illustrations (25 colour)
352 pages
978-1-84868-513-0

Available from all good bookshops or to order direct
Please call **01453-847-800**
www.amberleybooks.com

Also available from Amberley Publishing

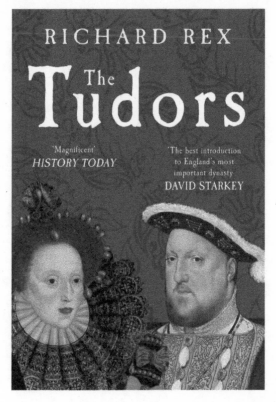

An intimate history of England's most infamous royal family

'The best introduction to England's most important dynasty' DAVID STARKEY
'A lively overview... Rex is a wry commentator on the game on monarchy' THE GUARDIAN
'Gripping and told with enviable narrative skill. This is a model of popular history... a delight' THES
'Vivid, entertaining and carrying its learning lightly' EAMON DUFFY

The Tudor Age began in August 1485 when Henry Tudor landed with 2000 men at Milford Haven
intent on snatching the English throne from Richard III. For more than a hundred years England was
to be dominated by the personalities of the five Tudor monarchs, ranging from the brilliance and
brutality of Henry VIII to the shrewdness and vanity of the virgin queen, Elizabeth I.

£9.99 Paperback
143 illustrations (66 colour)
272 pages
978-1-4456-0700-9

Available from all good bookshops or to order direct
Please call **01453-847-800**
www.amberleybooks.com

Also available from Amberley Publishing

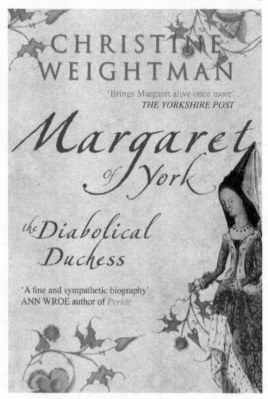

The amazing life of Margaret of York, the woman who tried to overthr
the Tudors

'A pioneering biography of the Tudor dynasty's most dangerous enemy'
PROFESSOR MICHAEL HICKS
'A fine and sympathetic biography... brings us impressively close to one of the most interesting - and importa
- women of the 15th century' ANN WROE
'A fascinating account of a remarkable woman' THE BIRMINGHAM POST
'Christine Weightman brings Margaret alive once more' THE YORKSHIRE POST

£10.99 Paperback
51 illustrations
256 pages
978-1-4456-0819-8

Available from all good bookshops or to order direct
Please call **01453-847-800**
www.amberleybooks.com

Also available from Amberley Publishing

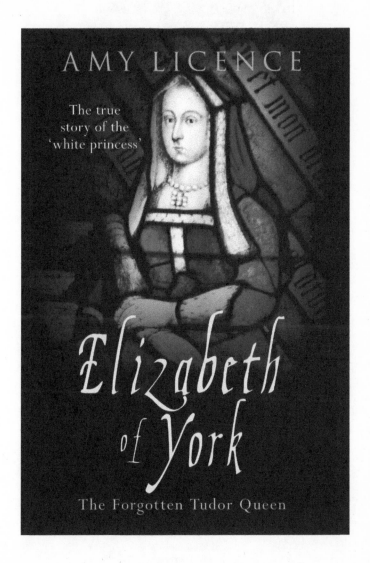

AMY LICENCE

The true
story of the
'white princess'

Elizabeth
of York

The Forgotten Tudor Queen

Available from all good bookshops or to order direct
Please call **01453-847-800**
www.amberleybooks.com

Also available from Amberley Publishing

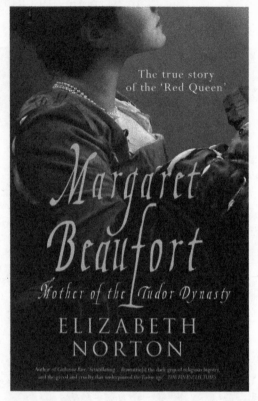

The true story
of the 'Red Queen'

Margaret
Beaufort
Mother of the Tudor Dynasty

ELIZABETH
NORTON

Author of *Catherine Parr*. 'Scintillating ... dramatic[s] the dark grip of religious bigotry,
and the greed and cruelty that underpinned the Tudor age.' *THE FINANCIAL TIMES*

Divorced at ten, a mother at thirteen & three times a widow.
The extraordinary true story of the 'Red Queen', Lady Margaret
Beaufort, matriarch of the Tudors

'Portrait of a medieval matriarch' THE INDEPENDENT

Born in the midst of the Wars of the Roses, Margaret Beaufort became the greatest heiress of her time.
She survived a turbulent life, marrying four times and enduring imprisonment before passing her claim
to the crown of England to her son, Henry VII, the first of the Tudor monarchs.

Henry VII gave his mother unparalleled prominence during his reign and she established herself as an
independent woman.

£9.99 Paperback
63 illustrations (39 col)
272 pages
978-1-4456-0578-4

Available from all good bookshops or to order direct
Please call **01453-847-800**
www.amberleybooks.com

Also available from Amberley Publishing

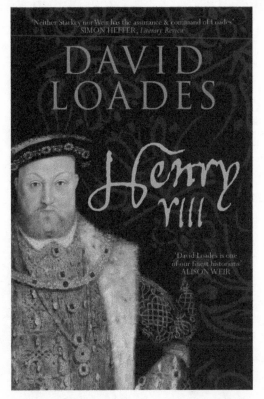

A major new biography of the most infamous king of England

'A triumph' THE SPECTATOR

'The best place to send anyone seriously wanting to get to grips with alternative understandings of England's most mesmerising monarch... copious illustrations, imaginatively chosen' BBC HISTORY MAGAZINE

'David Loades Tudor biographies are both highly enjoyable and instructive, the perfect combination'
ANTONIA FRASER

Professor David Loades has spent most of his life investigating the remains, literary, archival and archaeological, of Henry VIII, and this monumental new biography book is the result. As a youth, he was a magnificent specimen of manhood, and in age a gargantuan wreck, but even in his prime he was never the 'ladies man' which legend, and his own imagination, created. Sexual insecurity undermined him, and gave his will that irascible edge which proved fatal to Anne Boleyn and Thomas Cromwell alike.

£25 Hardback
113 illustrations (49 colour)
512 pages
978-1-84868-532-1

Available from all good bookshops or to order direct
Please call **01453-847-800**
www.amberleybooks.com

Forthcoming February 2013 from Amberley Publishing

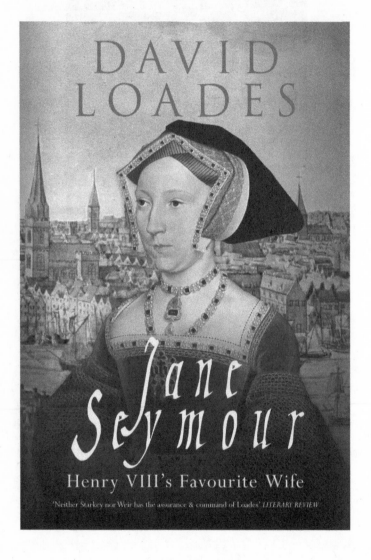

DAVID
LOADES

Jane
Seymour

Henry VIII's Favourite Wife

'Neither Starkey nor Weir has the assurance & command of Loades' *LITERARY REVIEW*

Available from all good bookshops or to order direct
Please call **01453–847–800**
www.amberleybooks.com

Available July 2013 from Amberley Publishing

The Tudor femmes fatales
who changed English history

B

The
Boleyn
Women

ELIZABETH
NORTON

Available from all good bookshops or to order direct
Please call **01453-847-800**
www.amberleybooks.com

Also available from Amberley Publishing

The tragic love affair that changed English history forever

Anne Boleyn was the most controversial and scandalous woman ever to sit on the throne of England. From her early days at the imposing Hever Castle in Kent, to the glittering courts of Paris and London, Anne caused a stir wherever she went. Alluring but not beautiful, Anne's wit and poise won her numerous admirers at the English court, and caught the roving eye of King Henry.

Their love affair was as extreme as it was deadly, from Henry's 'mine own sweetheart' to 'cursed and poisoning whore' her fall from grace was total.

£9.99 Paperback
47 illustrations (26 colour)
264 pages
978-1-84868-514-7

Available from all good bookshops or to order direct
Please call **01453-847-800**
www.amberleybooks.com

Also available from Amberley Publishing

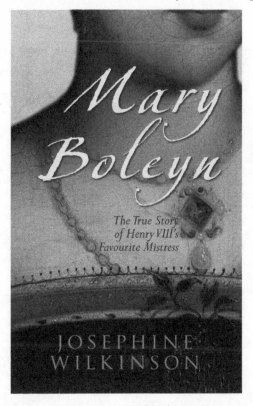

*The scandalous true story of Mary Boleyn, infamous sister of Anne,
and mistress of Henry VIII*

Mary Boleyn, 'the infamous other Boleyn girl', began her court career as the mistress of the king of
France. François I of France would later call her 'The Great Prostitute' and the slur stuck. The bête-noir
of her family, Mary was married off to a minor courtier but it was not long before she caught the eye
of Henry VIII and a new affair began.

Mary would emerge the sole survivor of a family torn apart by lust and ambition, and it is in Mary and
her progeny that the Boleyn legacy rests.

£9.99 Paperback
22 illustrations (10 colour)
224 pages
978-1-84868-525-3

Available from all good bookshops or to order direct
Please call **01453-847-800**
www.amberleybooks.com

Forthcoming May 2013 from Amberley Publishing

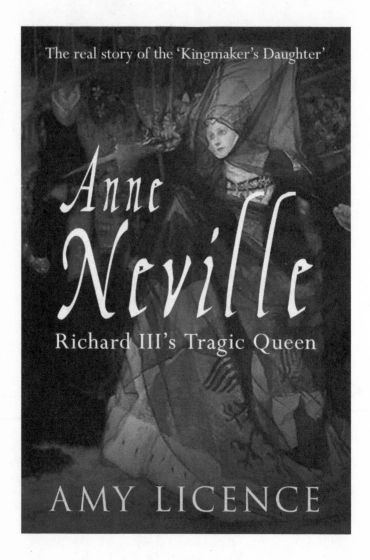

The real story of the 'Kingmaker's Daughter'

Anne
Neville

Richard III's Tragic Queen

AMY LICENCE

Available from all good bookshops or to order direct
Please call **01453-847-800**
www.amberleybooks.com

Also available from Amberley Publishing

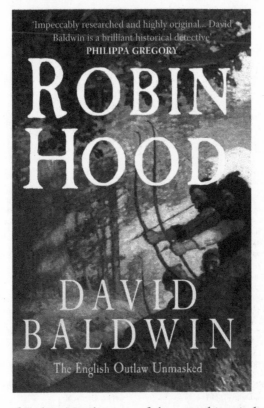

The identity of Robin Hood is one of the great historical mysteries of English history – until now

'Impeccably researched and highly original... David Baldwin is a brilliant historical detective'
PHILIPPA GREGORY

David Baldwin sets out to find the real Robin Hood, looking for clues in the earliest ballads
and in official and legal documents of the thirteenth and fourteenth centuries. His search
takes him to the troubled reign of King Henry III. His conclusions turn history on its head
and he reveals the name of the man who inspired the tales of Robin Hood.

£9.99 Paperback
76 illustrations (40 colour)
288 pages
978-1-4456-0281-3

Available from all good bookshops or to order direct
Please call **01453-847-800**
www.amberleybooks.com

INDEX

Index

Index